I would prefer a
baker !!!

Dad.

THE
UNDERWATER
BOOK

Proud as a peacock. This beautiful shot of a gurnard was taken in 30 feet of water on rough ground between Shoreham and Hove. This is the best of several pictures taken at the same time. The fish appeared not to be frightened by flash or the movement of the diver changing flash bulbs as long as this was done slowly. Sudden movements obviously upset the fish. Rolleimarin, close-up lens, Kodacolor-X, f 22/125, PF5 bulb. Tony Baverstock.

THE UNDERWATER BOOK

Edited by Kendall McDonald
for the British Sub-Aqua Club

PELHAM BOOKS

First published in Great Britain by
PELHAM BOOKS LTD
26 Bloomsbury Street
London, W.C.1
1968

© 1968 by British Sub-Aqua Club

Printed in Great Britain by
Ebenezer Baylis and Son Limited
The Trinity Press, Worcester, and London

All the contributors to this book are members of
THE BRITISH SUB-AQUA CLUB

All the photographs in this book were taken underwater
around the coasts of the British Isles by members of
THE BRITISH SUB-AQUA CLUB

Foreword

By H.R.H. the Duke of Edinburgh

BUCKINGHAM PALACE

Most children start with an urge to explore, some lose interest as they grow up, others just dream about it, but in a minority the urge grows in intensity throughout their lives.

The greatest thrill for any explorer is to be first, to see something or to find somewhere not previously recorded. This has always been pretty difficult to do. You can't climb Everest or walk to the South Pole on a normal budget and anyway it's been done before.

Diving underwater is the answer to the explorer's dream, particularly if he has only modest means, and since the invention of the aqualung people have flocked to learn the technique. It has opened a whole realm of exploration to amateurs and they have jumped at the chance.

Inevitably most of the "firsts" have gone and many of the easier discoveries have been made, but even so life underwater is so completely cut off from normal existence that diving will always remain an exploration and a special experience.

What gives it a particular interest at the moment is that we are living through the pioneer stages of the unfolding of a new science, a new technology and a whole range of new human occupations under water. Even a casual glance through this fascinating book is enough to show some of the remarkable possibilities for the future. This book also tells the story of the pioneers and the gradual development of equipment and methods.

The sea is the last unknown area of the world and there is so much to discover, so much to learn and such a potential for development that any progress can only be made by the closest collaboration between amateurs, scientists and experts. The accounts written by divers of the British Sub-Aqua Club in this book show very clearly what amateurs have to offer in knowledge and enthusiasm. What is more, their diving has not been in the warm limpid waters of the tropics but in the cold, tide-torn and frequently poor visibility of the seas around the British Isles.

Like so many worthwhile occupations, diving is dangerous only for those who have not trained and practised for it. Without any doubt the most important and valuable contribution made by the British Sub-Aqua Club has been the development of a comprehensive system of training and qualification and its strict supervision.

Anyone with the smallest vestiges of the urge to explore will feel a strange tingling sensation as they read this book. It will probably turn out to be the first step towards the hiss and bubble of an aqualung and the dim, slow-motion world under the sea.

CONTENTS

ILLUSTRATIONS

DRAWINGS

THE AMATEUR DIVERS OF BRITAIN

by Harold Gould

Harold Gould is Chairman of the British Sub-Aqua Club. Is
former president and chairman of London Branch. A Justice
of the Peace, he is an active First Class diver.

EVER since the evolution of true man there have been divers.
Somewhere, sometime, there must have been a first dive, a first
penetration of the surface of the sea. We shall never know who
that man was. We shall never know whether he went underwater willingly for experiment or food, or whether he fell from
some primitive craft like a dug-out canoe.

But even if the first man underwater got there by accident,
certainly there must have been later, deliberate, trips under the
waves. The proof of this is on record. The job of diver was
certainly in existence in Greek and Roman times and there was
then a flourishing industry based on diving for sponges.

From then on man's progress and desire to conquer the
undersea world are clearly documented. But there was no mass
exploration of the sea-bed. The men who went under the
surface were generally carrying on the occupation of diver and
not diving for pure pleasure.

The day of the pleasure diver came comparatively recently
and is largely due to the perfection of a "fool-proof" demand
valve in 1943 by the young Lieutenant-Commander Cousteau
of the French Navy and a Parisian engineer Emile Gagnan.
Their success brought sport-diving into being.

So the aqualung was then available and ordinary men and
women could dive in safety below the surface. But the aqualung
was still a heavy piece of equipment when compared with a
tennis racket. Its use might have stayed confined to a bunch of
very strong young fanatics who were prepared to hump it from

the nearest railway station to the sea, if it had not also been for the phenomenal growth of the ownership of the private car. With transport easily available getting the gear to the sea presented few problems and the day of the amateur diver dawned.

Nowhere in the world was this new sport welcomed as quickly as it was in Britain. Perhaps we have an instinctive feeling about the sea, perhaps we determined that our seas were just as explorable as the clear, generally calm, waters of the Mediterranean, where of course the aqualung had its natural home.

Today the British Sub-Aqua Club—the controlling body for the sport in Britain—has over 300 branches, has an active diving membership of over 10,000, and has trained nearly 50,000 divers since its inception in 1953.

In this book you will read of the exploits of a few of the Club's members, exploits which are all the more remarkable when you realize that these are true amateurs. They dive in their free time only—that is at week-ends, sometimes in the evenings, usually on their annual holidays.

Members of the Club come from all walks of life, have an incredible spread of full-time occupations, and are not confined to a narrow age band.

For anyone who is reasonably fit can dive. Age in itself is no bar. Surgeon Rear-Admiral Stanley Miles, who is one of the world's top experts on diving medicine, wrote recently in the Club's magazine, *Triton*:

"At what age should a man (or woman) stop diving? This question is repeatedly asked, but of course there is no real answer other than to say that age as such has nothing to do with ability or fitness to dive. . . . There are those in their forties who are quite unfit to dive and others still diving in their eighties. . . . The decision must therefore not be taken on age alone. Diving may, indeed, if of a gentle and supervised nature, even be of benefit to the aged."

Of course Admiral Miles will also stress the need for fitness—the fitter a man is the happier he will be underwater.

Basically, the would-be aqualung diver should have no evidence of heart-trouble or fits or attacks of unconsciousness, no evidence either of respiratory disease, his ears should be sound, and he should not suffer from claustrophobia. The wearing of glasses is, however, no bar.

Anyone who can pass such standards of fitness can be trained to dive. He or she will go to the nearest branch of the British Sub-Aqua Club and pass through the club's excellent training programme. And this training is really good. So good that the Club's instructional manual is the accepted standard for many countries in the world.

The Duke of Edinburgh is a Past President and now Honorary Life Member of the club and is no mere figurehead. He, too, went through a course of training in the use of the aqualung, following closely the Club's methods and tests.

Of course, there is an element of danger in underwater swimming—this is certainly part of its thrill—but the B.S-A.C. has a fine safety record, mainly due to its insistence on safety procedures. The stress throughout all training and in the open sea dives that follow is on safety and the National Diving Committee of the club while researching into such things as deep diving and the use of mixtures of gases, is constantly revising its safety procedures.

The Club was founded in 1953 by Oscar Gugen and Peter Small. It was a great blow when Peter Small died during the ascent from the Hannes Keller world-record dive of 1,000 feet. This sort of deep diving, however, is outside the Club's scope and researches and is the province of the world's navies.

But if the club's amateur divers are not penetrating to the abysses of the ocean, they are doing useful work in depths up to 200 feet. Some of their achievements set out here in this British Sub-Aqua Club book (an addition to their excellent manuals of instruction) are clear proof that it has all been supremely worth while.

DIVING WITH A
PURPOSE

by Alexander McKee

Alexander McKee is an expert on changing sea levels and
underwater archaeology. He lives on Hayling Island and is a
member of Southsea Branch. Is an author of books on underwater subjects, particularly farming the sea.

IF anyone finds a sunken church and village on his very first
aqualung dive, one may safely surmise that he must be a
character in fiction—schoolboy's fiction. But that, more or less,
was what happened to me in the summer of 1960, at nearly
forty years of age. I thereby skipped the novice diver's classical
progression from the stage of sheer wonder and delight in being
underwater at all—which may last two or three years—to the
next phase when, if the diver has achieved nothing, he considers the affair a waste of precious time and even more precious
compressed air. Possibly it may have helped inoculate me also
against spearfishing fever, which tends to infect divers in stage
two, and sometimes even in stage one. Being a historian by
trade, I naturally preferred to get my teeth into a documentary
problem, which this indeed turned out to be.

Oddly perhaps, the affair itself is now history, for it was to
prove the first sustained effort at underwater archaeological
investigation around the British Isles. But it was all so primitive
to begin with, and is so much overlaid with knowledge acquired
later, that I cannot catch the atmosphere of the time without
myself now turning back to re-read what I had written shortly
after the initial discoveries. The first one—which aroused sus-
picion merely and so triggered off the long sequence of investigation—occurred on 3 July, 1960.

I see that I was much concerned with water temperature.
"The onset of cold is very sudden; one minute, you are all right,
just a little chilled, but held fascinated by the underwater

16

scenery; the next minute, you are gasping, you feel sick in the stomach, at least half your swimming efficiency is gone, and you care dangerously little whether you live or die." How true—and how prehistoric. It seems I used to dive without a suit in those days, in swimming trunks only. For this reason, on this day, I was the first one overboard, and, this being my first boat trip with Southsea Branch of the B.S-A.C., was much concerned with technique. "Holding my mask in place, I jumped, hit the water, and submerged in a kaleidoscope of green sea and white bubbles. Rising once to the surface for air, I took a long breath flat on the surface, snapped my arms straight down as if trying to touch my toes, kicked my legs vertically in the air, and, driven under by the force of gravity on them, went for the bottom fast."

I did not expect to see it. The boat was at least one and a half miles out from shore in Hayling Bay, and my ignorance was such that I thought it must be at least 60 feet deep. But "I had been driving down for only a few seconds, when I saw a dark blur which became, in another second, the seabed coming up at me—and a small, surprised rock-fish getting the hell out of it four feet from my face. His heart must have missed a beat, to see this sudden arrival from the surface of a monster seven feet long (counting the flippers), with one great, glaring eye, and one great horn sticking up from behind its right ear. I went straight down past his tail, on to the deck—weed, lots of it, growing on something, presumably rock; but it didn't look like rock. Or, at any rate, the rocks were like no rocks I had ever seen before. With somewhat jumbled mind, I turned up for the surface, and with a few fin strokes, was there. There was a shout from the next boat, 'What's it like?'

"I took the snorkel mouthpiece out, and beat my fins together to take my mouth wide of the water. 'It's shallow!' I shouted back. 'About fourteen feet.'

" 'What's the vis. like?'

" 'Good.'

" 'What's the bottom like?'

"That had me. How was I to describe it? 'Well, it's . . . rock . . . sort of.'

"That settled the matter for them. This must be Church

Rocks. A series of heavy splashes announced their arrival backwards in the water—one of the easiest ways out of a boat, particularly with an aqualung on, is to fall in spine first. Soon, there
came at intervals across the waves, a roar like that emitted by
a spray-stunned seal; it was some diver barking in triumph. A
close look would reveal the glittering white of a plaice or brill,
or the darker colour of a lobster. If the diver tried to show it to
you—always an effort, for although a lobster in water weighs
hardly anything at all, it is pretty hefty in air—you knew it
must be a big one, two or more feet long; the captors of the
smaller lobsters swam steadily, silently and without ostentation
to the side of their boats."

My only serious purpose was to pass Test (3) of Group D—
"Surface dive to the 18–21 foot level wearing basic equipment".
Once I had achieved this feat three times. I could then go on to
Groups E and F—that is, aqualung training in the swimming
pool. As soon as the rising tide gave a minimum of 18 feet I
plunged madly three times, emerging twice with a fistful of
weed and once with a small rock. Now it was my turn to
trumpet in triumph across the water. Someone said "Oh, yes"
in a tired voice, as I boldly dumped the stone in the middle of
a lot of depressed looking lobsters, with a shout of "Group D!"
Subsequently, I wrote an embittered paragraph, to the effect
that "When French divers pass a certain test, they receive the
'accolade' of the free plongeurs, or whatever it's called; a
mystical, thrilling, enlightening, liberating, nature-communing,
death-defying experience, according to French journalist-divers.
Well, I had 'plonged' all right, but where was the mystical
experience? Obviously, to get any attention in these parts,
you had to clout the Diving Officer over the head with a heavy
rock."

Thus far, as described, it was a pretty normal Club trip for
the time; and not so different from much of what is done today
on such occasions. That is, almost entirely a waste of time. Only
if absolutely desperate for a dive, would I now even contemplate taking part in such an affair.

There was one difference, however. "When I climbed back
aboard, I found John Powell sitting in the bottom of the boat,
chipping at a piece of rock with a hammer. He and some of the

others had been down with lungs, and also curious about the rock, had brought up this second sample (the first sample, in the gloom, had turned out to be a crab which had obligingly grasped the head of the hammer and so delivered itself into his hands). There was a white flaky substance around the rock which might have been mortar; it certainly looked so, to our inexpert eyes." There was a girl geologist in the boat, Janet Lance, but she could not hold her breath long enough really to examine the "rocks" on the bottom. In her laboratory next day, she discovered that the rock was very soft and full of worms, but could find no trace of mortar.

Meanwhile, I went overboard for a last fling. "The tide was now running fast, and I was having more and more difficulty in getting down; the fact was, I couldn't clear my ears, and in the deep bits—for the depth varied by about 6 feet or so—the pressure pain in my ears felt like a road drill wielded by a demented dentist. Visibility was getting bad, with the increasing tide run; I jabbed at some yellow growth hanging to the side of a rock, and it burst into fragments. Actually, it was a sponge, but I was still under the impression that sponges were all Hans Hass and Captain Cousteau, and nothing at all to do with matter-of-fact British waters. Then, as I went down again, in about 20 feet of water, and after skimming along the bottom for a few seconds, began to turn upwards for my return to the surface, I saw it.

"It was a right-angled rock. So far as I could judge, the angles were exact and perfect; there was an inside angle and an outside one. The thing was like the corner of a wall. Later, I remembered what it reminded me of—the broken foundations of a house in the Möhne valley, below the dam which had been 'bust' during the war by Guy Gibson's squadron. It was just a swift, fleeting impression, and in poor visibility. You couldn't hang a coat on it, archaeologically. But having often explored the Möhne valley, I knew what building foundations really looked like after they had first been scoured by water and then overgrown with weed and grass, and I had photographs for comparison."

That was how it began. Some of it makes me smile now. I had honestly forgotten that I ever had trouble clearing my ears, and nowadays curse when I have to hang around on the anchor waiting for a novice to blow his nose. On a new site, the immediate identification by top-quality experts of the geological strata and the biological range are automatic procedures; any deviation from the normal is at once noted, because the "normal" is known. Occasionally, I have the use of really useful, ultra-expensive scientific instruments (NOT underwater television). I still do not much care whether a man (or a woman) is a "good" or a "bad" diver; I am interested mainly in their powers of observation and any special knowledge they may be able to bring to bear.

My immediate impressions at the time, written up the same night in my detailed dive log-book, turned out to be not so far wrong. "What we saw was consistent with a small village overwhelmed suddenly by an inrush of the sea many centuries ago. NOT coast erosion—which breaks up a building bit by bit. NOT a concrete fort or similar erection of reasonably recent date. NOT rocks either, unless a type none of us had ever seen before. Possibly the 'church' in Church Rocks is significant; but, of course, no church bell tolling—the highest part seen by anybody was a pinnacle about four feet high."

After writing up the log, while impressions were still fresh, my next act was to telephone the head of Portsmouth Museums Society. Was there any documentation for submerged buildings off Hayling Island? There was—I would find them in C. J. Longcroft's *The Hundred of Bosmere*. "It's amazing the heat this subject generates," remarked the Portsmouth City Librarian next morning. "There was an extraordinarily acid correspondence in the Portsmouth *Evening News* a few years ago. I'll look it up while you're reading *The Hundred of Bosmere*."

The gist of the story which emerged was that there had been a great inundation at Hayling around 1300, which had submerged the church and "almost all the hamlet of Eastoke". The church had originally been "in the centre of the island", so the inundation must have been great indeed; no mere matter of coastal erosion. This was followed by another great inundation around 1340. The best inundation, from my point of view, was one that had occurred later still, in around 1380, because a document which had survived made clear the actual process involved. The inhabitants were then claiming for relief of tax on the grounds of inundations old and new, and stated specifically that land which had been "overflown by the tide for five or six years then last past . . . could not be sown" (i.e., it uncovered at low water); but that "300 acres of arable land . . . were submerged by the sea and entirely destroyed within forty-three years then last past . . . and that there was then deep water there." Sea defences had been made, "of piles, earth, and turf . . . which were entirely broken down, destroyed, and submerged. . . ."

To my mind this could be read in only one way. There had been a rise in sea level, rather like a high tide extending over a long period of time. The effects had been postponed, and perhaps worsened, by the construction of sea defence walls. And this was what I wanted to know.

As far as I personally was concerned, the Church Rocks investigation was never archaeology. Properly speaking, archaeology is a method of studying history by stripping (and thereby destroying) the successive occupation layers of a site, on the principle that the layer which is on top must be the most recent, the layer at the bottom the oldest, and to date them from pottery and other artifacts found within the layers. Unless the stripping process is minutely recorded, much of the evidence potentially available will never be discovered. To do this on Church Rocks at the time was quite out of the question and in any case of questionable value. Even the church itself, if excavated, would tell us little we did not already know; there were, after all, on Hayling already two existing churches which had been standing before the original church had ever been submerged, and they were in a much better state of repair than the lost church could ever be.

I had only two questions to ask of the submerged site: why and how was it submerged? What were the causes? I do not know into which "box" these questions fit, but they were the queries I personally thought most pertinent. They were broad, because I was in effect inquiring into the entire 'church bells tolling under the sea' legend, and using two means—documentary research and seabed search—all concentrated on one particularly favourable site.

Work had been done on this general subject by British divers
—but it had been undertaken entirely in the Mediterranean.
Having once been involved in a Malta earthquake, I entirely
ruled out all Mediterranean evidence for the moment. It was
rendered totally unreliable because the earth's crust was
notoriously unstable and still affected by active volvanoes there,
quite apart from the fact that the divers were not date-conscious
and did not try to eliminate some at least of the volcanic factors
by this means. At Church Rocks, however, we could eliminate
earthquake effect entirely. The English Channel is not volcanic
and no more than slight tremors have ever been recorded; apart
from this, the documentary evidence showed that the inundations had occurred during the period approximately 1250–1425,
a matter of some 175 years, whereas the effect of an earthquake
is immediate and momentary, most of the damage being done
in seconds.

This left as the major alternative only the tilting or warping
of the earth's crust, an extremely slow, almost imperceptible
movement which, again, did not fit the documentary record.
Whereas volcanic action did not tally because it was too rapid,
this did not fit because it was too slow. It was true that the
south-east coast of England was believed to be sinking into the
sea from these causes, but there was evidence on Hayling to
show that its effect was nearly negligible. A large tract of land,
with a watchtower, on the Sussex side of Chichester Harbour
had been "overflown" by the sea in the 19th century, as reliable
maps showed, but, unlike Church Rocks, it was not "deep in
the sea" after 43 years; on the contrary, after more than one
hundred years, it still dried out at low water. Clearly, therefore,
any tilting of the land surface which was taking place must be a
minor factor; and further, the rise in sea level which was now
the only credible alternative, must have stopped long ago.

These theories were hurtful to Mediterranean divers and
destructive to the ideas of some geologists, mostly the out-of-
date ones, who still postulated a very gradual, continuous rise
of sea level due to the sinking of the land surface. My opinion,
on the contrary, tended to a tide-like fluctuation of sea levels.

By no means whatever could this effect have been local to
Hayling; and it was here that I parted company with the local

historians. They had tended, naturally enough, to consider Hayling in isolation. I, however, now made it my business to research the subject throughout north-west Europe, and discovered that the same stories of inundation disasters occurred on all obviously vulnerable sea coasts during approximately the same period. The evidence was of a gratifyingly diverse nature. Whereas on Hayling it was contained in Norman tax documents, in some of the Frisian Islands, notably Sylt, the references were in the parish registers of existing churches; whereas at Winchelsea the evidence lay in State Papers dealing with the planning of a new town to replace the submerged one, in the Zuyder Zee the water had actually been pumped off the drowned land and the sunken villages excavated in air by ordinary land archaeologists. The stories were all very much the same: and nowhere was there a mention of church bells tolling under the sea. On the contrary, the ruins had clearly uncovered at low tide for some time after the original inundations and a good deal of material had been salvaged. On Sylt, for instance, tradition associates an early altar screen, unmistakably dating from Catholic times, with no less than two sunken churches. Removed from the sunken church at List to the church at Eydum, it was then taken to Westerland church when Eydum was lost.

There were similar legends at Hayling. Both churches contemporary with the submerged church contain objects said to have been dredged up from the ruins or "washed up" on the beach: at St. Peter's a bell, at St. Mary's a Saxon font. The present vicar, the Rev. John Beaumont, MBE, found a third item—similar in basic design and decoration to the font, which had been carved from a Saxon or Viking cross; it was in use as a sundial, and the owners testified that their parents had bought it from a man who had discovered it on the beach. It proved impossible to take the story any further, but by then I knew for a fact that the ruins on Church Rocks had been "robbed out" for salvagable material, probably by the original owners, the monks. Instead of walls, I had found the trenches where wall foundations had been cut into a strata of natural rock, and the rock itself levelled for the laying of floors—which was why it had looked so odd at first sight and aroused my suspicions. Also, for purposes of geological testing, I had myself removed several large building blocks which were obviously much harder and of a quite different texture to the natural strata. These were mostly of Weald sandstone, which occurs naturally some twenty miles inland, but no nearer than that to Hayling. They are now lined up in my garden and I daresay that future historians will quarrel about their origin. For the record, one was raised to the surface by filling an oil drum with compressed air and then *towed* behind the boat and beached on the shore opposite my house, the other was lifted direct into the boat by four men, one of them the Vicar, who also took part in some of the diving operations.

All these operations, which went on sporadically for many years, while we were learning the business of undersea exploration, and learning to dive at the same time, confirmed the stories of the established local historians and also the ideas of the local archaeological society; later, they were reinforced by indisputable traces of marine sediments found on land, one of which was associated with the late Roman period, and bore out the theory of alternate rise-and-fall of sea level. For two modern, local historians, however, this research came at an awkward time. One of them, Major F. G. S. Thomas, deserved better.

He, too, believed in the sunken church but parted company with his predecessors on the extent of the inundations. He really could not believe that so great an area of land had been lost to the sea, and, accepting that the old church was "in the centre" of the island, tried to move the site of Church Rocks nearer to the shore, as this would also reduce the extent of the theoretically inundated areas. Our Church Rocks site he called "Fishermen's Church Rocks", and maintained that the real site of the church was only a few hundred yards off the present-day beach instead of two miles out to sea, where we were to find all the building material. He had some evidence for this, as various 18th and 19th century charts showed no less than three inshore sites marked as "Church Rocks".

When I made my first snorkel dive on the seaward site on 3 July, 1960, I had never heard of Church Rocks, let alone Major Thomas. But, in fact, he had launched a search for the sunken church much earlier than this, in the summer of 1955, in co-operation with the then Chairman of Southsea Branch, Mr. Frank Martin. They had finally located "Fishermen's Church Rocks", but eventually decided that there was no trace of building material there. It was my novice's luck to see that suspiciously right-angled "rock" before I had so much as even learned to use an aqualung! But it was hardly luck, that on the first occasion on which I did use an aqualung—without actually having learned to use it—I found two large slabs of building stone within ten minutes. This highly irregular dive was carried out on 14 August, 1960. I noted in my logbook, "Like flying. Delightful! I was so fascinated I didn't want to come up—indeed, I had forgotten about coming up; but I was, after all, living on borrowed air!" I think the hazards in amateur diving have been over-stressed. At any event, I have never had an "adventure" on Church Rocks and always used to reckon that the really dangerous bit was driving from Hayling into Portsmouth to get my bottles re-filled with compressed air. Now that they have installed traffic lights it's not quite so risky.

What does require explanation, however, is the ease with which some people could spot building material—or any other anomaly anywhere of an archaeological nature—and the total failure of most people to see anything at all. Except, of course, lobsters. And therein, I fancy, lies the heart of the problem. In the beginning I at any rate refused to take notice of any lobster I happened to meet and kept my mind fully concentrated on the work on hand. An eminent archaeologist once wrote, "In digging, you only find if you care to find, and according to the measure of your caring; or, as a famous and fortunate explorer once put it, you find what you go out to find."

All sorts of excuses can be made for failure. Underwater lighting, which contains no contrast and therefore tends to flatten out all the opposed planes of a man-made object. Underwater camouflage, the seaweeds, algae and sponges which break the outlines or cover them completely. The very poor average visibility on Church Rocks, and other local sites, which means that you all too often see only part of an object at a time, making recognition difficult. The excessive cover of laminaria weed which, when the tide turns, alters the entire aspect of an undersea landscape, so that momentarily you recognize nothing. The very short time at your disposal, with present day techniques. The specially difficult problem on Church Rocks, where the most important buildings were erected on a reef of natural rock, and those away from this outcrop were put up on an unusual foundation of heavy "erratic blocks" placed under the load-bearing points of the structures only, a method significantly paralleled on land at St. Peter's Church, which was built to relieve pressure on the original church.

But these are only excuses to cover lack of real interest and determination, not qualities which can be simulated. The proof occurred in the summer of 1966, when for the first time I was able to take a genuine archaeologist underwater with me. Miss Margot Varese was then one of a group of archaeologists or archaeological students working at London University who had been encouraged to learn to dive by Miss Joan du Plat Taylor, Vice-Chairman of the newly-created Committee for Nautical Archaeology. I had been able to give Miss Varese a full briefing on the Church Rocks problem, which included not merely the gist of the documentary story, but visits to most of the surviving structures on Hayling which were contemporary with the submerged church site, and show samples both of the natural Bracklesham Beds strata as well as the Weald sandstone and Mendip stone used in addition for building. Even so, conditions were difficult, with a dense weed carpet rippling in the current and visibility of three feet or less. I thought we should fail, but Margot found a "pathway" within minutes.

Anything less like the romantic idea of a submerged building would be hard to imagine. Under your nose, an area of sponges and algae surrounded by thick laminaria growth, which she could examine only section by section. You could see clearly for about 18 inches only. But her slow and careful examination showed a sand-and-shingle-filled trench with approximately straight-cut sides, 12 inches across, aligned north-south, and flanked to the east certainly by a flattened rock area which she considered to be most probably a floor. I found this place again a few weeks later, in 10 feet visibility, and could then see at a glance that she had been right in her provisional diagnosis—the trench was in fact a typical "robbed out" wall, the space partly filled up with shingle, and with obvious floor areas both sides.

Possibly a little knowledge goes a long way.

However, the scepticism shown by divers who knew Church Rocks well, but had never seen building material there, had one useful and gratifying result. Although photography in visibilities down to 4 feet had previously been thought impossible, locally at least, I was spurred into technical experiments (NOT involving a close-up lens, useless in the circumstances), designed to record exactly what I myself saw (a) in its natural condition, with camouflage intact, and (b) with part of the weed growth and algae scraped off to reveal the unmistakable right-angles and flat surfaces of rough-hewn stone. When achieved, this technique was a useful supplement to memory, not merely in regard to the exact shapes of building blocks, but in recording the exact order of events during a dive.

In the beginning, not a few people were horrified, even scandalized, at the very idea of setting out to investigate what appeared to be a vaguely Atlantis-type legend. Most of this was undoubtedly S.L.M.F.—Scholarly Lack of Moral Fibre. It is professional death to a scholar to be thought "unsound", or "wild", or to have anything at all to do with unfashionable theories or subjects. Fear of making a mistake must in the past have held many back, from the anticipation of deadly ridicule. On the other hand, it is said that a businessman who makes fewer than four mistakes out of ten decisions almost automatically becomes a millionaire and gets a knighthood into the bargain. In fact, we made only one error of magnitude, and this was in dismissing out of hand, because of the shallow depth, the entire "church bells ringing under the sea" story. We should have seen this before, because the very fact that any church tower or steeple could never be submerged by an inundation within the 15 to 25 feet rise of sea level which seems probable, should have suggested the possibility of the original story referring to the ringing of the bells of just such a half-submerged church. In fact this legend occurs only in respect of lakes, not the sea, where the structure would either collapse or be pulled down; and some future explorers might do worse than investigate lakes where such legends exist. Who knows what they might find?

Nowadays, the investigation of changing sea levels around the British Isles is a perfectly respectable proceeding, although in some cases the old ideas concerning a geological cause still confuse the issue.

In 1964, a 13-strong expedition organized by Guildford Branch of the B.S-A.C. and led by Mr. R. Kingsford-Curram, went to the Scilly Isles with the idea of checking the latest findings of land archaeology against the possibility of a rise in sea level. Archaeologically, the Scillies make no sense at all with the sea at its present level. In 1962, for instance, the site of a Roman trading post was discovered on the tiny, isolated island of Nornour, surrounded by a good deal of sea and an intricate array of treacherous rocks. On other islands there is evidence of agriculture, but no freshwater supply whatever to support it. Geologically, however, Scilly is a flat-topped mountain rising steeply out of the sea. If one postulates that sea level in Roman times was not less than 14 feet lower than it is today, then the plateau would have been dry land and all the scattered islands now visible would at once cease to be islands.

There has always been a good deal of evidence for this, in submerged structures visible from the surface which have been dated to various periods, including Iron Age and Roman occupation. And there have been the usual stumbling blocks, such as the submerged walls visible off the island of Samson, which could possibly be prehistoric fish traps built in the sea anyway. There are also stories of the "Lost land of Lyonesse" associated with that historically shadowy figure, King Arthur, who, in the Scillies, has succeeded in having an island named after him and an anchorage still called "Arthur's Harbour". One of the Guildford team's main objectives was to check on this "Harbour".

Their conclusion was, that it had been an anchorage rather than a harbour and that the main Roman trading port has still to be found. Kingsford-Curram wrote: "On our very first dive, off the southern tip of Great Arthur, we located the end of what we suspected was the harbour wall and I should make it clear right from the start, that this wall was a natural rock formation. It is now 15–20 feet below the surface on an average high tide, but it may be visible from the southern peak of the island at a low spring tide. I see it as a natural feature that was utilized and probably improved upon by man. I do not base this view on the horizontal (10 feet) and vertical (15 feet) surfaces that were so prominent. The wall is made of granite, a stone that is commonly found in cubic forms, with large flat surfaces and this, no doubt, accounts for its regular shape. I base the suggestion upon the absence of other rocks.

"All over the sea bed in the Eastern Isles, apart from where it is covered by drifting banks of sand, one finds jumbled heaps of granite boulders. These boulders lie just as they fell when the supporting land was washed away many, many centuries ago. Now the top of the wall has a clean horizontal surface (although deeply rutted in places) and there are no protruding, or loose, boulders anywhere along its length. I gained a distinct impression that the top of the wall had been cleared of obstructions. Similarly, the sea bed on the innermost side of the wall, except close in against the shore, was far less rugged than that on the outer side. It is quite feasible that some attempt had been made to clear and level the bed, because 2000 years ago it would certainly have been dry at low water. We tried to find evidence on the adjacent shore of 'harbour facilities', but met with no success at all. My conclusions are that the stone pier was a natural feature that was so situated that there was a safe and sheltered anchorage behind it. The probability is that those who used the harbour took simple steps to improve it, but that it was not the main harbour of 'Siluram' (as the island appears to have been called in 240 A.D.) and, consequently, did not receive sufficient use for a township to have built up on the adjacent shore. I am convinced that such a township existed."

This is the kind of evidence, and inference, acceptable to archaeologists although less dramatic than that required by editors and television producers. It is interesting that the legend of Arthur, who may have been a Romano-British general, dates to around the 5th century A.D., because there is a similar myth regarding an ancient Breton king whose palace at Ys is supposed to have sunk into the sea during the 5th century, at a point on the French coast directly opposite Scilly. Ys ranks with Lyonesse as a legend, but the coincidence of dates and the similarity of geographical position can hardly be ignored now. French attempts to locate Ys have been baffled by rich weed growth and the tendency of some continentals to give up when the water is cold and the visibility bad. With the Mediterranean temptingly on their doorsteps, one can hardly blame them. Mr. Kingsford-Currum speaks highly, however, of "Lyonesse". "The Scillies are a diver's paradise. I have dived all over the Mediterranean and in Ireland, but I have never found better visibility and diving conditions generally, or more interesting flora and fauna. There is only one snag—the natives are hostile. They want to turn the islands into a 'Millionaire's Playground' and unless you spend liberally, they don't want to know you." As Scilly has since become a "Treasure Hunter's Paradise" as well, investigation of those walls off Samson might well require support from a wealthy American foundation.

The next initiative was made by Major Hume Wallace, Chairman of Kingston Branch, at Selsey along the line of the famous "Beacon Cliff". The Selsey peninsula is quite clearly a drowned feature, and one of the first moves I made in the Church Rocks investigation was to hire an Auster from Portsmouth Aero Club and from it survey the general geographic area Eastney–Selsey, which is really one great bay sub-divided as Hayling Bay and Bracklesham Bay. Underwater, these bays are very different, because while Hayling is protected by the eastern edge of the Isle of Wight against the normal south-westerly gales, Bracklesham and Selsey are quite open to the full force and "fetch" of the winds. On 18 August, 1960, I opened the throttle and drove the Auster across the grass and when she lifted gained height over Langstone Harbour for a look at the wreck of the tug *Irishman*, as a guide to how much you could see down through murky water. It was quite remarkable how helpful this aerial view was. I then flew out to Church Rocks and made several passes over the target at heights varying between 600 and 100 feet. "Nothing at all to be seen but a dark, choppy sea stained with small streaks of white from breaking waves," I noted, and then turned east for Selsey.

With airbrakes out, I went round and round the Mixon, which stands above the submerged Beacon Cliff, watching a yacht running through the channel here which is supposed to represent the bed of the submerged River Looe and trying to match the actual scene with a description by Bede of the long-lost monastery which used to stand here. The exposed Mixon Bank fitted, but so did several other similar banks. The visibility, however, was extraordinary and you could see seaweed and shingle quite clearly down through the water. My impression was that the area was too eroded, too exposed, too large, and too dangerous for us to tackle at that time, considering that we were novices in all directions. On the way back I flew just out to sea off Sussex and noted the position of a great growth of weed, ship-shaped, in the shallows off Wittering. I did not dive this until six years later, when it turned out to be the wreck of the French schooner *Blanche*, stranded in 1910.

In detail, I learned nothing of great importance, but the overall view was very valuable, because the general shapes and altitude of the entire local coastline showed very great similarities to those of the North Frisian Islands, on the border between Germany and Denmark, which I had inspected from the air in 1951. The shapes and the inundation stories were similar, only my transport was different—on that earlier occasion I had been in a Meteor VII jet fighter travelling at near the speed of sound instead of trundling along in an old Auster with the brakes on.

In succeeding years, John Baldry and Roger Silver of Southsea Branch did some preliminary work on Selsey, especially Beacon Cliff under the Mixon, while Maurice Harknett and I spent a short period on a geological survey of Bracklesham Bay. The latter showed the full force of erosion, with the strata considerably mixed up, fossil palm trees being found in association with fossil mollusca at least 20 million years older. The most surprising features of that altogether freak landscape were the submerged cliffs, up to 20 feet high, capped by thin sheets of hard rock; possibly these were evidence of former coastlines, but it was impossible to date them. Geologists still argue as to whether the area has been under the sea three times or four times; about the only thing on which they are agreed is that the typical climate of this part of England is sub-tropical. The fossil palm trees in the Bay and the bones of prehistoric rhinoceros and elephant which have been excavated on the shore below highwater mark near the lifeboat station at Selsey are part-proof of this. I attended the last such excavation, in 1965, and kept in touch with other land archaeological work as a matter of deliberate policy. Archaeologists are agreed that what we still have on land in the Selsey area represents only the fringes of former Roman and Iron Age settlement; the bulk of it has been submerged, including the former Belgic capital. The coins from its Mint are still washed up.

But I had serious doubts as to the value of underwater exploration in this area at the present time, the basis of which was strikingly demonstrated in January, 1967, when the ordinary process of cliff erosion at Selsey exposed a Roman well. It also gave us for the first time the Roman land level—some 9 inches below the present topsoil. The well had been constructed of unworked stones found in the Mixon area, and the sea was in process of washing these away and scattering them along the beach, so that they were indistinguishable from the natural article which, so far as we knew, had never been used by man. It was shortly after this that Major Hume Wallace began his explorations at Selsey, a story he tells himself elsewhere in this book. One result was a meeting at Fishbourne, near Chichester, between Mrs. Margaret Rule, the archaeological conservationist at the Roman "Palace" site there, Major Hume Wallace, and myself. In the course of this we spotted, in the foundations of part of the "Palace", stones identical to those used in the eroded well at Selsey, which we now knew came from the Mixon area. This showed the extent of the underwater problem facing Kingston Branch, because it meant

---

A fantastic first! These are the first underwater pictures taken in Britain of basking sharks. A boat with divers on board approached one of these sharks off the coast of Devon while it was feeding on the plankton which reduced underwater visibility considerably. This visibility made photography difficult and the size of the shark—16 feet—also upset the photographer, Colin Doeg. He recalls taking the pictures—"finning backwards madly"—vividly, but cannot remember his exposure settings! Film was Tri-X. Camera: Nikonos. Behind the bubbles in the top picture on the right is another diver. In the bottom picture the shark's mouth is fully open acting as a sieve and straining the planktonic food from the water. The shark seemed oblivious to the divers presence, which, says Colin Doeg, "was just as well!"

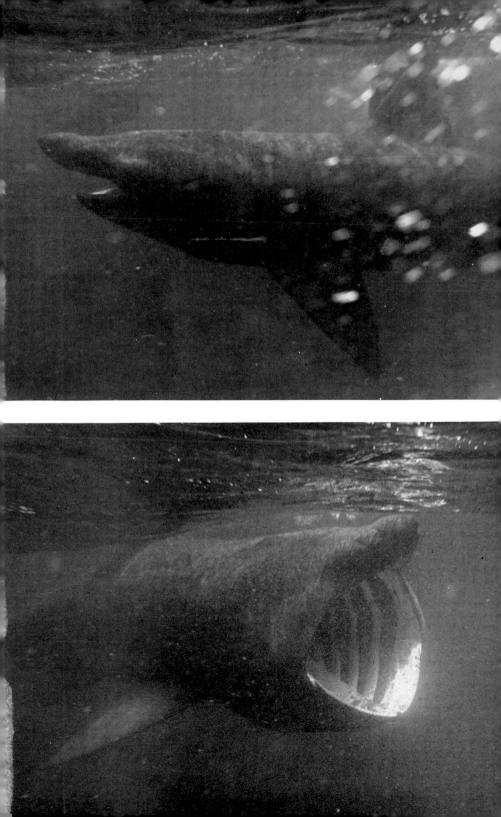

that the quarries on the Mixon had been in use from approximately 75 A.D. to the mid-19th century, with consequent disturbance of the site.

However, it was possible to compare notes on the extent of sea level charges which all three of us, separately, believed had taken place. The findings of land archeology in the area, as expressed by Mrs. Rule, would accept a rise of no more than about 14 feet. Major Hume Wallace, who then believed the cause to be geological in origin, had much the same figure in mind, although I understand he is now prepared to go to no more than 18 feet. My findings, based on Church Rocks, were the only vague figures. I supposed somewhere between 15 and 25 feet represented the rise in actual sea level which had taken place in the late Middle Ages; as far as Roman times went I had no facts, and therefore no opinion. The reason for my vagueness was that I knew that there were any number of variables. Firstly, I did not know the level of the land relative to the sea when it was inundated—it could have been very low-lying or even in parts actually below sea level to start with. Secondly, I knew that not merely sea level, but *seabed* level, varied also; the seabed was a fluctuating factor and you simply could not say that there were so many fathoms at such and such a spot, according to chart datum, because changes between one year and another could easily make a difference of 2 feet and might on occasion alter by as much as 8 feet. Thirdly, it was very hard in practice to say exactly what *present* sea level was. Those who live by the coast will know what I mean. We are continually astonished by some of the geologists, who speak of the oceans as if they were a bucket and the sea as if it resembled

---

Facing Top. A new kind of scientist. Taken underwater at Spithead by Alexander McKee this photograph shows Miss Margot Varese, who is an archaeologist first and a diver second. She has examined both the site of the wreck of the *Mary Rose* and the submerged church off Hayling Island. Trained by the National Diving Coach, Brian Booth, she had done only a dozen aqualung dives before taking part in these operations (see Chapter Two). *Bottom*. Photography at depth is often difficult due to reduced light. This picture of a wrasse was taken at a depth of 70 feet with natural light in the clear waters near the Eddystone Lighthouse. Tri-X. f8/60. Colin Doeg.

3

static water inside that bucket. The oceans are of course continually being affected by enormously powerful cosmic forces, and contain internal rhythms of which as yet we know little; but comparatively slight changes in oceanic circulation could have the most momentous effects locally, especially in the peculiarly semi-enclosed, restricted waters of the North Sea and English Channel.

It will require a great deal more than any of us have done so far finally to unravel the secrets of the vast mechanisms at work.

All the best wrecks are found on land, and ours were no exception. The most famous of them was the most important known wreck in the whole of north-west Europe, more interesting even than the Swedish galleon *Vasa*, deliberately discovered by Anders Franzén in 1956, as the result of a plan which he formulated in 1950 in his study and began to carry out in the sea from 1953 onwards. It really is as difficult as that, and the number of valuable historic wrecks which have been located as a result of a deliberate search can still be numbered on the fingers of one hand. If the adjective "valuable" is given its proper stress, then there are only three—Anders Franzén's *Vasa* (now raised and in a museum of its own), George Bass's statue-carrying Roman wreck (the latest of his discoveries off Turkey), and our own *Mary Rose*. Which represented the greatest triumph would be hard to say.

The *Vasa* was certainly the easiest, if such a task can ever be described as easy, but the technical means at Franzén's disposal were primitive. George Bass's search area was by far the largest, as he had no real "pin-point" position. Our own objective was uniquely troublesome, as she proved to be buried 20 feet down under mud—but we had the most intricate, efficient and expensive electronic equipment ever used in underwater archaeology, for the final, decisive strike. It was a far cry indeed from my first underwater discovery, made with the aid of swimming trunks, mask, snorkel, flippers, and a good, deep breath, only seven years before.

More important than any individual wreck, however, was the overall intention. When we began, in 1965, we did not know what such wrecks would look like in the Solent area, we had no idea what factors would have affected them; and nor did anyone else. The only information available was regarding Mediterranean wrecks, and even that was sadly out-of-date and unrepresentative, being little more than the early impressions of the aqualung pioneers. No real study had been made either of the few, mostly modern wrecks, we had so far examined. Our experience was almost entirely confined to submerged buildings. Consequently, the primary object of our operations was not to raise cannon but to erect principles. We frankly regarded ourselves as novices, with everything to learn.

About a dozen wrecks in all were considered (not all of them fresh discoveries, because it proved important to look again at hitherto unconsidered trifles). They covered the period approximately 1420–1920.

The oldest ship examined was Henry V's *Grace Dieu*, laid down in 1416, which had been surveyed and identified long before, in 1933. There is an enormous gap in the history of ship building which begins in 1066 with the Viking-type warships depicted in the Bayeux Tapestry and ends in 1628 with the Swedish galleon *Vasa*. After about 1700, the National Maritime Museum alone has no less than 25,000 ship and boat plans and some actual ships, such as the *Victory*, laid down in 1759, are still in existence. But the only significant evidence we have of the striking developments which took place between 1066 and 1628 are the scanty remains of the burnt-out *Grace Dieu* and the much richer story still to be extracted from Henry VIII's *Mary Rose*, which was laid down in 1509 and sunk in 1545.

Later, it became clear to us that the *Mary Rose* site was very much more important even than the above indicated; not merely was the hull and armament likely to be well preserved, but also the bodies of many hundreds of the officers and crew, from the Vice-Admiral downwards. In other words, a complete cross-section of Tudor military and naval society was likely to lie well-preserved in the mud and clay; a unique find impossible to duplicate on land. As soon as I realized this, I redoubled our already strict security precautions and, searching around for a phrase to describe this new conception in underwater archaeology, decided to use "closed community". This therefore took the place of the standard phrase "closed find", to describe a wreck in archaeological terms; a phrase with which by now I did not agree, as its definition, that everything found in a wreck must necessarily have been in use at a single moment of time, was open to wide misinterpretation, mainly because we are not the only people interested in the past. Some of our ancestors were, too, and a mass of Etruscan vases does not necessarily mean an Etruscan wreck—it could be somebody's collection wrecked on route to somewhere else. I have in my own "operational briefing museum" at home the handle of a vase from a real Etruscan wreck, around 700 B.C., but future archaeologists digging up my home would be inferring too much if they concluded that I actually used Etruscan dinner ware in the literal sense.

Because we had everything to learn, and might in our ignorance cause damage, we chose to begin operations on ships which, besides being of no great historic value, had been largely or partly blown up by 19th century divers. These were the *Royal George*, which had capsized at Spithead in 1782, and the *Boyne*, which had caught fire at Spithead in 1795 before grounding and blowing up off Southsea Castle. Both were three-decker line-of-battle ships similar to the *Victory*. Neither presented any great location difficulties. At this time, the *Mary Rose* was regarded very much as an off-chance, as there were no less than four different suggested locations for her, only one of which, a story that she was next-door to the *Royal George*, was in any way precise and therefore capable of rapid proof or disproof.

At the same time, again because we were ignorant, we incorporated into what I called Project Solent Ships a biological inquiry which entailed collecting marine specimens, specifically shellfish. The point about this is that while science has invented so far only very crude instruments for sampling what I may call the "Vitimin content" of sea water, shellfish are particularly fussy about their environment, and, to cut a long story short, once you have listed the shellfish in a particular area you know a good deal about the environment. This part of the project was directed by a local marine naturalist, Mr. R. V. Wells, and its relevance to a study of historic wrecks is obvious. Some of the materials in them are subject to corrosion, and the rate and type of corrosion must vary with the chemical constituents of the water; other materials are not so much corroded as eaten, and therefore both the rate and extent to which they are eaten will vary with the type of organisms present in the water, which will depend on the chemistry of the water, plus temperature, turbidity, and so on. In short, before you study the ship, you study the environment in which it lies.

There were other closely allied fields of study as well. One of the most important was into the operations and equipment of the early divers, who had worked on many of these wrecks before us. It would be valuable to know what artifacts they raised, what was the condition of those artifacts when raised, where were those artifacts now, and so on. We wanted to know what damage they had done to the various sites, and with what, and how. And perhaps also, locked away somewhere here, were clues to the real position of the *Mary Rose*. Later, I realized that a study of the battle of 1545, in which the *Mary Rose* was lost, might also provide clues to her position.

We went first for the *Royal George*, which had been dived on almost from the day she sank, culminating with Colonel Pasley's protracted attempts to blow her up during the five-year period 1839–1843. I doubted that he had succeeded entirely, but at least we were unlikely to cause any further significant destruction to the site, whatever we did. On the other hand, it was clear that the wreck might not be immediately obvious to the eye, especially in low visibilities, and so we paid great attention to establishing the natural environment away from the wreck. It was clay and mud, with a very thin scattering of light shingle —one piece only to the square yard approximately; very little organic growth; and a carpet of surface artifacts most of which dated to around 1900, the most modern being a fork and spoon both dated 1957, the oldest being a bottle of pop from the late 19th century.

The outskirts of the wreck showed scattered debris of a much older sort—a 32-pdr. cannon ball, rope rigging, and so on; plus odd mounds with a much higher shingle and organic content than the surrounding seabed, and containing part-buried artifacts. Ignoring several hundred items lying loose on the surface, I extracted a small pottery jar almost buried in one of these mounds, and this was subsequently dated to the late 18th century, the time of the sinking of the *Royal George*. The wreck itself, discovered on the third operation, also proved to be a mound, but quite twice as high as Pasley claimed to have left it. I should judge between five and six feet high, very extensive, with a high shingle and organic content, and with heavy and immovable lumps of concreted ironwork protruding in a number of places. This was contrary to Pasley's claim, but corroborated the complaints of fishermen, ancient and modern, who know where the *Royal George* is and avoid it like the plague. The alignment and the shingle content showed that this was the *Royal George* and not conceivably the *Mary Rose*. By now, I had the early divers' descriptions of both wrecks, and knew their alignments to start with. It would not be claiming too much to say that I "recognized" the *Royal George*.

Of course, all this is appalling from the point of view of the layman, who wants a romantic-looking wreck, sign-posted and labelled, moreover, for greater certainty. He is not going to get it. My favourite funny story concerns Pasley's five years work on the *Royal George*. The only artifact recovered with the name of a ship marked on it was a dog-collar owned by the late Midshipman Little and it was inscribed—H.M.S. *Victory*. Little had in fact died in the *Royal George*, but his previous ship had been the *Victory*. My second favourite funny story concerns the *Boyne*, which looks much like the *Royal George*, except that the mound is between 10 and 12 feet high, the shingle is larger and covers it completely, and there are very many dead oyster valves around. A Gosport mariner called Abbinett did the early salvage on the *Boyne* and recovered from her a field gun which had been captured by the Poles from the Swedes in a battle near Warsaw in 1702. Taking identification by artifact quite literally, this must mean that two continental armies fought each other 30 feet down off Southsea Castle. Consequently I actively dislike identification by artifact, particularly single artifacts, and prefer basics, such as position, size, alignment, etc.

My own test for artifacts was: are they buried, or are they not? And I liked to get a range of them, not just one. The small shingle mixed up in the *Royal George* mound might have been partly drift shingle held up in passage by meeting this obstruction, but almost certainly most of it was ballast from the lower part of the hull, as described by Pasley's divers. To find shingle under the sea would not alert a novice diver, or anyone else new to an area; it only leaps to the eye when considered in the context of the natural environment. The shingle on the *Boyne* was not ballast, it was drift shingle, in my opinion; but to understand why I think that, you too would have to see both ships. And also read the pioneer divers' reports.

As far as the *Royal George* was concerned, a great deal hung on the accuracy of identification. A rival team was in the field, and they also were looking for the *Royal George*, not to investigate it, but as a starting point to find the *Mary Rose*. If I had boobed in my identification, as a result of which I had searched the area around the wreck and declared it free of any sign of the *Mary Rose*, then my *Mary Rose* NIL RETURN would be wrong and, on that seabed, they would find her first.

Here, it is worth while considering briefly, for the benefit of those likely to be engaged in similar searches, the valuelessness of what should be reputable evidence. According to the eminent Naval authority Oppenheim, the *Mary Rose* sank in the Brading/St. Helens area off the Isle of Wight, and this was backed by an inscription in the *Victory* Museum in Portsmouth Dockyard, stating that she was "sunk in action with the French fleet off St. Helens". On the other hand Sir Robert Davis, the world authority on diving and the history of diving, stated: "The wreck was abandoned and forgotten until, during the *Royal George* operations, divers came accidentally upon the remains of the ship sunk 237 years earlier, lying but a short distance away." It seemed that Pasley's divers were meant and that, bearing in mind the limitations of search with helmet diving gear, the wrecks must lie within a few hundred feet of each other.

Now, I knew they did not (if I was right in my identification of the *Royal George* remains). I had eliminated Oppenheim (and the *Victory* Museum) earlier, on the grounds that the position five miles away did not fit a contemporary painting made of the battle and the sinking of the *Mary Rose*. I now eliminated Sir Robert Davis also, which left me with a news-paper statement ("between the *Royal George* and the buoy of the *Edgar"*) and an imprecise reference by a contemporary, the Elizabethan Admiral Monson, to the *Mary Rose*: "Part of the ribs of this ship I have seen with my own eyes; there perished in her four hundred persons." That meant shallow water. Contemporary accounts of the Tudor salvage operations rather implied shallow water, too, although they did not expressly say so. I turned the whole search towards an area in the shallows where, by intensive re-reading of the battle, I thought the *Mary Rose* might be. This was pure deduction. I knew she had to go from A to B, either via X or Y, and that she had sunk during a turn to port. I came up with several possible positions, one of which was less than 200 yards from where the *Mary Rose* actually is. If Scotland Yard could do with a good man. . . .

However, I very soon discovered that the seabed in this shallower area was extremely soft; and while the *Royal George* area would hold a wreck, here even a big ship was likely to disappear entirely from sight, leaving no surface trace. I had now also come across accounts by the divers who had really found the *Mary Rose*—not Pasley's men at all—but the actual inventors of the first workable helmet diving gear, the Deane brothers. John Deane had been working on the *George* at the time, in 1836, but had been called away to help a party of Gosport fishermen who had got their lines hung up again on a familiar but unknown obstruction. It was the *Mary Rose*, almost completely covered by sand, clay and mud, but with bits of timber still showing here and there, plus one gun. After this, it was clear that the Deanes, out of consideration for their business partners, the fishermen, would have left no surface trace of the wreck. I called off the search, to await the loan of electronic detection gear which Miss Joan du Plat Taylor was trying to obtain. I also fully explained to Miss Taylor my reasons for believing that the *Mary Rose* was in this area, and not near the *Royal George*.

This was the position at the end of the first year, 1965. In the spring of 1966 Miss Taylor called a meeting between ourselves and the rival group, in order to obtain co-operation, but this proved impossible. Apart from the fact that our methods varied and would not "mesh", they firmly believed the *Royal George* to be 650 feet south-west of the mound I had discovered, although they could produce neither mound nor artifacts in their esti-mated position. Being sure of this, they discounted naturally my NEGATIVE *Mary Rose* report for my *Royal George* area. We there-fore had to agree to disagree. They would continue to search to seaward of the 10 fathom line and we would operate in the area shoreward of that line. Shortly afterwards, John Towse and myself came across an absolutely authentic pin-point position for the wreck of the *Mary Rose*. The details I dare not give yet, but it was well inside our area, and a long way from the *Royal George*.

We therefore recommenced operations on a wreck which I was convinced was completely buried. The first stage consisted entirely of navigational exercises, to see how closely we could match a pin-point on a chart with the physical sea in fact, and then examine the seabed, and in particular to search for scour marks such as one would expect the gradual burial of a big ship to make. I found what I and Miss Varese both thought were such marks, in the right area, but I failed to convince most people, failed even to convince everyone that the *Mary Rose* was completely buried, although now I was sure that she was deep below the mud and clay, probably deeper than we could reach with our 3–4 feet long handspears. I stood by my opinion, if only on the grounds that for every dive the others had done, I had carried out three.

As an elementary instrument-detection test, I first used a compass. It was a splendidly simple idea in theory. A dinghy would be rowed across the site on a definite bearing which would be maintained by use of a bearing compass operated in the dinghy by Mrs. Margaret Rule, who had for some years been accompanying us, at our request, as archaeological adviser. The dinghy would tow its anchor just above the seabed and Margot Varese and I would hang on to this anchor, Margot prodding with a handspear and I watching "eyes down" on my own wrist compass for any significant waverings or variations which would indicate a mass of metal such as one would expect to find in a wooden warship. Surprising, maybe, but true. I thought there might be several hundred tons of it around. We dived and got started, poor Pete Cope at the oars of the dinghy being assisted by our flippers and the tide combined, and then there was one damn deviation after another. Each one was accompanied by a roar vaguely like an express train going through a tunnel, combined with a high-pitched whine, at an unmentionable distance above the backs of our necks. These were, of course, ships, the bane of diving life anywhere in the Spithead area, and as on this occasion we had four of them over us in 20 minutes, the dinghy crew forgot about bearings and just rowed like mad to avoid being run down. Still, we saw the scour mark.

The next time we tried a Wardle & Davenport magneto-meter, and that was even less funny. When you depend on a free loan, you cannot dictate the date, still less the tides and the weather. We got Force 6, Gusting 7, Force 8 Imminent. In these conditions we got a very strong contact on the fringes of the *Mary Rose* area and overboard went the marker buoy, followed by me. The wind was driving Maurice Harknett's motor boat away from the buoy—and me—and a strong tide was pouring into my face. So breathing madly I clawed my way forward towards the buoy, by following the marks left by the anchor as it had dragged across the bottom. After all that, the contact proved to be a buried, unmarked, uncharted cable which ought not to have been there at all. To give the instrument its due, it performed very well on two modern wrecks and a known "anchorage gash" area, by which time the Force 8 was no longer "Imminent", it was with us, so we went home to tea.

We got another magnetometer loan shortly afterwards, and this time both Miss Taylor and Peter Throckmorton, who identified a bronze age wreck off Turkey, were present. I knew of his work on buried Mediterranean wrecks, which were a great advance on the earlier efforts which used to pass for "underwater archaeology" in that area, and the main idea was that he should examine personally the very light sediments in the *Mary Rose* area. He had to do it in 9 inch visibility, which must have been damping after the Gulf of Taranto, but his verdict was a happy one: the qualities of the sediments were such that a big ship would sink deep into them very quickly, so giving extremely good preservation, possibly even of documents. We did our dive together on a magnetometer contact, which I

know now was the *Mary Rose*; but the dial readings were most
uncertain because of interference from at least one buried cable,
and we did not then feel able to place any reliance on it.

What was needed was a mud-penetrating instrument which
would not be affected by "gash" metal—a "pinger" or "boomer"
—which would also measure the amount of mud over the wreck.
John Mills of E.G. & G. International came down on 7 January,
1967, with the Edgerton "boomer", encouraged by five days of
flat calm and a fine weather forecast. But the weather broke,
unforecast, just eight hours too soon, and we went out of
harbour in near freezing conditions into heavy, breaking seas
which swamped the generator. We spent some five hours at
sea, the technicians trying to get the generator to work, and
occasionally succeeding, before it broke down for good and we
had to run for home anyway to avoid being swamped.

The best chance of all did not occur until the first week of
October, 1967, when E.G. & G. were planning a four-day
period of trials and demonstrations of a range of their equipment to potential customers. John Mills managed to arrange
that these should take place in the Solent area, based on
Southampton, which would enable some demonstrations to be
carried out if the weather was bad and a run or two over the
Mary Rose site if it was good and time allowed.

I was invited to spend all four days out with them, and it was
an extraordinarily interesting and valuable experience. They
were demonstrating two instruments operated in combination
with each other—sidescan sonar, which shows the patterns and
contours of the surface of the seabed, and the pinger probe,
which cuts down through the sediments to show their composition. In effect, as you steam along, you have a 500 feet
visibility view of the seabed on either side of the ship on one
instrument, and a deep cut into the sea bed, possibly to a depth
of several hundreds of feet, directly below your keel, on the
other. Both instruments record what they see on marked and
measured graph paper, which you may examine at your leisure
afterwards. A gale was forecast for the first day, but did not
quite measure up to expectations; calmer weather was forecast
for the second day, which turned out to be a full gale; and
on this day also an essential component of the pinger, the

hydrophone and hose, got happily wrapped round the prop of our 45-ton steamer.

I had the only aqualung on board, and if the *Mary Rose* was to be found that hydrophone had not merely to be cleared from around the screw and shaft but recovered into the bargain, and so I was for it. We tied up to a buoy off Fawley, with the tide ebbing at 3 knots and the wind blowing a full October gale. A 3 knot current is the underwater equivalent of a hurricane, and I had to hang on to first, the rudder, then the screw, with my left hand as I made two strategic cuts with the knife held in my right hand. I got the hydrophone and hose back, although the hose had been chopped beyond repair by the screw, but the job took a full 25 minutes.

On the third day a full gale was forecast, but did not arrive, although it was pretty lumpy in the Needles Channel; and the forecast for the fourth day was also wrongly pessimistic. The wind was very light and from the best direction for the *Mary Rose* site—north-west. Unlike magnetometers, sonar instruments will not work well in noisy conditions, such as those created by a rough sea or masses of shingle being moved over the seabed by a big spring tide, which was just what we had. On this day there were about twenty potential customers on board, including the Home Office, Police, oil companies, and a Dutch geological institute. Late in the afternoon, all demonstrations concluded, John said I could just have time for one or two quick runs over the *Mary Rose*. With such an audience, I felt a trace of "first night nerves"!

Coming from Bembridge, it was necessary to turn on to the standard "run-up" bearing by turning through more than 120 degrees and being used to conning motor boats over the course, I did not allow sufficiently for the larger turning circle of the steamer. So on the first run we passed in front of the bows of the *Mary Rose* instead of directly over the hull. This proved to be fortunate, because at a range of 200 feet the sidescanner picked up a beautiful picture of the wreck, to the astonishment of all concerned, not least myself. It implied that the sidescanner had penetrated the sediments, something it is not designed to do, and had never previously been known to do.

The next run was on the usual "marks", and on this occasion

both sidescanner and pinger simultaneously picked up the wreck. By this time, the customers were nearly climbing on each other's backs to get a look at the recording paper coming out of the machines. The sidescanner gave a less clear picture from directly above than it had from the side, which was interesting and valuable knowledge; and the pinger, although not in the best of health, showed that the wreck was 20 feet below the seabed. The use of both instruments together showed where the pinger cut was made—aft of amidships on a wreck at the right position, on the right alignment, and of the right size and shape to be the *Mary Rose*. It took us until late that night to work out, provisionally, why the sidescanner had picked up a buried object. The E.G. & G. team had never met this before, but what they had investigated before were geological features. The wreck was an un-natural feature which had been inserted into the seabed, disturbing the sediments and leaving clear scour marks—a depression with two mounds. Possibly we had a new principle here, because John Mills is now of the opinion that there was virtually no penetration of the sediments.

Later, it occurred to me that this principle, if principle it proved to be, was the direct equivalent of O. G. S. Crawford's work in aerial photography connected with the location of archaeological sites invisible from the ground. In the early days of underwater archaeology in U.K., gushing references to Crawford used to stick in my gullet, because the copy-cat is unlikely to succeed in a new environment; but now most probably the laugh was on me. Anyway, the next stage ahead is for a thorough two-day survey of the site, with this time the pinger working properly. We cannot air-lift the mud off to expose the wreck momentarily for final and formal identification, until we have a law to protect the site from predators. In this connection, it needs to be pointed out that during the "runs" across the target, we never stopped; the steamer was on the move all the time. Knowing the surrounding skylines like the back of my hand, I had no trouble at all in getting improved "marks"; but no one else aboard could ever return to that spot by design on the basis of what he saw.

By this time, nearly three years after I had first planned Project Solent Ships, we could no longer regard ourselves as novices. Some of the sidelines, especially in historical research, had turned up trumps. By historical research, I mean original work, the uncovering of a mass of new evidence, unknown and unpublished. I have space to refer only to the highlights, which were mainly connected with the pioneer divers, in a helpfully logical sequence.

Firstly, all histories of the development of diving gear will have to be rewritten, on the basis of this new evidence. In 1825 Charles Anthony Deane patented a smoke helmet which, by 1828, he and his brother John had developed into an efficient "open" diving dress similar to those now used in American Marinelands. With it, they went into the underwater salvage business, working on many historic wrecks, including the *Mary Rose*. I uncovered first, their full correspondence with the authorities regarding this, plus the correspondence and findings of the first Mary Rose Committee, set up in 1836. I uncovered, second, a diving manual which they wrote in that year, describing "Deane's Patent Diving Apparatus" in exact detail. I located, third, a portfolio of watercolour sketches which John Deane had commissioned to be made of the most important artifacts recovered from these wrecks, but which had been lost sight of since 1839. I discovered, fourth, by studying this portfolio and also the researches of people connected with Colonel Pasley, that the biology of wrecks, the deterioration of various materials, the presence of concretions, the nature of galvanic action, and so on, had been intensively studied in the 1830s and 1840s. Consequently, all the standard works which state that underwater archaeology began with the discoveries at Antikythera in the Mediterranean in 1900, will have to be amended. Underwater archaeology began at Spithead in the early 1830s, and the men who carried it out were not primitive sponge-divers using helmet diving gear, they did not really understand, but the men who had actually invented and proved that helmet diving gear in the first place. The work of 1830–40 was far superior to the Mediterranean work of 1900 and, indeed, to any work done in the Mediterranean up to about 1958.

Lastly, by putting together the results of our own Spithead researches for the years 1965–67 with the recorded findings of the pioneer Spithead researches of 1832–44, we collectively wiped the floor with most of the so-called Mediterranean "experts". I exclude, of course, the Americans, whose work was beyond reproach and in many respects well ahead of ours. The mistake most of the Mediterraneanos had made was the most human one of concluding that the world's horizons were bounded by the Mediterranean; more culpable was the work of British and other copy-cats who had gushingly accepted their dictums without thought. One of their oft-repeated dogmas was that wrecks in shallow water very soon break up and that therefore the only well-preserved wrecks will be found in deep water. Of course, this is true of certain shallow, rocky coasts, of which Durdle Dor is a good example, where seabed and wave action combined must act like a mincing machine. But we showed that it was anything but true of gently sloping sandy coasts, especially where the basic bottom was clay or mud; the long slopes gradually broke the force of the waves and the soft seabed often preserved a substantial part of the ship. We can now point to eight such examples, four of which occasionally uncover at low water of exceptionally large spring tides. You can't get much shallower than that!

The other, and more important, establishment of a new principle was founded on the destruction of the early Mediterranean dictum that wood in the sea lasted only twenty years (subsequently amended to read: "Except, of course, in the Baltic, where there is freshwater and no teredo"). But this amendment was forced by Anders Franzén, as a result of original thought on the *reasons* why wood disintegrated. His pioneer researches led the way and pointed to the right approach. The second genuinely thoughtful investigation was that on the composition of artificial fishing reefs carried out by the California Department of Fish and Game. These showed, conclusively, that in Southern California, wood was destroyed within three to five years, mainly because of the appetite of two marine boring worms, *Bankia cetacia* and *Teredo navalis*, the former sometimes exceeding 1 foot in length. They arrived at much the same figures for motor car bodies, although the cause of deterioration here was more directly the chemical content and temperature of the water, of which the existence of shipworms is an offshoot.

When we began we took notes of the fact that wood in Southern California waters lasted three to five years, in the Mediterranean no more than twenty years (as confirmed by Throckmorton conclusively), and much longer than 300 years in the Baltic. So we asked the question: "What is the figure for the Solent Area?" Not, repeat not, the figure for British waters. The reason was that we already knew, from first-hand investigation, that there were no less than four different underwater environments *within* our own small area; and heaven knows how many outside it! This was where the mollusca count came in, plus certain heretical observations and actions of my own. I actually noted the condition of wood in wrecks of various dates and worse, I took samples for examination by marine biologists. And blushingly, I offer the result: No *teredo*. No *Bankia cetacia*, either. Only the poor little gribble, not a shipworm at all, but a deformed crustacean. The worst enemies of wood could not get a footing in the Solent, because the environments were adverse. I was on the way to proving a new principle: study the environment, then you'll have some idea how long the various materials in your local wrecks will last.

For check purposes I located, or identified, or otherwise investigated the following: French barque *Monte Grand*, wrecked Bracklesham Bay, 1920; French topsail schooner *Blanche*, wrecked Bracklesham Bay, 1910; bucket dredger *Withern*, sunk Langstone Harbour, 1909; "composite" barque *Caduceus*, wrecked Hayling Bay, 1881; and a supposed "Convict Ship" in the Langstone Channel, probably more than 100 years old. In all of them, the wood was still in reasonably good condition, although attacked by gribble and in the case of a cleat from the "Convict Ship", very fragile. This latter I was unable conclusively to identify, so the dating is uncertain.

The really staggering figure was produced by two trawlermen who habitually use aqualungs. In September, 1967, they got their nets hung up on a wreck which they investigated by diving. The structure appeared so interesting that they brought two of the frames and planks back to harbour and notified Southsea Castle Museum, who notified me. The skipper, Mr. K. Cope, told me that he thought there was a fair chance of this wreck, in his judgement, being very old, possibly 16th or 17th century, and if so, they would be glad to carry out further investigation. I took one frame and one plank for drawing and photographing and showed them to Mr. W. O. B. Majer, of the Society for Nautical Research. His verdict was: at least 200–250 years old, possibly 300–400 years old. Part of the frame had been attacked by gribble, but the rest was in good condition and therefore may expose above the seabed only occasionally. For this reason, the data obtained by the pioneer divers at Spithead was important.

In 1836, the *Mary Rose*, after 291 years, still had woodwork showing (although this too might occasionally have covered); in 1844, the *Edgar*, after 133 years, was standing 13½ feet high above the seabed, both gundecks intact, like the *Vasa*, but, unlike the *Vasa*, the condition of the wood was fragile in the extreme; in 1839, the *Royal George*, after 57 years, was standing between 33 and 36 feet high (she was a three-decker); and in 1840 the *Boyne*, after 45 years, was standing between 8 and 10 feet (having burnt to the waterline and suffered a magazine explosion). There was enough information here to give great food for thought, but it was still possible for a scientific writer in 1967, to state that in the sea all organic material disappears after forty years; granted that this was a welcome 100 per cent increase on the old dogma-figure of twenty years, it demonstrates how Mediterranean-fixated British underwater archaeology still is, at least on the theoretical side.

Of great interest from this point of view also was the wreck of the *Grace Dieu*, for when I visited her in May and September of 1967, some 550 years had passed since her building and nearly 530 years since her destruction. Yet her timbers still appear above the tidal waters of the Hamble River, near Bursledon, at the low water of spring tides in the spring and autumn. Quite a good survey was carried out by wading and walking in 1933 and some members of that original team, including Major-General Prynne and Lieutenant Commander Naish of the National Maritime Museum were re-surveying her when I arrived in Maurice Harknett's dinghy on the second occasion. I had some questions to ask of the wreck. The usual answer is: "Oh, she is protected by the mud." This did not wash really, because of the numberless sea squirts I observed festooned on the ribs. Some shellfish can live under mud; sea squirts, however, require some sea water, and were a living refutation of too casual theories. Nor did the investigators show any interest in the shellfish which they dug up from under the mud during their excavations. I collected several specimens of a large, unusual clam and showed it to Mr. Wells. So far from being an ordinary beast, it had never been reported from the Hamble River before and proved to be the American clam, *Venus mercenaria*, which was first reported in British waters only in the late 1950s, and is an American national delicacy. Obviously, it was spreading up the Hamble from Southampton Water.

The *Grace Dieu* site was unusual because it appeared to be a boundary area, and a fluctuating boundary at that. Although tidal, a stream led fresh water draining off the fields almost directly to the wreck, and this mixture might well discourage many ship-eating organisms, as well as the acid quality of the water and mud, caused by the galvanic action resulting from the mass of metal junk lying about everywhere. While good for wood, it was merciless on metals and I was able to ascertain that steel corroded after only a year in these peculiar conditions. That mud might well repay chemical analysis.

The return that night from the *Grace Dieu*, however, proved to be the ultimate in British underwater archaeology, at least for Harknett and I. We had launched the dinghy from Moody's boatyard, downstream, with just enough water to float us out for the first quarter-of-a-mile. When we returned, this being an enormous spring tide, there was not enough water for that last quarter-mile and we were not prepared to wait half-an-hour or so. So we "dinghy-sledged" back to the quay, putting most of our weight on the back of the dinghy and using our feet as propellers. As my feet were bare, and there were some nasty sharp objects in the mud, I quite missed the poetry, romance, and adventure normally associated with underwater exploration, at least in the public mind. I defy even a French diver to make that proceeding sound glamorous (although the technique we used is a perfectly serious one usually employed for rescues over mud).

A disagreement had arisen as to which exactly was the most sternmost part of the wreck, impossible to resolve to everyone's satisfaction because the stern is way out in the river and only Harknett had thigh-boots. I therefore suggested to Maurice Young, the leader of Southampton B.S-A.C.'s archaeological group, that they might care to survey it by diving at high tide of a neap tide. I knew they had already done a good deal of mud and river work on Roman remains in Southampton, besides a search for the wreck of the frigate *Assurance*, wrecked on the Needles in 1753. Their historical research, carried out by John McKie, had been a model of what such work should be, and the Needles area was thought to be virtually un-divable, due to the very fast currents (up to 8 knots) and the extremely short slacks (20 minutes). They discovered that there was a further hazard—fresh water, flooding out underwater from the Isle of Wight chalk, meets the sea water and—bingo!—a dense white cloud results, reducing visibility to inches only. After a few dives, they bitterly nick-named the Needles "Sea Area Clammy Death"!

Anyway, they were not likely to be offput by the uninviting *Grace Dieu* site and on 8 October, 1967, they were able to report to the Committee for Nautical Archaeology: "A search was carried out in twelve feet of water with a visibility of six inches (which is usual for this area), working from a search line twelve feet long, thus giving us coverage of a 24 feet diameter circle centred on what I took to be the sternmost extremity of the wreck. Nothing of real interest was found, however, except several large pieces of rock (not local) which I believe to be ballast from the ship. No large timberwork was observed, other than that identified as frames, which is by no means conclusive, as there may quite well be large amounts of it buried under the mud. More diving and probing might prove this to be the case.

"Mr. McKee's remark about Henry V's fish farm is no exaggeration either; to carry out a search in extremely murky water with your face only six inches above the bottom can be quite an unnerving and hair-raising experience when small flatfish suddenly take off within inches of your nose. I would agree with Mr. McKee wholeheartedly when he says that he is of the opinion that the wreck may contain a number of artifacts and that a full scale excavation of the site may prove to be rewarding. In my opinion, provided enough local interest could be aroused, the whole thing could be completed in a very short space of time." The same idea has occurred to the National Maritime Museum, and provided that sufficient money can be raised to conserve the remains, the hull of the *Grace Dieu* might well go on exhibition in Southampton. It would be an easier proposition than raising the *Mary Rose*, for exhibition in Portsmouth, and be an excellent rehearsal for that costly feat.

Compared to the historic ships of Henry V and Henry VIII, the two most famous underwater explorations of 1967, those to the Scillies and to the Shetlands, were of no great importance. They concerned, respectively, the *Association*, a three-decker wrecked in 1707, and *De Liefde*, a Dutch East Indiaman wrecked in 1711. Both ships are from a fairly well known period and both, from their situation, come into the category of "Humpty-Dumpty Wrecks"; in short, not all the Queen's divers and archaeological men will ever put those two ships together again. So perhaps not too much has been lost, and certainly a great deal of publicity has been gained, from the frankly treasure-hunting aspect of these searches. Unfortunately, however, the publicity has been of the wrong sort and the Press generally is still under the impression that these performances represent underwater archaeology. What professional archaeologists will think of that, is enough to make one shudder.

In fact, both groups did start off with a vaguely archaeological purpose. And both did well in locating the approximate site early. *De Liefde* was found in 1965 by Lt.-Cdr. Alan Bax and some coins were raised, but the most thorough search took place in 1967, lasting ten weeks. Diving conditions were ideal. At a depth of 100 feet, visibility was never less than 40 feet and often in excess of 100 feet; even in 125 feet, the divers could always see the surface above them. On the other hand, the hull appeared to have broken up, the artifacts distributed widely and then in many cases covered in rock falls or enclosed in concretions resembling brown coal. The whole area was a maze of gulleys and rock falls, with some of the rock-faces solid with sea urchins. Even to map the remains seemed pointless, as the position of artifacts was fortituous, bearing possibly no relation to their original siting in the ship. And as this was a lone wreck, there would appear to be little chance of mixing of artifacts.

It was otherwise with the *Association*, which arrived on a popular rock in the Scillies at the head of a fleet, not all of which escaped disaster. The Scillies ranks as one of the most notorious accident black spots in the English Channel, rivalling the famous "Back of the Wight", and is not above collecting oil tankers when the occasion serves. Consequently, it is hard for anyone to claim that they have definitely found the *Association*, because although they may have found one or two pieces from that wreck, these may well be mixed up with the remains of many other wrecks and, unless excellent records are kept, it will prove impossible to differentiate.

A large number of rival teams were involved in the search and two at least did intend to map the area and did in fact make a start. But as the Ministry of Defence (Navy) was selling salvage contracts like hot cakes to all and sundry with a pound or two to pay and a bit of high explosive in the bank, their good intentions were literally blown to pieces. The amateur divers of the Naval Air Command Sub-Aqua Club, having located what they thought was the *Association* (although there seemed to be insufficient artillery around for a three-decker), were betrayed by their own publicity people, who trumpeted their triumph to the world. Rough mapping had hardly started when up came a rival treasure-hunter, the ex-Admiralty helmet diver Roland Morris, who had long had an option on the *Association*. All he had to do was note where they were diving, and then go down himself. Even had there been an exclusive rights contract to the *Association*, matters would still have been difficult, because how could anyone prove that any site in that area really was the *Association*? The Press were quick to pour in at the news of treasure and consequently the term "underwater archaeology" is now synonymous in Britain with loot and a bit of quick bang-bang. It will probably not be long before someone steals into Portsmouth Dockyard at dead of night and blows up the *Victory* in the hope of plunder—and serve the Navy jolly well right if they do.

One unexpected result of the "Solent Ships" project was the establishment of a couple of experimental lobster farms. Chasing creepy-crawlies round the rocks is perfectly all right when you have nothing better to do, but when underwater time is limited and valuable, you tend to resent this necessary diversion of effort. It is necessary, usually, because of family pressures for sea food. "While the old man's out wasting his time on old dead things (archaeology) he might just as well get us some live things to eat," fairly well expresses the feminine reaction to diving as a hobby. Every modern miss, alas, is an unrepentant cavewoman under the skin, albeit much lazier. Skinning skate, sole or plaice is too much like hard work for them, and what is required to keep them happy is something which can be cooked in its skin, preferably by hubby. For this unscientific reason, the first lobster farms were set up, both in U.S.A. and U.K. One sees now why cavemen always dragged cavewomen off to their caves by the hair; the latter were too tired to walk.

What was necessary was a stock of live lobsters suitably concentrated and of the right age groups for cooking, from which sufficient specimens could be collected in a few minutes when required. This philosophy is probably in the mainstream of science after all, because most inventions, from slaves to machines, had a marked distaste for manual labour as a prime motive of the inventor. We certainly had that necessary qualification. We had the other qualifications also—knowledge of the local underwater environments and of the habits of lobsters and crabs on a face-to-face, person-to-person basis. In this, we were well ahead of State science, starved of funds as usual.

The first controlled experiments in lobster stocking, so far as we knew, had been carried out by members of our own branch, Southsea B.S-A.C., in the late 1950s and early 60s. The point about the lobster and the crab, and many other sea creatures as well, is that their survival depends largely on the possession of a secure base or home. Caught in the open by a predator, they have little chance of making a successful defence. Consequently, or so we thought, to increase the number of homes available must increase the number of lobsters. To do this is not comparable at the moment with breeding lobsters, but it does conserve the stock at market size; no doubt we will work down to the little 'uns in due course. Success in this line is far more important than it would be on land, because although a cow may have many calves, the number does not approach 10,000, which is what the female lobster gives birth to at one sitting, more or less.

Food for thought lay in the results achieved by John Towse and his chums on a rock area off Haslar, near Portsmouth, in a single year of a small-scale experiment. Simply by snorkel diving, without use of aqualungs, they had ascertained that there were 14 natural homes for lobsters just offshore, plus some accidentally placed man-made homes, to which they added some of their own, making a total of 7 artificial homes, as against 14 natural.

In a single year, 1963, operating only in their lunch-hours, they took 44 lobsters from the 14 natural homes and 39 lobsters from the 7 artificial homes, plus 4 lobsters found in the open away from cover. The highest number of lobster taken from a single home was 17, this being an accidental man-made object. The largest male taken was of more than 10 lbs, the largest female more than 4 lbs, and the average weight was over 2 lbs. The average shop lobster is only about 1 lb. Four divers only were concerned, operating for only 45 minutes at a time, at mid-day, when the tide and weather were right, and without the aid of breathing apparatus.

As this was a natural rock area, it was not disturbed by trawls and artificial homes could be added at will; as it was not a traditional lobster ground fished by professionals, they were the first-comers and in effect it was theirs. Consequently, what Harknett and I were looking for was something similar, a virgin area un-trawled and un-fished, to make similar experiments of our own. The obvious thing to do was to find wrecks which no one else had located, as these provide the basis for a farm, already stocked, and to lay down further homes to see if we could by this means preserve additional lobsters which otherwise would fall victim to predators. In short, to increase the numbers of the desired creature, not just to hunt or trap it. We did in fact become more enthusiastic about the experiments than about the lobsters themselves; and hoped to go on experimenting, and getting a mass of relevant facts and figures, for at least a year or so until, as was inevitable, pirates saw us at work, made a note of the location, and plundered it; an unethical, but at present legal, proceeding.

Two of the wrecks we found seemed suitable for experiment. One was the wooden barque *Caduceus*, on the Hayling side of the Solent; the other was a concrete barge on the Isle of Wight side of the Solent. The *Caduceus* was a low-profile wreck, rather exposed to south-west winds, but excellently stocked with lobsters—Harknett took seven of them, totalling 22 lbs, in the first 20 minutes of the first day. The concrete barge was a solid, high-profile object in the protected lee of the Isle of Wight, but being too roomy produced on average, in its natural state, two lobsters only at a time, albeit large ones up to 10 lbs. We therefore put more effort into the *Caduceus*, laying down ten motor car tyres, a heavy drain-pipe affair, and a large number of ridge tiles, in collaboration. Harknett alone laid down a few ridge tiles beside the concrete barge. Apart from taking legal size lobsters and crabs, we left the environments untouched.

We discovered that a colony of bass habitually slept under the broken decks of the *Caduceus*, screened by the weed, using this as a base for their raids along the coast. As far as we knew, the detection of this habit was a new discovery and we left the bass in peace in order to study their habits. For the same reason, we did not molest the conger up by the bow, although congers are supposed to prey on lobsters and certainly prey on crabs, quite apart from the fact that it might well compete for food with the lobsters and crabs. At this stage, it was of much more importance to establish the conger as predator or competitor than rudely to assume that he was, and kill him off. That would come later, only with proof, and only then if we were satisfied that the relationship was purely destructive, which it might not be. The first batch of artificial homes provided a surprise—within a short time they filled up with large prawns; and we began to consider whether it might not be necessary to think about providing an increased food supply for the extra lobsters we hoped for next year, and if first-quality mussels, transplanted from a nearby site, would be acceptable to our 'herds'. As an experiment, we also transplanted a pregnant lobster found on Church Rocks to our new "farm", to see if she would settle in. This was the situation when the winter brought the operations of 1966 to a close.

Our habit of being successful in searches for new wrecks, and then keeping them "secret" in order to study the natural environment and experiment with it in a controlled manner, rather than throw them open to every mad spear fisherman and mighty underwater hero in the business, caused some resentment. Some mighty underwater heroes were mightily upset. We therefore slaved to get Harkett's boat early in the water in the 1967 season, long before anyone else was afloat. On 4 April we succeeded and set sail for a slice of suffering. Harknett's new suit was so smart that he could go to a wedding in it, but I looked like an exceptionally tatty tramp, all patches and mends, and was clearly going to feel chilly.

We made straight for the *Caduceus*, and were horror-struck by what we saw in 3 feet visibility. With foreboding for our tied-on tyres, I had watched from shore the winter swells sweeping the wreck site, but not under any circumstances had I conceived that we could lose the heavy drain-affair or the ridge tiles, which I personally had stuffed securely in under the decks, really wedging them tight. Yet gone they were, all of them. And there was a lot more of the wreck showing than we had ever seen before. Clearly, the site had been scoured down about 2 feet. I subsequently ascertained that this lowering of the seabed level had taken place around the same time, early 1967, on the "Convict Ship" in Langstone, the *Blanche* in Bracklesham Bay, and on Church Rocks also.

In early February, however, the trend must have been the other way, for a shore dive to the "Convict Ship" showed that she was buried at that time. It was not until later in the year, by discussing the matter with Frank Martin and Mr. K. Cope, that I knew for sure what had happened. The lowering of seabed level at these points had much exposed the wrecks, so that lines-of-travel which previously were clear were now continually resulting in snagged nets. Our first "farm" had been broken up by the trawls, against which we had thought the wreck structures would give protection.

Even more depressing, momentarily, on that first April dive, was the discovery that the *Caduceus* was now uninhabited... No lobsters, no edible crabs, no shrimps, not even a bass. We had discovered, the hard way, and at the high cost of nearly 14/-

for lost nylon line, one half a principle : sites exposed to winter wave swell will be deserted in winter. A little lobster I caught during the summer by Portsmouth Harbour entrance best illustrated this. I took him ashore to show to some children, then put him back. When on shingle, in the area of the mildly-breaking waves, he could not move; was quite helpless, swept back and forwards like a piece of driftwood or an old bottle. I had to dump him deeper out before he could swim.

Our hearts in our neoprene bootees, we up-anchored and set off over the icy grey seas for the Seaview "farm" in the lee of the Isle of Wight. I did not bother to dive. Normally, only two lobsters came from this wreck per visit and that would suffice only for Harknett. That is, if there were any there at all, which I now doubted, for early shore dives by myself and other people had produced nothing from many known lobster-bearing areas. In fact, there proved to be eight lobsters there, many of them tucked safely into Harknett's ridge-tiles. Statistics-wise, this gave an increase of some 400 per cent above previous average. And we had another half-principle : lobsters in winter will gather in a high-profile protected area, safe from winter gale-surge. The full principle we were postulating now became, therefore : lobsters do not necessarily seek deeper water in winter, as is widely believed by both fishermen and divers, they merely seek *protected* water, still water, and depth is merely one way of providing this. A high-profile sunken structure, acting as a breakwater, will serve equally well.

My first thought was to transfer all farm experiments in future to such structures in the lee of the Isle of Wight, and leave the more open area of Hayling Bay, with its many wooden wrecks, alone. And then the pirates came, rustling our stock, with shrill whoops of rodeo triumph and flourishing of sextants.

The experiment, as such, was in ruins. What we were after, was not so much lobsters now, as facts and figures; with the "farm" wide open to raiding, these would be incomplete and therefore valueless.

We therefore cry "murder". If we could legalize our claim to parts of the seabed, we would plead, "Me'lud, the defendants did slaughter our statistics, maliciously, with malice afore-thought . . . We ask, me'lud, for nothing less than that they be reduced to the ranks of snorkel-class divers and be branded forever on the flippers."

I, at least, could afford such leniency. Indeed, I was almost smug. In a book I had just published, *Farming the Sea*, I had predicted that just this sort of thing would happen, if occupation of the seabed was not legalized on the lines of the contracts for North Sea gas. I had also made the rather unfair remark, that, so far, no State seafarm had ever been raided by pirates, because there was nothing there yet worth nicking. The implications now were infinitely pleasing. The raid was a sort of back-handed compliment to success.

WRECK DIVER

by Derek Cockbill

Derek Cockbill is Diving Officer of the British Sub-Aqua Club.
Has been diving since 1957. Born in Sheffield, he has lived for
many years in the West Country. Is this country's greatest
authority on wreck diving and was in charge of the largest
piece of amateur marine salvage ever completed in this country
on the S.S. *Maine*.

OF the many facets of underwater activities there is probably
none which stirs the imagination of the amateur diver more
than that of wreck exploration.

To explain its fascination is difficult and defies logic; a ship
sinks, its life's purpose ended to become one of many hundreds
lying in the dark waters around our coasts, forgotten for the
most part, disintegrating slowly and to the unimaginative, just
a rusting pile of scrap.

Even in life many of these vessels were only coastal tramps
with little of the glamour surrounding their more elegant ocean-
going sisters and so in death one would imagine they have little
to commend them. And yet in the alien surroundings of their
watery grave, whether large or small they assume a new per-
sonality with an aura of mystery which from the first contact
acts like a magnet, converting the mere aqualung diver into a
wreck-hunting addict.

My conversion came during 1961 when in the early part of
that year Torbay Branch—B.S-A.C. met to discuss its diving
programme for the coming season. To date our diving had
followed the pattern of many other diving groups, the main
objective being crab and lobster hunting but it was felt we
needed something more to stimulate interest and after much
discussion it was decided we would attempt to locate and
identify as many wrecks within the 20 fathom line along
the South Devon coast as possible with the ultimate object
of recording the history and untimely end of each vessel

found, with "before" and "after" photographs where available.

We decided to base our operations in the Salcombe area for two main reasons. The first was that the waters west of Start Point promised better underwater visibility at the depths we expected to operate (we could tackle the more hazardous diving conditions in the murkier waters east of Start when we had gained more experience of wreck diving conditions) and we realized the deeper the wreck the greater the chance of it being reasonably intact. At depths greater than sixty or seventy feet the pounding effect of storms is minimal nor are wrecks at this depth affected by the "wetting and drying" action of the sea which accounts for the rapid deterioration of those in tidal waters. The other consideration was due to the fact that this area had taken a heavy toll of shipping over the centuries and would therefore afford us the greatest scope.

And so a start was made and I became responsible for the initial research which logically began with direct local investigation and an examination of large scale Admiralty Charts of the area on which all known wrecks in open water are charted. From the charts we were able to pinpoint two or three wrecks lying within reasonable steaming distance of Salcombe which I felt were worthy of immediate investigation whilst from the local lifeboat and other records (not to mention the many local legends), we were able to establish rough locations of a number of wrecks which had run aground and broken up on this rugged coastline.

As the diving season approached discussions took place as to which sites we should investigate first and it became apparent that old habits die hard as the majority were in favour of visiting areas where we might find evidence of those wrecked on shore rather than those in deeper water. The reasons for this view was that in shallower water our air endurance was greater than at depth and in the event of our not locating a wreck—then there was always the delectable crab and lobster to fall back on!

One particular wreck I was most anxious to find was known by the local fishermen as the "railway line wreck" (for a reason we were never able to establish). It was shown on the chart to lie in an average depth of 100 feet, standing clear of the seabed by approximately 40 feet about one mile from shore midway between Bolt Head and Bolt Tail. However, on every occasion during the early part of that 1961 summer my suggestion that we attempt its location was overruled for some alternative inshore site and although we successfully located and identified a number of inshore wrecks they were badly broken up with little more to offer than twisted ribs and shattered plates, like some weed-grown underwater scrapyard.

One Sunday morning in June, however, we spent an abortive morning in search for the final resting place of the ill-fated *Ramilles*, a 74-gun Man O'War which ran ashore in a gale close to Bolt Head in 1760 with a loss of 700 lives. It was unfortunate that the area was also the haunt of a colony of grey seals which, judging from the extremely poor catch of crustacaea, had made serious inroads into the stocks of these delicacies much to the annoyance of the foraging diving-party. With half a day's diving gone and precious little to show for it, morale was at a low ebb so my plea for a crack at the "railway line wreck" was greeted with apathetic approval—if only to humour me— and so the anchor was raised, and we steamed for the site about a mile distant. The sea was mirror calm and, as we approached, the area we could see the surface was disturbed—which we assumed was due to some large obstruction disturbing the flow of the flood tide over an otherwise flat sand and shingle seabed.

Steaming ahead of the tide, we dropped our anchor and drifted, hoping as the anchor swung suspended just clear of the seabed, it would foul some part of what we were sure must be the wreck. Suddenly the anchor warp stiffened, bar taut, in the strong tide and we knew we had hooked something. Quickly we donned our diving gear and, waiting only until the tide had slackened sufficiently to allow safe diving, we dropped into the water and headed down the anchor rope—a thin white line disappearing into the abyss below and beyond. The water became gradually colder as our depth gauges approached the 80 feet mark and still the water around seemed as black as night when, below us, a grey form suddenly began to take shape before our eyes—and in a moment we were on the upper structure of what seemed to us to be a monstrous wreck.

In pairs we left the anchor, which had conveniently snagged the guard rail, and gradually worked our various ways fore and aft, to find the ship virtually intact apart from the super-structure (which we eventually learned had been dispersed to reduce the wreck as a hazard to navigation), lying on an even keel as if still steaming towards the shore.

I shall never forget that first sensation of drifting along the upper decks, a short, thick grey marine growth covering every part; dropping through an open hatch to the gloomy bowels of the ship, the engine and boiler rooms now dark and for-bidding, occupied only by the slowly drifting wrasse, pollack and pouting, seemingly unconcerned by our presence. On the fo'c'sle the anchor cables lay on the deck, disappearing forward to support the port and starboard anchors still in their hawse pipes, and through the deck to the forward chain locker deep in the forepeak. Finning over the bow, we turned to face the vessel as if to see it steaming straight at us and, as we followed the old-fashioned upright stem to the seabed fifty feet below, we could not escape the feeling of awe that this once proud vessel still retained a ghostly dignity in its silent resistance to the slow, inexorable erosion of the sea which would bring about its inevitable disintegration.

Our return to the hot, sunlit surface brought a barrage of questions and cross-examination from those who had been unable to dive and, although we might have been guilty of some slight exaggeration here and there, our excitement was infec-tious and no one spoke of anything else but how soon we might return to the site. The fever of wreck-hunting was upon us all.

In the weeks that followed all other forms of diving were for-gotten, and we dived many times on the wreck, collecting such small items as a brass plate engraved "Seaman's W.C.", a fork bearing the stamp of the Atlantic Steamship Co., a brass door lock stamped with the name of the Glasgow manufacturer and the following week—the key to fit it. We became familiar with every part of the ship from the 4·7 gun on the poop deck to the Seamen's quarters in the fo'c'sle, and with each dive the fascination was renewed.

It was on one such occasion towards the end of the summer that the Skipper of the *Princess*, which we charted for these trips from Salcombe, idly commented that a vessel of such a size might well have a bronze propeller which could be of considerable value, but as we had already examined the spare prop bolted to the after well-deck and found this to be iron we presumed the large four-blader underneath the counter stern would be of the same material. However, a closer examination would not come amiss and so armed with a hacksaw and torch, two of us dropped over the side and descended to the deck. Following the contour of the massive stern to the rudder, we were soon able to discern the silhouette of the now-still propeller blades, and we quickly dropped to the seabed alongside. It was particularly gloomy here, what little light we had on the upper deck was now obscured by the stern looming menacingly above us but in the light of the torch, the first cut of the hacksaw revealed a dull gleam of gold—it was bronze.

From that day forward the talk in the Club was of nothing but salvage and during the winter months that followed plans were formulated and in spite of lack of equipment and experience, the money to come from what we were convinced would be a successful conclusion was virtually "in the bag". When I look back on the trials and frustrations of those months that followed I go hot and cold with the thought of how near we were to utter disaster so many times.

On the research side I had not been idle and facts concerning a number of wrecks we were currently investigating were gradually building up including our "railway line wreck" which proved to be the S.S. *Maine*, a 3,600 ton cargo steamer built in 1907 and originally named *Sierra Blanca*. She was *en route* from London to Philadelphia with a cargo of 500 tons of chalk, goat-hair and ferrugreek seeds (no mention of railways lines in this manifest and is it likely that we would be exporting such a valuable wartime cargo?) when she was torpedoed at 8 a.m. on the 23 March, 1917, off Start and badly holed in No. 2 hold on the port side. Help was at hand, however, from a mine-sweeping Flotilla returning to Plymouth from Dartmouth and an attempt was made to take her in tow and beach her but at 12.15 p.m. the same day she sank only a mile from shore to lie undisturbed for 43 years.

Face to face with a baby lobster. Lobsters often go for a walk. This youngster chose the rocky area off Peacehaven, near Newhaven. Photographer Tony Baverstock spotted him, sank to bottom and remained still. Intrigued, the lobster moved forward and right into focus of the close-up lens of Calypsophot camera. Depth 30 feet. Flash, f22/125.

Above. Fish that have not seen divers before often come close enough to touch. Penny McDonald sits on the seabed beside a sunken Mulberry unit 40 feet down, two miles out off the Sussex coast while photographing pouting with a Siluro camera. Black-and-white from a High Speed Ektachrome transparency, f16/60. Kendall McDonald (see Chapter Five). *Below.* Portrait of a stinger! Jellyfish, photographed at St. Abbs, Scotland, with Nikonos held at arm's length! Tri-X, f16/30. Colin Doeg.

Our main concern at this stage was to trace the name of the owners of the wreck and if possible arrange its purchase, as this is the only satisfactory way of ensuring the full benefit of any salvage operation. It was only after a great deal of correspondence that we unearthed the Insurers who, having paid the owner's claim for a total loss, now held subrogation rights for the vessel. After much delay and bargaining we were able to purchase the *Maine* outright for £100. It was ours at last!

The next major problem was to separate the propeller from the wreck and, during the following season, after much planning we were successful in doing this, using submarine blasting gelignite. However, due to winter weather fast approaching, our only attempt to lift the propeller that year was unsuccessful.

To dismiss a whole season's diving in one paragraph is easy in retrospect, but in fact those months are engraved on my heart as being the longest—in part rewarding as well as the most frustrating—I have ever experienced. One gratifying outcome of the use of explosives was the removal of every vestige of marine growth on the propeller, revealing the manufacturer's name and job number from which they were able to trace details of its weight and dimensions as $6\frac{1}{4}$ tons and $17\frac{1}{2}$ feet respectively. As a result of these inquiries, the manufacturers also made us a very attractive offer for its scrap value should we raise her. This made us even more determined to succeed.

After carefully considering the various methods we might adopt, we finally decided to err on the cautious side, in view of its value, and hire a lifting vessel capable of winching and transporting the prop to Plymouth, which was the nearest port where cranage was available for loading it on to a truck. Following much discussion, we were successful in obtaining permission to hire an Admiralty mooring vessel, the *Barbastel*, when it was next in the vicinity of our site. We realized this would prove more economical than hiring it to make a special journey—as it was we had to accept a charge of the order of £20 per hour.

Our chance came when the *Barbastel* was due to lay racing marks for the Naval College at Dartmouth and would thus pass close by the *Maine* on its return journey.

The day dawned bright and clear and, again using the

Princess, we rendezvoused with the *Barbastel* at 10 a.m. at the site.

During the previous week, in appalling diving conditions, we had shackled a heavy lifting hawser to the propeller laying the hawser along the sea bed to which we connected a thinner wire and a marker buoy to the surface. The idea was for the *Barbastel* to anchor close to the buoy, pick up and winch in the thin wire until the heavier lifting wire was over her bow—when it should then be able to lift the full weight of the propeller clear of the water—and steam for harbour. We imagined our presence would only be that of spectators, but fate was to take a hand; the marker buoy and thin line were hauled aboard the *Barbastel* and winching commenced but before they were able to secure the heavy lifting wire the *Barbastel* was suddenly swung to starboard by a strong gust of wind, with the result that the whole weight of the vessel was thrown on to the thin lifting wire—which stiffened like a bow string and parted, allowing the heavy hawser to fall back into the water.

It is impossible to describe the feelings we experienced during those first few moments after the enormity of this quirk of fate dawned upon us. I am sure I aged ten years in as many seconds. With the lifting vessel on hand and a successful outcome just within our grasp, there was only one course of action to take. Without further ado, two of us kitted up and dived with a line to locate the end of the heavy hawser. We discovered that, in dropping back into the water, it had coiled itself about the stern of the *Maine*—in appalling confusion—but we eventually located the end and attached our line. This was hauled up by the small crabbing winch in *Princess*, with everyone praying it would not snag on some part of the wreck. Mercifully there were no complications and when we had hauled as much of the hawser as the small winch would support, a line was thrown from the *Barbastel* to *Princess* which we secured to the end of the hawser, now only a mere twenty feet below the surface. With the *Barbastel*'s line secured, the *Princess* was cut free and we stood off to watch with bated breath for the lift to be resumed. For what seemed like a lifetime we stood there— too far away to see what progress was being made—when, suddenly, a blade broke the surface and we all went wild. The fruits of two years' labour and frustration hung just above the water before our eyes and we realized with indescribable relief that we had "made it".

The propeller was eventually bought by the original manufacturers, J. Stone & Co. Ltd., and transported to London for scrap and, although we felt it deserved a better fate than the melting pot, I believe a piece has been preserved by the Company to mark an unusual resurrection. We eventually received a cheque for £840 which, after deducting £400 for expenses incurred including the purchase price of the *Maine* we were able to make a clear profit £440 plus a 3,600 ton wreck now lighter by 6¼ tons.

We still dive regularly on the *Maine* and, with every visit, there is something new to fascinate. I hope we may continue for many more years. It was our first real wreck—and it has given us a great deal of pleasure and excitement, not to mention a little profit!

Although I have made much of the thrill of wreck diving, the research into wrecks holds an equal, though different fascination for me—and it is not until one starts to dig into the past that one realizes the many widely varying sources of information that are available if one is prepared to delve deep enough.

The trade routes around our coasts are well-travelled paths and the progress of vessels following them, with cargo and passengers for all parts of the world, are well documented and recorded, particularly so if some fate should befall them.

For the wreck-hunter to be successful in his quest for the exact location and identification of a wreck it is essential to study as much information as is possible to obtain and, as well as contacting the more obvious sources—such as the Hydrographic Department of the Admiralty, The Shipping Editor, Lloyds, London, E.C.3, the Ministry of Transport and Trinity House—there are many others which can prove equally rewarding, dependent upon the age and type of vessel. These include such possibilities as the local lifeboat, museum, Customs and library records; Shipping and Mercantile Gazettes; Master's deposition before a public Notary; records of official inquiries into wreckings, etc. Indeed, the possibilities are almost endless. One of the fascinating aspects of pursuing such inquiries, if you are prepared to be diligent, is the variety of information that comes to light. With it, a picture can be built up of the vessel and the cause of the loss—which may help a great deal in its eventual location and positive identification. Local knowledge, sometimes correct but more often notoriously inaccurate, can nevertheless be a most useful guide—provided every effort is made to obtain documentary proof to substantiate the heresay. The truth of these remarks was to be borne out during our next venture.

Flushed with the success of our efforts on the *Maine*, we decided to turn our attention to the investigation of another large wreck in the area, supposedly sunk during the First World War according to local gossip, on which Salcombe fishermen occasionally snagged their "pots". No one seemed to know its name so, along with another dozen "unknown" wrecks, it was cheerfully designated the "coal-boat" (a fairly safe bet for a small coastal tramp of that era!). With a wreck charted in the vicinity and officially recorded as "unknown", the picture was further complicated by the added information from the Hydrographic Department that the charted position also covered a smaller wreck of an earlier date.

A great deal of digging revealed the information that the *Riversdale*—a 2,800 ton cargo boat—was torpedoed in the bow and beached near Prawle Point on the 18 December, 1917. In an attempt to refloat and tow her stern first to Plymouth the for'ard bulkhead collapsed and she suddenly sank, with a loss of two lives. Although these facts were confirmed by the Hydrographic Department there was insufficient evidence to confirm that the *Riversdale* and the "coal-boat" were one and the same.

We had full details of the *Riversdale*'s construction and, even though it was the type of vessel "built by the mile and cut off to length" as required with little to distinguish it from its contemporaries, we were still hopeful of finding some confirmatory clue as we steamed out of Salcombe estuary and headed for Prawle Point one bright summer Sunday morning in an effort to locate and dive on her.

Arriving in the area after a half hour's steam, we used the time-honoured method of coastal navigators for pinpointing their position at sea when in sight of land by lining up the "marks" given to us by the local fishermen to form transit bearings. The point of intersection should, we knew, put us over the wreck and, with an echo sounder for confirmation, its location should be relatively easy. Unfortunately, as is often the case in searches of this sort we were not immediately successful and, although we varied our position slightly, the echo sounder refused to draw that sudden vertical trace on its sensitized graph paper which we had come to recognize as a sure sign of some alien structure on an otherwise level seabed.

Haphazard searching is a time consuming and usually unrewarding pursuit and so, after a few minutes of this aimless exercise, we again took up the original position we had been given. Having prepared a large buoy and line suitably weighted, we tossed it overboard to give us a datum point. From here we began a circular sweep, steaming in increasing circles around the buoy, with the echo sounder ticking away in the hope of passing over the wreck. Suddenly, from a steady depth recording of 150 feet the trace leaped to 110 feet, fluttered uncertainly for a few seconds, and plunged back to its original level. For a brief moment we had passed over our objective. Quickly we turned and retraced our path, steaming at a snail's pace, until the trace was repeated on the sounder. The engine was then reversed to steady us, and the prepared anchor secured to a wire warp to prevent loss by chafing was tossed overboard. For a moment we drifted then the wire stiffened . . . we were "hooked"!

Quickly we "kitted up", and two of us were soon in the water and heading down the anchor rope for the wreck.

The depth recorded on the echo sounder was deeper than the chart had lead us to believe, but we hoped to be anchored somewhere in the superstructure—which would mean we would make contact with the wreck at about 120 feet—but as we headed deeper into the gloom and our depth gauges registered 100–120–130 feet there was still no sign of her. Suddenly we hit the shingle bottom to find no sign of a wreck—except a single piece of angle iron ahead of us, into which the anchor was snagged. We could not understand it, having seen the profile of the wreck traced so clearly on the echo sounder, but as my eyes became more accustomed to the gloom I was conscious of a shadow looming above me. Turning my head to the left and looking upwards, I saw the huge bulk of a ship's hull towering above me whilst to my right, separated from the main structure by some 10 or 15 feet the bows, cantered over at a drunken angle as if severed by some gigantic knife. By some fluke the anchor had passed through this gap in our efforts to hook the wreck, missing its 360 feet length by inches only. By good fortune it had hitched into a stray piece of metal which had fallen clear to the seabed.

Quickly we finned for the main deck and found her in exceptionally good condition for 50 years' immersion, the ship lying on an even keel with parts of her superstructure still intact. On her stern a small gun still pointed skywards, but our vision of a double jack-pot was soon shattered when we found her single propeller made of cast iron. Time and air were running out and, unless we were prepared to suffer the discomforts of stage decompression on a shot rope, there was time for no more than a brief investigation. However, we headed for the surface reasonably happy with our new find, though disappointed no positive proof of its identity was found—other than the significant state of the bow section, which was consistent with the fate of the *Riversdale*. As each member of the diving party reported his observations we became more convinced than ever of the identity of the vessel . . . but the positive proof escaped us.

It was on a dive later in the year, whilst examining the superstructure, it was discovered that the ship's helm was made of solid brass. Although only some 2 feet 6 inches in diameter, we felt it would make a very suitable addition to the club's collection of "wreck souvenirs"—and so armed with a pair of "Stilsons" and sundry other tools a diving group headed once more for Prawle Point and the "Coal boat".

The removal of the helm presented no problems, and it was not long before the marine-encrusted prize was hauled to the surface and safely lifted inboard. As we had anticipated, it was a fine specimen and all agreed it was well worth a thorough refurbishing. Within a week every trace of its long immersion was removed and, with diligent polishing, it was soon fully restored to its former gleaming glory. We all examined it with great interest, particularly the four letters "H.Q.M.R." amateurishly centre-punched into one of the spokes. These we assumed were the initials of some bored helmsman who, having little to do one quiet watch, had passed the time away recording his existence for posterity, except that his second initial appeared to be "Q", unusual to say the least and a fact that stuck in my memory.

By this time I had amassed a great deal of information from a variety of sources, on a large number of vessels in the area—too much for me to memorize and in urgent need of cataloguing and indexing if the full benefit of all we had learned was to be of use to us in the future. With this in mind, I turned to the specifications of all the wrecks of interest to us which I had obtained from a retired Merchant Navy Captain whose hobby and life had been ships. Then began the analysis of the material to hand. Working through this mass of information I started typing a record card for the *Riversdale* and it began . . . single screw steamer; built by J. Blumer & Co., Sunderland, 1906 . . . Signal Letters H.G.M.R. . . . SIGNAL Letters H.G.M.R.? The coincidence was too much—I rushed down to the club store, where the helm was now proudly displayed, and examined again those erratically punched initials in the spoke. The second letter wasn't a "Q" but a poorly formed "G"—these were not the initials of some long-forgotten sailor, they were the *Riversdale* signal letters. What a fantastic discovery—and from our point of view what more proof could we wish for?

My probings into the fate of the *Riversdale* had unearthed the fact that all British vessels which were sunk on or after the 20 August, 1917, were either wholly or at least partly underwritten by the Government—and the *Riversdale* was no exception. We decided that such a vessel should also belong to Torbay Branch and, after further correspondence with the Ministry of Transport, we were able to agree a satisfactory purchase price for her. In due course we received a most impressive blue-ribboned document informing us of our ownership of the *Riversdale* for the sum of . . . £5 0 0.

With two merchantmen totalling 6,400 tons of wrecked shipping to our credit, it is not difficult to imagine our thoughts turning to higher things. The next wreck to come within our scope of interest was the *Empress of India*!

Lying in Lyme Bay in 140 feet of water, this 14,300-ton Victorian Battleship was an out-dated warship even in 1913— when she was towed to her present position to be used as a target ship during Naval manœuvres in the November of that year. It was unfortunate that, instead of confining the shelling to her superstructure, as was the object of the exercise, some over-zealous Gunnery Officer aimed a little too low for comfort, damaging her below the water line to such an extent that she "turned turtle" and sank. As a memorial to this untimely end, the well known Lyme Bay Bell buoy was positioned in her immediate vicinity to mark her final resting place, but at the onset of World War I the incident and the *Empress* were virtually forgotten.

Some older readers, however, may recall that during the Second World War there was a joke which took the form of a question supposedly posed by a Black-marketeer who asked "Pssst—want to buy a battleship?"

Accordingly, I wrote to the Admiralty suggesting this possibility, but apart from a brief acknowledgement of my letter I heard nothing for several months. I had almost given up hope of hearing anything further on this matter when one morning I received a very official and bulky envelope in the post from the Director of Naval Estimates in Bath, enclosing a Tender Form for the *Empress of India* together with the Admiralty's Conditions of Sale. It would seem my inquiries initiated a search by the Admiralty into the possibility of their disposing of this long-forgotten asset and although we would have dearly loved to "put in a bid" one of the many conditions quoted was that "the Purchaser disperses the wreck to the satisfaction of the Admiralty within 12 months of the date of purchase". We, of course, realized that the conditions laid down were part of a standard procedure for Admiralty tenders and all clauses would not necessarily apply in every case, but nevertheless I was diffident in committing Torbay Branch to the dispersal of 14,300 tons of armour-plated battleship—however unlikely the possibility of such a clause being enforced. In the circumstances we therefore reluctantly declined to make an offer in

Seventy feet down in a Welsh lake—the wreck of an aeroplane. A Westminster branch diver surveys the crumpled remains, which are of an R.A.F.
plane of between-the-wars vintage. Despite extensive inquiries no details
of the crash have ever been discovered by the divers who found the plane.
Tri-X film (developed for 25 mins. in Promicrol) f5.6/25, Russian Zenith
camera in housing. Leo Zanelli (see Chapter Eight).

Above. Sea hares mating. These six-inch long slugs (*Aplysia punctata*) are aptly named "hares" when you look at the great long "ears". This picture taken only a few hundred yards off the coast at Bognor, Sussex, shows only two of the hares who were there in great numbers. Tri-X. Calypsophot camera. f11/60. 30cm. close-up lens. Kendall McDonald. *Below*. Funny things flat fish. Tony Baverstock, who took this very close-up picture at Newhaven in 25 feet of water, finds plaice easy to approach in clear water and not frightened by flash. Yet on dull days and dirty water they are apprehensive and difficult to approach closely. f22/125 with flash. Calypsophot camera, PF24 bulb, 25cm close-up lens.

this instance and our dream of being the first B.S-A.C. Branch to own a battleship was shelved.

We heard eventually that the *Empress* was bought by a German salvage firm and, although some material was removed during a short salvage attempt in 1963, its bulk still remains undispersed 50 feet proud of Lyme Bay seabed in 23 fathoms of water.

Although I have dealt with the fascination of wrecks and wreck diving at some length I think a comment here on some of the hazards involved might serve as a timely reminder to the potential wreck-hunter before taking the downward plunge.

In the first place, all normal safety precautions—dive planning procedures and equipment—are essential, but special emphasis should be placed on the following points.

As far as equipment is concerned, there are certain items which are very necessary. A knife, well sharpened for cutting away any net or line in which you might become entangled. Gloves to protect the hands from rusting plates, frayed wire hawsers, etc. A torch for illumination and attracting your "buddy" diver. A "buddy" line is also very useful in poor visibility and a guide line is absolutely essential if you intend to explore confined sections of the wreck.

Before entering the water it is important to assess the diving conditions likely to be encountered on the wreck, such as the state and strength of the tidal stream, the possible visibility which will depend upon the nature of the seabed, tidal strength, depth, water clarity, weather, etc. It is important there is sufficient visibility for contact with your "buddy" diver to be easily maintained—on no account should wreck diving be carried out alone. Tidal streams should be slight but sufficient to disperse any silt which may be disturbed whilst finning on the wreck. In fact, one should aim to dive just before slack water if possible—in order to take advantage of dead water at the end of the dive and your return to the surface.

Once on the wreck, it is important to orientate oneself before moving off and plan so as to return to your point of departure. Prior knowledge of the ship's design is a real advantage in this respect. Moving about the wreck should be done slowly and with extreme caution, taking care not to brush against parts of the wreck and to handle the structure carefully. Avoid stirring up silt which reduces visibility rapidly, and keep a sharp look out for snagged nets and fishing line abandoned by anglers. These can easily become entangled in your equipment.

Allow plenty of time for your return to the surface—a last minute snag delaying your departure with empty tanks could be embarrassing.

To sum up:

1. Be sure of your equipment and check it thoroughly before entering the water.
2. Consider all the factors in your pre-dive planning.
3. Never dive alone.
4. Take it easy.

With common diving sense as the basic ingredient, a fascinating wreck dive is assured.

Since the early wreck diving days of Torbay branch we have investigated, located and dived on some 30 wrecks around Britain and the thrills experienced on our first exciting dives are still as real today as they were at the time of operations. We know that thrill will never fade.

DIVING IN AN
EFFLUENT SOCIETY

By Dr. David Bellamy

Dr. David Bellamy is a lecturer in botany at Durham University.
Is an authority on the effect of pollution on sea life. Was
Scientific Officer of Durham City Branch of the British Sub-
Aqua Club and led the largest underwater investigation into
pollution ever carried out in this country.

"POLLUTE the sea? ridiculous! how could we ever pollute
that lot?" That is what people think. But since Eve first
polluted Adam, some 110 billion human beings have lived off
this Garden of Eden called Earth. They have each lived for
about twenty-five years and each has produced about a half a
gallon of urine per day throughout their life. In round or rather
in square figures, this means that 1,000 cubic miles of human
urine has been produced and got rid of. When similar figures
are computed for that other product of our bodies the spectacle
is just too revolting, but when compared with the gross volume
of the oceans which is 330 million cubic miles, you can see that
it is a mere spit in a very large bucket.

If it was just human excreta there would be nothing to worry
about. For a start most of the waste products of our bodies are
broken down and re-used long before they get into the sea.
Even if the whole volume mentioned above had got to the sea
and was still there, the total dilution factor is so great that it
would represent only three parts in every million. However,
we must remember two points; first, the world's population at
present stands in excess of three thousand million, which means
that out of every 100 people that have ever lived, three are
alive today and all are doing their bit. Second, man is a gre-
garious animal and likes to live *en masse* in great concrete conur-
bations, so the pollution problem on account of human sewage
alone, is getting critical in some places.

Unfortunately, it isn't just sewage, but all those other

by-products of our affluent, or should we use the word effluent, societies, which find their way into our estuaries, into the sea, and often on to our beaches. To name a few, domestic waste, coal washings, fly ash, contraceptives, toxic chemicals including detergents, oil, radioactive waste, and all that other sad jetsam of our age which we already seem to take for granted, cluttering the tide pools which were once full of fascinating living things.

This chapter, which may at first sight seem so out of place in a book of this type, is going to be primarily about those fascinating living things and the effect pollution can have on them. It will be mainly concerned with the inshore marine fringe, in which both divers and pollutants are most concentrated and it will focus attention on the important scientific observations which can, and must be made by the amateur diver, if we are ever going to understand the complexities of life on the borders of inner space.

The inshore marine fringe with its marked zonation of environmental factors is without doubt one of the richest habitats for life on earth. Only the diver can fully appreciate this fact, a fact which the sea jealously guarded until the invention of a glass screen gave men clear vision underwater. When we don a mask and take to the sea we are privileged to enter this, the last great stronghold of nature; with an aqualung we have the possibility of becoming, at least for a short while, part of it. The land explored and exploited in part to destruction; the open sea charted but unexplored, yet already its stocks of great fish and mammals exploited, some almost to extinction; the inshore fringe now waits its turn, will it be sensible utilization or exploitation? Conservation or destruction?

Man is already beginning the process of violation. Spear fishermen seek out and kill. The engines of the combines churn the great kelp beds of the coasts of north America, reaping a rich harvest of alginates, and the effluvia from twentieth century civilization pours from foul estuaries to lay waste stretches of this productive hinterland.

It was across this fringe that evolution faced its most difficult task. It was here that animals and plants first tested their land-legs in the struggle for existence, a struggle which left a diverse flora and fauna perfectly adapted to the myriad niches of the inshore fringe. To begin to understand the effects of pollution on this wealth of life, we must begin to understand something about the life itself.

Passing down from the splash zone, especially on a gently sloping rocky shore, it is often very obvious that the seaweeds, the marine algae, occupy distinct zones. What is more, within each distinct zone the animal populations may themselves be very distinct. Below low water mark the zonation continues, but becomes less marked, great kelp beds eventually giving way to sparse communities of more delicate brown and red seaweeds. With increasing depth the abundance, even of the red seaweeds, diminish until only animal life, life which is not directly dependent on sunlight, remains, brittle stars, peacock worms, sea cucumbers, and the like. Three main factors appear to determine this zonation: (1) exposure to air, (2) exposure to wave action, and (3) diminishing light intensity and spectral range.

The process of organic evolution has fitted each plant and animal to a particular environment niche, to put it very crudely to a particular way of life within the inshore marine fringe. This can best be illustrated by reference to some actual examples.

First, the seaweeds; it is immediately obvious to anyone visiting the seashore in the temperate regions, that there are three main kinds of seaweed, green ones, brown ones and red ones. All of them contain the green pigment chlorophyll, the pigment which is of prime importance in the process of photosynthesis, the process by which light energy is changed into chemical energy in the form of sugar. The process which feeds the whole living world. Light must be absorbed before it can drive the photosynthetic mechanism. Chlorophyll absorbs light predominantly at two wavelengths, 6550 Å in the red end of the spectrum, and 4350 Å in the blue end of the spectrum. Seawater also absorbs light, absorbing the rays of longer wavelength more readily. Therefore, the deeper a plant or animal lives in the inshore fringe, the less red light will they receive and the more will they have to depend on blue light for vision or for photosynthesis. One way for a seaweed to get over this problem is to have in addition to chlorophyll a range of pigments, which will absorb other wavelengths. Thus, the red seaweeds are red because they contain phycocrythrin, a red pigment which absorbs blue light very efficiently, and red seaweeds are often the most abundant plants found in deep water.

The second example is one of the most abundant animals found on the seashore, the common or public-bar mussel. Mussels do not always live in little glass jars, they may be found in enormous numbers on what must be classed among the harshest environments on earth, fully exposed rocky shores. Here they must be able to withstand the full force of the elements. When the tide is in, waves and surf are the order of the day, when the tide is out the mussels can be dried and baked under a summer sun, or frozen solid on a frosty winter night.

Yes, the mussel can live and thrives where few other animals bother to try. Fixed to the rock by tough threads they can weather any storm. In adverse conditions it must be useful to have a shell in which to retire, a shell which can be held tight shut by very strong muscles. However, when the tide is in and the mussel beds are underwater, the muscles are relaxed and the shells opened to allow feeding.

Mussels are filter feeders and in order to collect sufficient food they must pump large volumes of water through their shells. A large mussel can shift four pints an hour, which is enough to earn it a place of honour in any public bar. The water passes into the shell and through the gills where all particulate matter is strained off. Mussels have gills and just like fish they use them to obtain oxygen from the water, but the gills are also perfectly adapted for food collection. All particles in the water are collected by the gills to be passed forward towards the mouth. You can imagine that not only food but all sorts of microscopic junk is strained off. The heaviest particles, like sand and silt, simply fall off the gill *en route*. Nevertheless, a lot of indigestible material arrives at the head end, but before it can enter the mouth it must cross a peculiar structure known as the labial palps. The labial palps are highly efficient "sorting bays", which direct only the choicest small particles towards the mouth, the larger pieces of intractable matter passing in the opposite direction to be ejected from the shell. Next time you feel like grumbling about a gritty mussel, just remember the mussel did its best. These are just some of the many ways in which that "simple" animal, the common mussel, is perfectly adapted to its own way of life.

Not only are the organisms, the plants and animals themselves perfectly adapted, but so are the communities, of which they form an integral part. Take one as an example, that most striking feature of the underwater world around the coasts of northern Europe, the kelp beds.

The great kelp plants are like the trees of a forest, their stipes (trunks) and haptera (roots), often covered with a host of epiphytes, red seaweeds, sponges, sea squirts, bryozoans, polyzoans, anemones, hydroids, in fact, a complete cross section of the living world. The rocks in between the kelp roots are not bare but are covered with an equally bizarre array of life, and every crevice and crack houses a multitude of animals from minute larvae to that most sought after of all beasts, *Homarus vulgaris*, the lobster.

It is a fact that a single kelp plant during each year of its maturity, can produce more than 1 million new potential kelp plants. At that rate it wouldn't take many years before the oceans were solid with kelp. They are not, so we know that something must be keeping the numbers in check. Among other things the answer is the grazing animals, limpets, winkles, sea urchins and the like, which spend their whole lives browsing over the rock surfaces, and the next time you find one look at the business end of a sea urchin and perhaps you will realize just how efficient they are. The numbers of these browsers are in turn kept in check either by lack of food or by the carnivorous animals, sea birds, lobsters and star-fish. Yes, life on the seashore is a pretty bloodthirsty business; everything works to rule, and the rule is survival of the fittest.

Fit or not, when they die the remains of all living organisms, plants and animals alike, are rapidly broken down and eaten by a whole host of scavengers. The fine detritus that remains feeds another great group of organisms with which the fringe abounds. These are the filter feeders, one of which has been described above. This group of animals includes such delicacies as the mussel, the clam and the oyster. These in their turn form part of the great food web of the inshore environment, a very small part of which is harvested to feed man.

The whole complex of the environment and the living organisms is a working unit which we call an ecosystem. The kelp forest ecosystem described, is limited in the British Isles to a zone between 1 metre and 40 metres below low water mark, the width of the zone depending upon the slope of the shore. This ecosystem harbours a fantastic wealth of life and due in part to its complexity, the system is maintained in a balanced state. Sunlight trapped by the process of photosynthesis is the driving force, the energy flowing through the food web. The struggle for existence is the struggle to get a fair share of the energy, the struggle helps to maintain the system in a state of balance. ANYTHING WHICH WILL UPSET THIS BALANCE CAN CHANGE OR EVEN DESTROY THE SYSTEM, AND THIS IS WHERE POLLUTION RAISES ITS UGLY HEAD.

Pollution is caused by pollutants; as far as we are concerned, pollutants are any substances which find their way into the sea and upset the natural balance of the marine ecosystems. Pollutants may be conveniently divided into four types, TOXINS, CLOGGERS, SUSPENDED MATTER and NUTRIENTS.

The term toxin is self-explanatory. Toxins are substances which are poisonous to living organisms, if concentrations of such substances get too high in the inshore zone then animals and plants will die. For instance, cyanide is produced as a by-product of certain industrial processes; if it gets into the sea in any amount—CAPUT. It is not only the by-products of industry, but the actual manufactured article that is often at fault. Research has dreamed up an enormous number of new toxic compounds such as the organochlorines, DDT, alkyl benzene sulphonate, etc., which are sold as constituents of herbicides, insecticides and detergents. They are produced to do very necessary jobs which they do very well, but many of them eventually end up in the sea. Diluted by the enormous volume of sea water, they are of little direct significance.

However, we have seen that the filter-feeding animals like the mussel described above, pass enormous volumes of water through their bodies in order to obtain enough food. Toxic substances can be concentrated to appreciable levels in the body of say an oyster, so that when a carnivore eats half a dozen, he gets a lethal dose. This is given the fancy name of concentration through the food chain.

It is not, however, a new thing, the North American Indians knew only too well what would happen if they ate mussels after there had been a red sea; the consequence was a violent gut ache and off to the happy hunting ground. So the coastal tribes posted look-outs to watch out for the sea turning red and warned the tribe not to eat mussels. Modern research has shown that the red seas are caused by the rapid multiplication of a microscopic planktonic plant called *Goniaulux*. A by-product of the life processes of *Goniaulux* is a highly effective nerve poison, a nerve poison which only works on vertebrates, animals which like ourselves have backbones. The mussels feed on *Goniaulux*, concentrating the toxin, which is quite harmless to them but lethal to man.

At the present day man is releasing more and more bizarre chemicals into the environment. Some are not directly toxic but when partly broken down by the life processes of animals, plants or bacteria, well, who knows. There are some 'look-outs' who are studying the build-up of toxic chemicals through the marine food chains with No. 1 in mind. Few people bother about their effect on the marine life, and remember it isn't just the loss of a few animals that we have got to worry about but the effect on the balance of the ecosystems.

From toxins to cloggers, again a straightforward case. An oiled seabird is a disgusting sight and a sad reflection on modern humanity. However, it is not only seabirds, but a whole cross section of marine life which is wiped out in this way, their gills and other respiratory and feeding surfaces clogged up by our waste, which is dumped with all good faith, into the sea. We must include in this category much of the intractable matter which when first dumped, spend some time in suspension; domestic waste, fly ash, coal washings, effluents from quarries and cement works, all can clog and kill the filter feeders. However, a more subtle change; while the matter is still in suspension it cuts down light penetration through the water, thereby precluding the growth of photosynthetic plants, whatever sort of pigments they may have. Similarly, deposition of these substances on the mucoid surfaces of the plants will have a direct shading effect, and deposition on the rock surfaces can so drastically alter them that the growth and development of spores and larvae is impossible. If regeneration is stopped in this way the whole ecosystem can break down.

We will leave the fourth category of pollutants for a bit, but it must already be obvious that pollution is a complicated business. The best way to understand this is to look at some case histories.

First, the *Torrey Canyon* disaster. The oil alone slaughtered a fantastic number of seabirds, despite frantic efforts of a great band of dedicated conservationists. In the waters of the inshore marine fringe, life went on as usual. Limpets and whelks were seen crawling about quite happily on the surface of the oil, the marine algae, even if smothered, showed little sign of damage. However, as soon as detergent was used to remove the oil the whole picture changed. The detergent was toxic, very toxic, and many animals were killed outright. The oil emulsion so produced was no longer an inert something to be crawled over, it became part of the marine environment, rapidly ingested by, clogging up and killing many animals. In the worst hit areas deaths were recorded at depths in excess of twenty metres and wholesale slaughter of the bulk of animal life from the splash zone to a depth of ten metres below low water mark.

However, even those seaweeds which had been bathed in concentrated detergent, were not too badly affected, and with all the grazing organisms gone they "had a ball". Shores which had been almost devoid of plant cover rapidly changed colour as fast-growing green seaweeds produced a thick blanket over everything; tens of thousands of sporelings sprang up on the bare rock between the adult kelp plants—the balance had been destroyed and the ecosystem responded. The main problem is not, when will all the animals return, for return they will. The main problem is how long will it take to restore the balance, will it be the same balance?

Was it right or wrong to use detergent? We can't really say. If the oil had been left, more seabirds would have died a terrible death and the balance of the ecosystems would have been altered from the other end, less predators, therefore more grazers. Was this potential loss balanced by the number of birds that died through ingesting toxic detergents by eating dead and dying limpets? The answer is, we shall never know. What we do know is that this short-term acute pollution has not only wiped out millions of living organisms, but has altered the ecological balance of many miles of coast.

From acute to chronic pollution. The *Torrey Canyon* disaster was a short sharp shock, what about long-term pollution? One of the best places to study it are the shores of north-east England. The coasts of Northumberland and Durham have long been known for their marine flora and fauna, which has been actively studied for the past one hundred and fifty years. The stretches of this coast which are affected by the outflows of the Rivers Tyne, Wear and Tees, have been polluted since the time of the Industrial Revolution. Industrialization and urbanization of the southern part of this coastal strip has concentrated human activity to produce what must be one of the most polluted coastlines in the world.

Sewage, coal washings, household and industrial waste, effluvia from heavy industry, chemical industry, you name it the Durham coast gets it. The concentration of feacal bacteria, the trade mark of human sewage, can reach levels in excess of one hundred thousand coliform bacteria per hundred millilitres of seawater on beaches which are not only used, but are advertised as holiday attractions. In some regions of the world bathing is stopped when the coliform count reaches only two hundred and forty bacteria per hundred millilitres. There is, however, little cause for alarm because there is no direct evidence of any disease being caught by bathing in polluted seawater. Eating shellfish from polluted water can be a very different matter but shucked oysters with coliform counts of several thousand are not sneered at by the gourmet.

Whatever else the coliform counts of these beaches means, it warns that they are heavily polluted and we know that they have been polluted for a very long time. When we look at the inshore marine ecosystems along these coasts, the facts are grim. Comparison with the detailed records of the mid-nineteenth century shows that out of ninety-seven types of seaweed recorded as of common occurrence on the Durham coast in 1860, only forty-one can be found in 1960, and of these only twenty-seven can be called common. This compares with a net increase in the number of species recorded for the unpolluted stretches of the Northumberland coast.

In north Northumberland the zone of attached seaweed extends from the splash zone to depths in excess of twenty-five metres. On the Durham coast even where there are rock platforms at lower levels the seaweed beds extend to a maximum of only four metres below low water mark, and many rocky shores are almost devoid of seaweeds. All evidence indicates that the main cause is suspended matter cutting down light penetration. The fact is that for much of the year only two metres below the surface visibility is nil, the research diver often has to work by feel and he feels some mighty funny things.

There is also some evidence that the loss of seaweed types from the littoral zone, where the shading factor would not be such a problem, could be due to toxic substances but much more research is necessary to prove it one way or the other. We do know what we have lost and we do know that the Durham coast is almost a seaweed desert compared with the coasts both north and south. The question is, does it matter? Reduction of the abundance and diversity of the seaweed flora of a strip of coast, who cares apart from those "funny people" who collect seaweeds like stamps?

Well, there is one case where it did matter, and matter in a big way because it hit someone's pocket; in fact, it hit the pocket of a multi-million dollar industry, the kelp industry of North America.

The coasts of California sport not only some of the largest of suntanned vital statistics, but also the largest of all the seaweeds, the giant kelp *Macrocystis pyrifera*. This gigantic plant, which reaches lengths of fifty metres, is harvested as a source of chemicals, and for use as fertilizers or food additives. Drastic reductions in the extent and the productivity of kelp beds near pollution infalls were noted from about 1940 onwards, and a large research programme was initiated in 1957 to investigate this decline in detail.

The account of the investigation by the Institute of Marine

Resources of the University of California and the Californian State Water Quality Control Board, will always remain a classic in the literature of inshore oceanography. This work describes how pollution has upset the balance of the giant kelp forest ecosystems in two main ways. One, by the reduction of light penetration due to increased water turbidity. The second, and most important, due to an increase in the number of grazing organisms, especially three types of spiny sea urchin. Populations of these avid browsers had built up in excess of the norm, destroying adult kelp plants and preventing regeneration of the forest. Under normal conditions the urchins would either starve or have to move on to fresh fields. However, in the polluted waters the urchins can feed on edible pollutant, their numbers are therefore maintained and kelp regeneration is impossible. This has been proved to be the case by experimental removal of the urchins by bombing them with quick lime; in treated areas dense kelp forests have soon developed.

A quotation from one of the main accounts of this work seems apt at this point. "However, an evaluation of kelp beds as a resource must also include their contribution to sport and commercial fishing. While this contribution is believed to be substantial it cannot at present be estimated reliably." This statement basically means that there is a hell of a lot of work to be done before we can even hazard a guess at the role which our seaweed beds play in the overall balance of inshore marine life.

Just how many animals depend on the kelp forest for shelter? Just how important are the seaweed beds as nurseries for the shellfish and fish which are an important source of protein in a world, two-thirds of whose population live on the brink of starvation? One thing that is very clear is that if we destroy them before we find out, we can never recreate them in order to find out. There is a fantastic amount of work to do.

Whenever anyone talks about mass starvation the optimists always look towards that hypothetical cornucopia, the sea. "Nothing to worry about," they say, "the sea can supply all our needs." If sea farming is ever going to be a large-scale reality it is going to be the euphotic zone, including that part of the inshore marine fringe which we have been discussing, which will form the bulk of our new farmland, and fantastically productive they could be. One hectare of kelp forest at the three metre level in the unpolluted waters of Northumberland can net sixty kilograms of dry matter per day. (A figure that compares very favourably with that for a good field of wheat which is thirty-four kilograms per hectare). A comparable hectare of the polluted Durham coast can produce only fourteen kilograms. This loss of production potential is even more serious when it is remembered that those all-important nutrients, phosphate and nitrate, which farmers must "pour" onto their fields to maintain fertility, are being poured into the polluted areas.

Before we can attempt to farm the inshore marine fringe, we must understand a lot more about the natural ecosystems we find there. If we don't do the necessary research work then any scheme to farm this fringe could be just another groundnut scheme, another catastrophe.

This is perhaps the real reason for including this chapter in this book, a book which will be read by divers, because it is the amateur divers who have got to do some of the work.

During the last century the development of an extensive public transport system brought about a flowering in the knowledge of the flora and fauna of our countryside, and it was the great band of amateur naturalists that made the bulk of the records, not the few trained professionals. In the same way the development of the use of the aqualung must lead to a similar flowering of the knowledge of our inshore marine ecosystems. Professional inshore marine biologists who can dive are pretty thin on the ground. The inshore marine fringe is vast and the amount of simple observational work which has got to be done is enormous.

Inshore marine biology looks to the "horde" of amateur divers who are fed up with harpooning flatties, making urchin lampshades or even chasing the elusive mermaid, and who are asking, what can we do? Well, here is the answer. The right questions can be asked, tasks can be evolved and this great task force put into action to help collect the vital data.

Can it be done? Yes, it can. "Operation Kelp" got off the ground with the help of the British Sub-Aqua Club, through

Triton, the club's magazine, and was completed successfully during the 1967 diving season.

A simple method of giving a moderately accurate picture of the productivity of "kelp forests" was essential. So these are the instructions that were given to divers.

The diver would need apart from his normal diving gear:

1. A pair of kitchen scales.
2. A pair of kitchen scissors.
3. A crowbar.
4. Two old pillow cases or two carrot sacks.
5. A square frame made of anything you like but IT MUST BE EXACTLY ONE METRE SQUARE.

What would the diver have to do?

1. Learn to identify *Laminaria hyperborea*. The main thing to note is that the stalk is rough to the touch and it usually has a lot of small red seaweeds growing on it. IF IT HAS GOT A SMOOTH STALK WITH NOTHING GROWING ON IT, LEAVE IT ALONE AS IT IS THE WRONG ONE.

2. At your favourite diving site, choose three areas of kelp forest, one at about 10 feet below low water mark, one at 20 feet and the other as deep as you can find it. Measure, as accurately as you can, at what depth below mean low water mark the kelps are rooted. This part, it was suggested, could be done during normal club diving activities. D-Day for Operation Kelp was to be the first convenient day for any particular club after 20 July, 1967.

3. On D-Day the diver was told to do the following:
   With his diving party to go, with square frame, crowbar and diving knife, to each of the chosen kelp forests in turn.
   a. Choose the part of the forest where the plants are densest.
   b. Place the frame within the densest patch.
   c. Remove all the kelp plants inside the frame. They must be removed whole, including the root-like portion (using the crowbar) and place them in the pillowcase or sack. Take them back to the shore.
   d. Repeat the process on a second square metre in the densest part of the kelp forest.

    e. The crops must be kept wet. Do not let them dry in the sun, keep them in sea water.

Then the shore party were to take over:

    a. Carefully scrape off all encrusting animals and plants which are growing on the kelp plant.

    b. Measure the length of the stalk and record this on forms supplied.

    c. Cut each kelp plant into three pieces—blade, stalk, hold-fast.

    d. Shake the water off each piece in turn and weigh as accurately as possible. Record the weights on the form.

    e. Finally, cut the holdfast down the middle into two equal halves, count the number of branch levels and record.

From this the divers ended up with the vital data from two one-metre square crops at three different depths. From this I expected to be able to calculate standing crop and production figures.

I added the rider that we couldn't guarantee that it would work—but it was at least worth a try.

And if any criticism of the operation can be raised then it must be criticism of the scientific reasoning behind the operation, not the work of the divers concerned.

The result of "Operation Kelp", although useful, will not go down in the annals of marine biology as a piece of classic research.

They will, however, be remembered as an example of how a group of over two hundred and fifty people from many walks of life, participated in an experiment and carried out a set of detailed instructions to the letter. What was the reason behind "Operation Kelp"? The work mentioned above on the effect of long-term pollution on inshore marine ecosystems along the north-east coast of England, had shown that kelp forest production—in the polluted waters of Durham, was only 10 per cent that of the unpolluted coasts of Northumberland. The question remained, was this anything to do with pollution? "Operation Kelp" gave the background count, as it were, of kelp performance from stations all round the British Isles. The production levels along the Durham coast stuck out like a sore thumb,

A plaice on a bed of mussels. Taken with Rolleimarin, close-up lens
and High Speed Ektachrome, black-and-white from transparency. With
flash. Depth: 25 feet. f22/125. Tony Baverstock.

they were not part of the overall pattern of variation in production.

But the collection of data on this scale was unique. Twenty-five clubs provided a task force of 262. 152 man hours were spent underwater, 7,052 kelp plants were harvested, giving a total crop weight of one-and-a-half wet, slimy tons. The total length of kelp measured was 3.5 kilometres, 21,150 weighings were put on record as were the cursings of at least 20 wives who found something nasty drying in their ovens at Regulo 1.

The theory behind the operation was simply that as a kelp plant gets older, it gets bigger. The stipe (stalk) and holdfast (root-like portion) grow for a number of years and can be aged. The lamina (blade) of the plant is produced afresh each year. So simply by weighing the various parts of the plants of known age, growth curves can be constructed from which comparable figures of performance can be calculated. This is exactly what the operation kelpers did—collected, measured, aged and weighed 7,052 kelp plants.

The overall trend was obvious, a decrease in individual performance, measured as stipe production, passing from the North-East to the South-West of the British Isles, with a subsidiary decrease passing up the English Channel.

Now we plan to use the amateur divers in another way—the setting up of ten experimental "kelp farms" around the coasts of the British Isles. And from the willing help we received on "Operation Kelp" I know that we are going to find just as many divers keen to join in.

Man, for the first time in his long history as a destructive force within nature, is beginning to realize that his continued existence depends in part on a full understanding of the balance that is nature. Man is a part of the great natural ecosystem the

---

Facing Top. Cheeky chappie in hiding. This butterfly blenny used a piece of old pipe as his hiding place in Bournemouth Bay in 30 feet of water. Rolleimarin, close-up lens, Perspex screen diffuser over flash, f16/125. Philip Smith. *Bottom.* Edible crab on a sandy bottom covered with worm casts. This picture, taken in Chapman's Pool, Dorset, shows clearly wave ripples in sand. Tri-X f5.6/125, Nikonos camera. Depth: 12 feet. Leo Zanelli.

biosphere, the sum total of life on this planet. The ecosystem is already so out of balance that two-thirds of the human race are living on the brink of starvation. Man's numbers will eventually be controlled.

Will it be mass starvation, atomic warfare for what food is left, pestilence due to pollution of our environment, or will man prove himself to be the fittest and do it by some form of balanced population control, backed by sensible utilization of all natural resources? If it's going to be the latter, and time is very short, then there is much work to be done to understand our effect on these natural resources.

THE MULBERRY THAT
MISSED THE INVASION

by Kendall McDonald

Kendall McDonald is author of books on diving and is on the
Executive Committee of the British Sub-Aqua Club. Has been
actively concerned with underwater swimming since 1953 and
is a prize-winning underwater photographer. Is a Bromley
Branch member.

SHE shouldn't be there. She should have played a vital part in
the wartime Allied landings in France. All 200 feet of her
should have been in position off the coast of France just after
D-Day, 1944, instead of lying broken in a jungle of weed 40 feet
underwater two miles off the Sussex coast.

This then is the story of the Mulberry which missed the
Invasion. For 20 years she lay on the seabed, forgotten by all
except perhaps the occasional fisherman who saw a dark shape
below the surface and lost both his tackle and his anchor in the
tangle of concrete and steel rods, valves and cables that she
had become.

How did she get there in the first place? An already yellowing
Press release from "Supreme Headquarters, Allied Expedi-
tionary Force, Public Relations Division", dated 15.10.44,
which I found in the cuttings library of the London *Evening
News*, tells the story. Between two thick red lines are the words:
"Unpublishable, unbroadcastable, and untransmissible before
2330 GMT OCT. 15, 1944". It was headed "Prefabricated
Ports" and starts like this:

"During the administrative planning of the invasion it
became clear that, even in the best possible case of all the French
ports falling into our hands undamaged at an early stage of the
operation, the quantity of stores to be landed for the main-
tenance of the force would exceed the port capacity. This meant
that stores would have to be landed over the beaches while the
ports were being improved. It was generally estimated that the

quantity to be landed in this manner amounted to about
12,000 tons and 2,500 vehicles of all shapes and sizes per day,
and that this would not be reduced for at least 90 days during
which many interruptions by bad weather might be expected.
In June 1943 the Chief of Combined Operations held a meeting
in London of Commanders, both British and U.S. with the
representatives of the British Service Ministries to hear reports
of the equipment that was being provided for the operation."

So really my Mulberry unit was being planned as far back as
June, 1943. The wartime Press release goes on: "The plan
originally accepted was that two artificial ports, one in each
sector, British and U.S., should be made, each consisting of a
breakwater formed of concrete caissons. The size of each
harbour had to be roughly the same as Dover. The execution
of the work was placed in the hands of the Ministry of Supply
on 24 September, 1943 . . ."

Then the equipment for the operation had to be built and
assembled. One of these assembly parks was at Selsey East. The
concrete caissons were towed there from construction sites and
then sunk by a system of valves to the seabed to await their
part in the invasion. It is interesting to note that vast quantities
of rubble from the bombed sites of London and other cities
were used in the concrete work. For example in the last three
months of 1943, a quarter of a million cubic yards, about
225,000 tons, were delivered to the riverside construction sites.
And the cost was colossal too. The floating piers, pierheads and
concrete breakwaters cost about £15,000,000. The story of the
success of Mulberry is well documented elsewhere. One estimate
was that it saved over 100,000 casualties.

What were the concrete "ships" really like? I don't think I
can do better than go back once again to that wartime Press
release for the answer: "These caissons were made in six
different sizes to suit various depths of water up to five-and-a-
half fathoms. The largest size had a displacement of 6,044 tons,
the smallest a displacement of 1,672 tons. Length of the largest
210 feet. When floating the whole looked rather like a Noah's
Ark without its roof, while, viewed from above, the cross wells
made it look like an egg-box, as there was no deck.

"Each caisson contained crews quarters for use during the

passage, the crew being partly naval for handling the ship, and partly from Royal Engineers (or Seabees) for carrying out the operation of sinking. At a late stage, Bofors guns, 20 tons of ammunition, and rough shelters for a gun's crew were placed on the top of most caissons as additional A.A. protection of the harbour.

"Caissons were towed empty across Channel by one large tug (about 1500 H.P.). On arrival they were manœuvred into position with the help of small tugs, and then special valves were opened, allowing water to fill the ship and sink it in place."

The caissons were towed at an average speed of 4 knots, some travelling 100 miles to their final position in the harbours. But some did not make it. Only one was lost on the long tow across the Channel when a gale—the worst in June for forty years—came from the North-East on D-Day-plus-13. But others never got started.

The trouble was that the idea of sinking the Mulberry units in parks on the seabed at places like Selsey was excellent—if you didn't want the units up again in a hurry, and providing the valves worked as perfectly in operational conditions as they did in drawings. But when they wanted to get the units up, however, it was not so simple. Valves didn't have wires fixed to them that they should have, suction pipes did not fit into pumping outlets, and the only answer to the problem was to mount a massive salvage operation. In his book *Up She Rises*, Commander Frank W. Lipscomb describes, through the eyes of one of the salvage officers concerned, what Selsey East Bay looked like then: "There, sure enough, were dozens of these monstrosities, sitting on the bottom, and moored to them were other fantastic pieces of equipment floating on small pontoons . . . The whole area of the bay, for three miles offshore, was cluttered up with concrete and steel equipment resembling nothing I had ever seen before, ashore or afloat."

In the end this massive salvage job was completed in time—but only just. Some of the units were never raised, some leaked, listed and were dumped, one was rammed and sunk by a small tug just as it was being taken over for the Channel tow, some wouldn't come up as they had broken their backs on the bottom.

Mulberry was a success without them. The war moved inland into France and Germany. And some of the Mulberry units that were left behind crumbled and sank beneath the waves. Once under the sea they were forgotten.

For some years I have kept a small fishing dinghy at Bognor Regis Yacht Club. The club has several members interested in diving, and though it is first and foremost a yacht club and devoted to the interests of its sailing members, the club committee have always followed an enlightened policy with regard to all water-users whether on or below the surface.

So a great number of my sea dives in this country were within dinghy range of Bognor and though visibility underwater was often down to a matter of inches, I usually managed to find something of interest to photograph. In fact close to Bognor is another Mulberry unit that missed the Invasion. This one is well-known not only to aqualung divers, but also to yachtsmen and holiday-makers.

This is the Mulberry which can be clearly seen from the beach at Pagham. Often as not the top of this one with its towing bollards and huge cleats is well clear of the water making the beacon marker clamped to it unnecessary. The beacon itself has now been bent right over at an acute angle by heavy seas.

This Mulberry is a good dive for beginners and on a calm sunny Sunday it is rather like Piccadilly Underground down there as strings of divers follow the man with a torch into the gloomy inner compartments. In fact on one occasion to my shame I "lost" the novice who was with me, and I was just getting really worried when one of the "underground trains" of divers went past me. The last one on the line looked familiar —it was my beginner happily following the flippers of the man ahead and firmly under the impression that he was sticking to me like a leech!

But no one should sniff at the chance of a shallow water dive on this abandoned unit. It is not uncommon to see a decent lobster lurking in the overhang where the tide has scoured the shingle away from under one sunken concrete wall. The growths on the "wreck" are worth much more than a casual glance. Some gorgeous plumose anemones decorate the walls inside the "cathedral" where the light streams down through the beams at the north-east end closest to the shore and there are some very fine examples of "dead men's fingers" (*Alcyonium Digitatum*) on a nearby wall.

Big mullet (*Mugil chelo*) feed on the bootlace weed around the outer edges and if frightened will rush for shelter in the holes where the sea has broken the concrete into large caves into the interior chambers.

It is a small unit—probably the smallest kind called C.1—and has one big disadvantage for the underwater photographer. The lower portions are usually covered with a fine silt, probably renewed by each storm, and the slightest disturbance is often enough to cloud the immediate area for some considerable time. This unit was one of those parked closest to the shore in the Selsey East area.

During a period of research into the likelihood of there being any shipwrecks just waiting to be discovered in the immediate neighbourhood, I kept coming back again and again to the Mulberries. It became obvious that these lost units were the nearest I was likely to come to any diveable wrecks in my immediate corner of the Sussex sea. The chart of the area has "Obstn" (Obstruction) marked in many places on it. Most are in the exact area where the Mulberry units were parked in wartime.

So I decided to concentrate on these so-called "obstructions". Several divers from Bromley Branch decided to join me in pinpointing the units that were never raised or broke their backs before they could be towed to France. There should be a lobster or two to be found if nothing else. But first we needed more information. A call to the Admiralty went something like this:

"All these obstructions around Pagham are they all Mulberry units?" "We can't honestly be sure—the majority probably are."

"Are the positions exact?" "They are more likely to be approximate. No inshore survey has been done there for some time."

From this conversation we suspected that the positions of the unraised Mulberry units on hastily made wartime charts had been transferred as accurately as possible to the main chart and for safety reasons the whole area designated as unsafe for navigation. (An interesting minor point soon arose: The Admiralty marked the Mulberries as "obstructions", but were obviously mildly concerned that perhaps they should be designated as "wrecks", as they were after all intended to float and be towed like barges.)

Then a chance meeting with one of the pilots of the rescue helicopters that are often to be seen whirling along the Sussex coast added to our confusion. He said that he knew of one dark shape in the sea well out from Bognor that must be a sunken Mulberry unit because of its square shape. But that was the only one he had seen from the air and he would surely have seen others which should have been in shallower water if the chart positions were correct.

The best bet therefore seemed to be the one that the helicopter pilot could vouch for. Though there was a chance that we could see it from a boat if the tide was low enough, we would obviously do much better if we used the Branch's echo-sounder and kept a sharp eye on the tracing it made of the seabed underneath us.

So that's what we did. The morning of the hunt was sunny with a slight south-westerly breeze giving a little chop to the sea. We took the small Pagham Mulberry as a reference point— in fact we refuelled the little 3 h.p. Johnson outboard in the shelter of the concrete mass rather as the big ships of the invasion fleet used the other units that did finally make the trip to France. From there we headed more or less directly out to sea. Every now and then Reg Dunton would check our position with a sextant, but the trace of the echo-sounder continued more or less straight and level with a slight tendency to increasing depth as we headed further and further out.

The "wreck" we were aiming for was marked on the chart as having a warning beacon in position but we knew from talking to local fishermen that no such beacon exists today. Finally, according to the sextant, we were over the "obstruction". But there was nothing there. The echo-sounder trace stayed depressingly level. We swept in towards the promontory of Selsey Bill. Still nothing. Then out to sea again. Still nothing.

Whose eyes really are as big as their stomachs? Pouting fry at Kim-meridge, taken in 12 feet of water. HP4, with Rolleinar close-up 3 lens. Philip Smith.

We seemed a long way out and stopped to refuel again—a sloppy business without the shelter of a Mulberry. We were beginning to think about chucking it in when suddenly the echo-sounder pen went mad. Up, up, up it climbed, then dropped just as steeply, leaving a great inked pinnacle on the paper. We all looked instinctively over the side and through the clearest water we had seen for weeks was a great dark shape. Thick fronds of weed (*Laminaria saccharina*) could be quite clearly seen. We had certainly found an obstruction with a capital "O". But was it a Mulberry or just an isolated clump of rocks?

It is difficult to say why but just looking through the water gave us the impression that whatever was down there was man-made. It was big, longer than broad, and somehow the angles seemed too sudden and sharp to be natural. A clump of rocks would surely spread out more gradually.

The thing to do was obviously to dive down and have a look. We sat and looked at one another—for ridiculous as it sounds we had left the diving gear behind! All we could do was to take an accurate position with the sextant and also take some visual cross-bearings on shore "marks". Then we headed for home, promising ourselves a dive at the spot the very next week-end.

But diving in Britain is not like diving in the Mediterranean and it was two months before I could get out there. The weather wasn't altogether to blame—though it certainly seemed that the British week-end syndrome had set in—fine all the week and then howling gales and rain at the week-end. Finally, however, on one Sunday morning everything went right. The tide was right. The sun shone. The week-days preceeding had

---

Facing Top. A cross conger. Philip Smith located this conger in Bournemouth Bay in 30 feet of water when the visibility was about 8 feet. Using his Rolleimarin, Ektachrome X film and flash with PF1B bulb hand held off the camera, he took three or four shots (f16/125). The conger put up with the first two bulbs and then decided he didn't like the flash at all. He started moving out at the photographer. And this was the result. *Bottom.* Whelk out for a walk. Taken in Swanage Bay when the visibility was down to four feet. Calypsophot camera with 20cm. close-up lens. Tri-X. Colin Doeg.

been settled. There was no wind to speak of and the sea seemed reasonably calm.

John Messent, another Bromley Branch diver, kept his 15-foot boat at Bognor Yacht Club too and I see from my log-book that the other divers, split between his boat and mine, were Reg Dunton, Ray Weddle, David Rose and Malcolm Inch. The ones who hadn't been on the first location trip were clearly dubious about the chances of good visibility and I hardly expected it to be as clear as it had looked from the surface that first time.

It seemed to take ages to get to the right spot, but once we were there there was no mistaking it. A great dark shape could be seen from the boats and both anchors smacked right into it. The tide was very slight and soon everyone was kitted up and rolling over backwards into the water.

It was a Phoenix unit. There was no doubt of that from my first sight of it through my mask. My first impression was that it was lying on its side. We were anchored nearer to the shore end and as I pulled myself down the anchor rope I could see from high up that the rope disappeared into a tangle of the long brown shapes of *laminaria digitata* and *saccharina* weed. Iron bars heavily encrusted with spongy growths and others stained red with rust criss-crossed the structure.

Then I realized that my first thought was wrong. What I was looking at and into was a series of compartments. This was the top of the Mulberry and the rods and bars were part of the strengthening of the concrete or part of the valve gear. Right at the end one stout metal upright rod, covered like the others with growths, but also bearing flag-like green seaweeds, could have once held the beacon marked on the chart, but that is only guesswork.

After checking that the anchor—the rope went over one iron beam and down into the gloom of one of the compartments—was firmly hooked in, I rose up, finned over the great fronds of weed and then dropped down the left-hand side to the seabed. My depth gauge showed something just under 40 feet, which told me that if this was indeed a Phoenix Unit Type A1, which stood 60 feet tall, then at least ten feet of the unit must be sunk into the sand and shingle bottom.

But it was there on the bottom in the shadow of one of the great walls that I had my first surprise, the first indication of what a paradise of marine life this was going to be. For suddenly I was surrounded by fish. Big fish. All looked at least two feet long. None showed the slightest fear of me. For a moment I held my breath—I was sure that my bubbles would scare them away—and started using my Nikonos underwater camera as though I had a hundred feet of film in it.

The fish were pouting (*Gadus luscus*). But pouting such as the shore angler or the angler over the rocks inshore never sees. They were huge and nearly all were beautifully marked with light bars down their coppery sides. It gave them a sort of zebra look. Then my eyes began to sort things out and it was clear that there were some differences in the fish.

The older, bigger ones, often bore no such stripes, but were a uniform golden-brown. But what surprised me most was that far from my bubbles frightening the fish away, the rush of air as I breathed out seemed to attract them. It got to the ridiculous state where I was almost unable to take pictures because there were too many fish too close! I touched them with my hands and could even push them gently out of the way. I could have sat there on the bottom for hours, but I felt that if this was just a sample there could be far more to see elsewhere. I moved on.

The pouting in a school of about a hundred were still wheeling around me and ahead of me as I finned along the walls of the wreck. A perfectly round hole in the concrete wall at my right hand caught my eye. The rim was metal and it lead into a dark interior. Part of a pumping valve? I couldn't tell.

I moved on again and stopped suddenly. A wall ahead of me seemed to be covered with balls of cotton-wool. The concrete loomed above and shut off the sunlight. It seemed almost twilight and it wasn't until I came closer that I could see clearly that I was looking at an area about 50 feet wide by 30 feet high —was this the bow or stern?—completely covered with dead men's fingers, white puff-balls that are really animals. Most had their tiny polyps fully extended.

I took one or two pictures of this extraordinary sight and swam on. Now I came out into the sunlight and met the first diver I had seen since descending to the sea-floor. This is some indication of the size of the Phoenix. I recognized Reg Dunton. He was prodding hopefully into one of the compartments— broken open sideways here—with his lobster hook. The Mulberry appeared much more open and smashed at this end. Either it had sunk deeper into the sand or waves had broken it up more. At any rate the whole character of the scenery changed as you finned along. As it became more open and flattened, the growth changed too. The long fronds of laminaria petered out giving place to pod weeds, or sea-oaks (*Halidrys siliquosa*) which grew out from the sand.

I realized afterwards that this cannot be right. Only very small weed can use shingle or small stones as its anchor. The fact that this forest of sea-oaks, looking very much like woodlands in miniature, could flourish there and grow to a height of three feet or so proves that it is using something buried under the sand for its holdfasts to cling to. And this "something" there could only be part of the wreckage. Certainly there is no doubt that this seaward end is more broken up. Lying on their side like two giant wheels almost touching the seabed are two of the unit's towing bollards. Here the unit seems to have twisted and snapped in the middle.

Is this the Phoenix unit that Captain Liscomb says in his book was rammed and sunk by a small tug just as she was being taken over for the long cross-Channel tow? It is far enough out at sea for this to be so. But back to my dive . . .

Other fish had joined the few pouting who now seemed to be brave enough to leave the shelter of the monstrous mass of the less-damaged portion and travel further with me. These new fish were even bigger, but shyer and their long green very streamlined "fish" shape marked them out immediately as pollack (*Gadus pollachius*). There were dozens and dozens of them, but they seemed to prefer the more open water. Even so by all the standards I have ever applied to being able to get close to fish, these were the opposite of any I have ever met underwater. They kept just out of reach, reacting swiftly to the slightest aggressive movement, and altogether much more powerful swimmers than the pouting. But as some indication of their lack of real fear one of the larger ones let me nudge him twice with the measuring stick I use for close-ups with the camera! They had obviously, like the pouting, never seen man before.

I took a picture of Reg Dunton with the fish behind him, felt the wind-on stiffen, and knew I was out of film. On such a day with the visibility in the open well over 30 feet, I could have used up film after film. A glance at my pressure gauge showed me however that I would soon need more air.

I turned and started swimming gently back down the side of the wreckage towards the anchor rope. When I think of it now I can still remember how beautiful it all was. It was like being in a giant outdoor aquarium with the sunlight slanting down through blue water as opposed to the usual English Channel blurry-greenery.

As I moved along half-a-dozen common starfish (*Asterias Rubens*) caught my eye on a patch of shingle at the foot of a steeply sloping wall. Each one was humped up in a balloon shape very unlike their usual flat star spread. All were eating. It was an undersea self-service store. As I watched I saw that the slope of the wall was covered with mussels and barnacles. Some dog whelks (*Nucella Lapillus*) were moving over the barnacles. They were white shelled whelks so presumably, as the whelk tends to change its colour according to what it eats, the barnacles and not the mussels were their food supply. In slow, slow motion one of the whelks moved too close to the slope of the wall and slid down on to the shingle where the starfish were humped over previous victims of just such a fall. But it was probably mussels which came the starfishes way by this food chute for all around the six diners were empty mussel shells.

On that dive the starfishes lunch-counter was the last of the sights I saw. I was so busy watching the starfishes keeping up the pressure on the shells of their prey that I ran out of air just there.

I think we were all shattered by the success of the dive. Certainly I remember thinking that such a place should be kept undamaged by man. What a place for a student of marine growth! Here was an accidental vast experiment, if such a student cared to make use of it. Precise calculations of the rate of growth could be made as everything could be worked out from the date of sinking when virgin concrete and metal went down to the seabed. I wasn't high-minded enough to say to myself that I woudn't take a lobster from the unit if one showed himself! But I don't think anyone except perhaps the novice spear fisherman could shoot those pouting—that would be the closest thing to murder there could be because I felt that those fish somehow trusted you.

Since then I have made dive after dive on the lost Mulberry. Each time the entry in my log-book gets longer and longer. We have found that you have to dive out there as much as two hours before slack water to get perfect conditions. The tide is never really a great nuisance to the diver because he can always shelter behind the mass of the Mulberry. But it does affect the visibility. When the tide is running it brings with it a great deal of suspended matter and though you can still study subjects close to, it does ruin the larger picture which has grown a feature for us of these dives.

I am sure that it was these later dives that brought the things I saw into direct conflict with the things I read—no matter how eminent the source. One thing the amateur diver has to remember is that he is seeing things that very few people, if any, have ever seen. Most books to which divers go as sources for information are written by men who have never seen the seabed, never seen fish in their natural state, never seen any form of marine life behaving as it does in the sea. Most of these eminent authors are not too proud to admit this. They are inclined, however, to let the evidence of a few trawled up specimen lead to a fishy conviction, to let the way a fish behaves in an aquarium become the way it behaves in the sea. They forget too often that the coloration of a fish as it lies at an angler's feet or is smashed on the deck from the "cod end" of a trawl, may not be the subtle colours of the undersea.

The diver then must use these books for identification, but after that he should proceed with caution. Fortunately we shall not long be without "proper" books. The marine biologists, for example, together with more and more marine experts are using the aqualung to see the objects of their study in real life.

This criticism of marine life reference books is not made with any sense of pride, nor would anyone in this book want to set

out to "Challenge the experts". But it is important that what
the diver sees should be written down. All this may seem to be a
a long way from my sunken Mulberry, but in fact it isn't.

Those clouds of pouting which rush excitedly all round us
when we dive there are not the pouting of the reference books.
If you look them up you'll often find them under "Bib". *Gadus
luscus* is their Latin name. "Rarely over a foot long," says one
book. Most of *my* pouting are over a foot long. "When first
caught," says another book, "it has a beautiful iridescent copper
colouring with dark cross-bands . . ." So far so good, but what
would the author say if I told him that in their natural state
there may indeed be some fish marked exactly as he says, but
my fish are dark-brown with *light* bands round them.

Which brings me to my main problem. Down in the dark
places of the tangled wreckage of the Phoenix are another sort
of pouting altogether. There in tunnels bordered with dead
men's fingers and in permanent shadow are big dark-copper
coloured pouting with no bands on at all!

Not all these un-banded fish are in the dark places but they
do seem to favour the gloomier spots. It is wrong to attribute
human characteristics to animal or fish behaviour—that I
know. But you would think that these were the old ones not
wanting to rush out and play in the bright lights with the
young adults. There is not the slightest doubt in my mind that
these fish are older than the others—they tend to be bigger,
they look underwater about two feet long, but the most com-
pelling reason for this feeling of age that comes on very strongly
at the sight of them is that they have a sort of glaze about them
particularly round the eyes. The eyes are bulgy and old—just
as an old conger's eyes are old. Their coppery-brown skin is not
the skin of a thrusting young adult, but has been scratched and
these marks show dully in the narrow places they glide in and
out of at the diver's approach. They, too, are not frightened
of you, but give more of an air of caution than the great shoals
of the others.

None of my books mentions the extraordinary use by pouting of the pelvic fin which together with the barbel gives a
tricycle undercarriage effect when seeing from below. These
two fins—if they can really be called that—reach out like soft

little forked hands at the slightest disturbance of the seabed that could mean the uncovering of food.

The impression of hands is too strong to ignore. In fact these "fins" and the way they are used give a strong indication of being sense organs in the same way that the barbel beneath the lower jaw is used for food detection.

The "friendliness" of the pouting surrounding this sunken wreckage really sums up the diver's dilemma. There is no doubt that these pouting could be "tamed" to the extent that a diver could literally have them feeding out of his or her hands. Two divers can, as my wife, Penny, and I have done, round them up, condense the shoal, almost pose them for photographs as required. But where are we then? What contribution can our close contact with these fishes make to a study of fish behaviour? What can we find out? What is wanted?

Here is the central problem. Shouldn't divers be in such close contact with the marine biologist that the expert can tell the amateur what he wants to know? Of course the simple solution is for the marine biologist to become a diver. This solution is far better than attempting to teach the diver to become a marine biologist. Amateurs such as I cannot hope to be able to spare the time to study up to the standard required. Must we then leave the whole thing to future generations of biologist divers?

It seems a fearful waste. I do not pretend to know the answer, but all I can say is that we must not allow the amateur diver to be put into the situation which some archaeological experts seem to want. One of them (a very eminent man) actually told me—"I wish you divers would not find the ancient wrecks, because time is immaterial—qualified archaeologists will reach them in the future and you are merely interfering!" As the stupidest statement of the century this takes some beating. But it reflects a train of thought among some experts.

It is fortunate for marine archaeology that some are not so short-sighted. In that field I prefer the attitude of Joan de Plat Taylor of the Institute of Archaeology who says in effect: "Find the wrecks, report them to us and then when the excavation or recovery work starts we'll see that you are in on it. If a artifact is something that we do not need we will let you keep it."

Sea spider, alias the spider crab. This fine specimen was pictured by Geoff Harwood at Abereiddy, South Wales, with his Agfa Flexilette with electronic flash, f11/125. Ektachrome-X at a depth of 30 feet.

The approachability of fish underwater would seem to bear a direct relationship to their knowledge of man. Certainly these pouting had not the slightest fear of the diver—probably due to the fact that they had never seen one before. Taken near Selsey in 30 feet of water on the wreck of a wartime Mulberry unit (see Chapter Five) on High Speed Ektachrome in Nikonos camera set at f16/60 with PF1B flash bulb. Kendall McDonald.

In other words while we are in the state that all experts are not divers and many more non-experts are divers, we must work together. At the moment, except in the field of archaeology and to some extent geology, there is a vast need for co-operation between the amateur and the expert.

Many keen divers find their experts and dive for them and willingly accept guidance from them. What is really needed is a central clearing house to which divers can take their problems and to which the experts can take their problems and requests too. The British Sub-Aqua Club has tried to set this up with their scientific liaison work and in the future this may well be the nucleus of some such common bond.

One scientist who realizes the value of such co-operation is M. W. Robins of the Department of Zoology at the University of London. He recently enlisted the aid of divers by an article in the magazine of London Branch of the B.S-A.C.—*London Diver*—for his researches into the distribution of "Dead Men's Fingers".

He wrote: "Dead Men's Fingers is the rather lurid name given to a colonial soft coral found in British seas. This name, however, does give a good indication of the strange, fingered form of the animal, its size and colour. It is probably familiar to most divers in our waters as white, puffy clumps standing about six inches tall, which occur on algae-free rock faces and pier piles.

"A closer study of this stationary and rather plant-like animal in its environment will reveal that it is strewn with small sea-anemone-like polyps standing above the general surface. In a large and fully expanded specimen, it will be seen that each polyp has eight tentacles and that these have further, very fine side branches. The animal feeds on plankton and fine, suspended organic gubbins in the sea, so such an array of food-catching polyps with many branched tentacles provides an efficient trap for such material. The mass of the colony is not calcified as in the true corals, but is fleshy. However, it contains many small calcaneous rods which give it considerable mechanical strength.

"The trouble with Dead Men's Fingers is that there are several types which have not yet been fully described and furthermore, their distribution is imperfectly known. Divers could add greatly to our knowledge with respect to the geographical range of these animals. There are three types which can be distinguished on the basis of their colour and their general body form. They are:

"1. White Dead Men's Fingers (*Alcyonium digitatum*). This has few (say up to four on average) stumpy branches or fingers; the polyps can retract completely within the substance of the colony. This is the most common type and can be found all round Britain's coasts. It has depth range from 0–100 feet.

"2. Pink Dead Men's Fingers. This resembles the former species in body form and the ability of its polyps to retract, but differs from it in being pink in colour. Its distribution is very incomplete: it is known that they occur in deep water trawling grounds of the North Sea.

"3. Red Dead Men's Fingers (*Alcyonium glomeratum*). This differs markedly from the two types described above. The form of the colony is more branched (with up to say ten branches) and the fingers are more slender; it is orange-red in colour and the polyps cannot retract into the substance of the body. It is not as ridged as the previously mentioned types and perhaps as a consequence tends to be found in sheltered positions such as rocky clefts and overhangs. It has a depth range of 30–100 plus feet. It has been recorded in the Scilly Isles, Cornwall, and Pembrokeshire and thus would appear to have a S.W. distribution.

"As the white form (*Alcyonium digitatum*) is well-known from many points around the British coasts, there is little need to record it from other localities. The reverse is true of the pink and red (*Alcyonium glomeratum*) types whose range can be deduced only from a few localities where they are known to occur.

"I would greatly appreciate further records of localities where the pink and red dead men's fingers occur. The animals can be recognized whilst diving on the basis of the description, but absolute proof of identity can be best established in a laboratory. For this purpose they can be preserved in 70 per cent alcohol (meths) or better still be brought back alive in a thermos flask two thirds filled with sea water."

I have mentioned earlier the wall of dead men's fingers on the sunken Phoenix unit. It was after reading Robins' request that I realized that I had seen—as I had drifted slowly up that incredible growth-covered overhang—red and pink growths among all the others. Realized too that in another part of the wreckage altogether I had seen a pronounced red cluster in one of the deep compartments. Had I photographed them? Out came all my colour slides of the Mulberry and on two of them red growths showed clearly. Was this what Robins wanted?

It is difficult to put into words how heartening it was to find an expert who was interested to the point of being willing to go anywhere to see my slides! If only most specialists reacted the same way to the amateur.

After studying my slides, Robins reported on them. It was not exactly what he was looking for—it was another specimen entirely. My pink dead men's fingers were *Alcyonium digitatum norvegica*. Said the doctor: "The pink form is said to predominate in Norwegian waters, but is known to extend to Plymouth although it is comparatively rare at that position. It is possible that the proportions of the two sub-species varies from North to South in the British Isles. If this is the case one would expect a high proportion of pink forms in Aberdeen, for example, but a low proportion of pink forms in the Channel. There is also a possibility that the pink form is adapted to the still waters of the Norwegian fiords and occurs in this country in specialized ecological niches, such as the inside of your Mulberry harbour where there is not much movement of water."

He went on to say that he felt sure that his research problem would be solved with the help of amateur divers.

Even if it was not a sensational discovery—even if it was the wrong kind of specimen—such co-operation, with enthusiasm on both sides, does prove what discoveries joint operations could bring.

Certainly contact was made and I know now that on my next dive on the Phoenix I shall be endeavouring to produce for Robins actual specimens.

My exploration of the Mulberry unit is presenting me with question after question. Lobsters are of course of interest. I like lobster. And provided I can capture them I have not the slightest hesitation in eating them. But my liking for lobster (cold with mayonnaise) is not the entire sum of my interest.

Here again, as in the case of the pouting, not everything one reads fits in with what the diver sees. Lobsters, says one source, rarely venture far from shelter and not at all in the daytime.

But I have met lobsters in the daytime in good visibility water hundreds of yards from the nearest rock shelter.

The bigger the lobster, says another source, the more sluggish his behaviour.

Yet a really big specimen—he looked nearly three feet long and on estimate was well over ten pounds—was the fastest thing underwater I have ever seen. As I dived down on him from behind he spotted me and claws flashed across in front of my mask in swinging hooks that for speed would not have disgraced a featherweight boxing champion. In a moment I was the one being attacked and I must say that I now have a healthy respect for the speed of a big lobster's reactions. (It is worth noting that this aggressive defence is not an isolated reaction—another diver told me that exactly the same thing happened to him in deep Devon waters. He, like me, reports that it was not at all funny at the time.) And yet some small two-pounders that I have taken from the compartments of the Mulberry by hand, put up very little resistance, nor were they very active.

The lobster's colouration is sometimes an electrifying bright blue. Others, older, are duller and vary from a deep black to a tired grey. Largest of all the lobsters taken from the Phoenix unit so far—for the place is honeycombed with impossible tiny tunnels and overhangs—is that lifted by another Bromley Branch diver, Reg Dunton. This veteran measured over 29 inches in length (from claw tip to tail) and weighed over ten pounds. He was more sluggish than the youngsters. His age, estimated by Dr. Norman Jones of the Marine Biological Station at Port Erin, Isle of Man, from a description of his size was "something between 15 and 20 years old". As Dr. Jones had no way of knowing that the lobsters came from a sunken Mulberry unit that must have "died" in 1944, his estimate has some independent corroboration.

There was considerable evidence too with Reg Dundon's lobster that he had not moulted for some considerable time. Not only was there a slipper limpet (*crepidula fornicata*) attached to the underside of the "crusher" claw, but the carapace was covered in growths, including two which looked like a woman's earrings—tiny green cones swinging from equally small hold-fasts. These could have been some sort of algae or a hydroid with a fleshy bryozoan growing on its end.

The subject of lobsters is a tricky one for the diver. Increasing pressure is being applied to authority suggesting that the diver either robs lobster pots or take so many lobsters and crayfish from the sea that he is depriving the lobster-pot fisherman of his livelihood.

This pressure is applied by professional fishermen through their organizations in the hope that the Ministry controlling such affairs will slap a complete ban on skin-diving in the seas around our coasts. This, even such partisans realize, is rather a remote hope, so they aim at a slightly diminished target—a complete ban on the taking of shellfish by divers.

What is it all about? Why should apparently sound members of society seek to extend governmental control to the very seas from which they draw their own livelihood? Why attempt to make "the freedom of the seas" a mockery?

The reason, I am sorry to say, is founded in ignorance, boosted by greed and fed by inflammatory statements from men in positions of trust who should know better.

The truth is, of course, that the average fisherman knows perfectly well that the amateur diver is not going to spend his precious time underwater in trying to extract a lobster from a lobster pot. Given the worst will in the world, such an undertaking strikes me as hazardous in the extreme. I have seen a lobster trapped in a lobster pot underwater. I have looked into such a pot. All I can say after a quick survey—for having come upon such an isolated pot I was anxious to clear the area altogether due to the fear that I too would be accused of robbing pots—is that I would rather you put your hand in than I. Once hauled to the surface the force of gravity pins down the lobster, but to represent the removal of a lobster from a pot *underwater* as a simple two-second operation frequently indulged in by divers is just moronic. If it were a regular practice of divers then I would suggest it would be easy to spot-the-diver at any gathering—he would be the one with various fingers missing!

No, the reason for trying to blame the amateur diver is to get at another sort of diver altogether. I refer to the *professional* crayfish diver, who is registered as a professional fisherman and cannot be stopped by anything short of a complete ban on divers taking shellfish of any kind. This is the diver the professional lobstermen fear and he is confused in their minds with anyone who dives beneath the surface.

I should think that the professional crayfish diver in the West Country does indeed make much more money than the traditional pot fishermen. Few would argue with this. Yet Ministry of Agriculture, Food and Fisheries research proved that the diver-fisherman is not depleting stocks of crayfish. The reason for this is fascinating. And boils (an apt word for shellfish discussion!) down to the amazing fact that *we do not know where the crayfish breed*. Experts believe that the immature shellfish are born and live somewhere off the coast of Cornwall and Brittany, but it is only the mature fish that migrate to our shores.

Divers who are familiar with the Devon and Cornish waters have rarely reported seeing a young crayfish—yet they have reported seeing lines of crayfish coming in from the greater depths. And lobsterpot fishermen conveniently forget in their arguments that the diver-fisherman is bound by exactly the same rules concerning the landing of immature fish as they are.

Even so emotions run high. Reports come in all the time of a state of almost open warfare between the fishermen and the divers. One Devon fisherman in all seriousness told me that the divers had ruined the scallop fishing.

When I expressed genuine concern—divers do not pretend that all of them are angels—I forgot what a mobile creature the scallop is and how like a set of flying false-teeth he looks when swimming away from danger. "How have they done this to the scallops?" I asked. In all seriousness he replied—"They took 'em in the middle of their breeding . . ." Divers may not be angels, but they can't work miracles either!

Even if some of the reported actions of divers are so ridiculous as to be a laughing matter, the effect of the fishermen's campaign should not be underestimated. Many people now believe that the amateur diver does rob the pots of the honest toiler of the deep and such accusations—produced without concrete evidence—are difficult to refute.

Sooner or later some way must be found to solve this problem for I fear that unintentionally this brooding violence will end in some ghastly tragedy—a diver on the surface cannot swim away from a boat driven carelessly near him. Lumbered with his aqualung and out of air the diver could easily be killed as a result of an action that starts out as merely an attempt to scare him.

I have tried here to stress that their are faults on both sides. A diver often swims close to pot-markers despite the British Sub-Aqua Club's advice not to do so. A diver has been known to flaunt lobsters near men who have just hauled their pots to find the whole line empty. A diver has been known to take more lobsters than he wants and leave the others swirling dead in the shallows of the sea near a fishing port. Divers in the past have sold their catch to pay for air and their accommodation. But that at least should now stop with the B.S-A.C. ruling that no diver may sell his catch, whether of shell-fish or fish he has speared.

But the pot-fisherman is not entirely blameless. I have dived for lobsters and I have put down pots for them. And my pots have been hauled, emptied, smashed or have just disappeared— and I have strong evidence that it is pot-fishermen who have done it. They seem to believe that no one else has any right to anything in the sea but themselves.

This attitude must change. The divers are here to stay and both divers and lobsterpot men will have to learn to live together in the end. A ban on the freedom of anyone to use the sea will solve nothing.

It was because of the damage and loss of my own pots, as mentioned earlier, that I struck on a new method of putting down lobster pots. Obviously my pots with their clear surface markers were no problem for anyone to find. But if there were no markers . . . ! Supposing I put the pots down by hand underwater, then no one could find them. But there was the obvious snag to the new art of underwater lobster-potting. If they couldn't be seen from a boat on the surface how was I going to find them? I puzzled about this for a long time and then realized that if I could find one central spot on the seabed and placed my pots round that then it could only mean a short search underwater before I found them again.

It is easier said than done. After a while I found I could locate a certain big rock underwater by means of shore marks—and I put my pots down around this, carefully placing them in likely spots. (A lobster often leaves empty mussel shells outside his hole, one half of the shell is usually intact, the other in fragments where he has cracked his meal open.) I had some success with this method, but the effort involved made it less and less interesting. When the visibility was really bad, despite quick location of the main rock, recovery of the actual pots was a long and tiring business.

On visits to the sunken Phoenix we tried this method too, but it just wasn't worth while there either. I think we got one lobster in a whole season by this method, probably because the lobster population had quite enough food there without bothering to go into an intricate trap.

On one dive I thought I had discovered the lair of a monster lobster—what I saw gave me quite a fright. I was used to looking for a few empty shells outside a hole, but in one of the compartments of the Mulberry I found a mound of empty mussel shells some nine inches deep and three feet wide. My imagination raced into action thinking of the size of a creature which could have piled up food litter to this extent.

I still haven't found out the reason for the mound of shells. They lie in one corner of a gloomy compartment the mouth of which is covered with a heavy laminaria growth that dangles down like those bead curtains on the doorways of bars and shops in Southern France. I have looked carefully all round about in the weed cover and can still see no obvious lobster hole or hiding place. Neither can I see the hiding place of an octopus which might have helped to create such a pile of reject shell. What carries them there? Is it just tide and currents? Then why only mussel shells? Has mussel after mussel fallen in when ripped off the outside in winter gales?

It seems unlikely. But there they all are in a great mound devoted exclusively to undamaged, but empty, shells. Do mussels, like elephants, creep away to die in a secret grave-yard? The whole thing is just another mystery of this par-ticular part of the sea and only makes one realize how little time there is in a bottle of compressed air down among the life in the sea.

Probably I shall never know the answer to the mussel shell dump for sure, but it does raise another question in my mind. Supposing after thousands and thousands of years, the archaeo-logists of the future find the remains of this concrete structure and while excavating find my pile of mussel shells. Will they then assume that the inhabitants of this concrete structure lived on mussels and that they have discovered a rubbish dump close to the living room? A ridiculous suggestion, yes, but doesn't it throw the tiniest bit of doubt on all the mounds of empty shells that some archaeologists identify on a sea-shore of long ago as evidence of the eating habits of primitive man? Could not some of these mounds have collected in the same strange way as mine?

What other creatures live on my Phoenix unit? Well it would never do to forget the conger (*Conger Conger*). The slate-grey head of one that slid out from under a growth-covered piece of concrete looked like that of a Great Dane, except of course for the cold eyes. A late afternoon, early evening, dive is the time to see the congers. They start to stir then ready for the night's hunting, but in the pod-weed forest at the south-western end of the unit you can sometimes find them swimming slowly along in full light in the middle of the day. But it is the overhang covered with dead men's fingers and the large dead-white anemones (*Tealia Felina*) that marks out the real conger territory. Down there in the gloom is the sort of tumbled territory that the congers love.

Out beyond the weed is the flat floor of the mud-sand-shingle plain of the rest of the local seabed. On this, if your eyes are sharp or the "seabed" moves, you can find a decent sized sole (*Solea Solea*) or two. Sometimes a plaice (*Pleuronectes Platessa*) settles on a grey mud patch and his own camouflage gives him away. The orange spots stand out like beacons on the grey background and sighting is simple. Yet the same fish half-buried in sand or shingle will fade from view.

Swinging in from the plain like so many grey-blue bombers come big bass (*Morone Labrax*). The Mulberry is obviously a favourite spot of theirs. Alert, suspicious, powerful, they are difficult to approach. One diver stalked one through the weed until it spotted him. Then the big bass, which looked over three feet long and must have weighed over 10 lbs, shot up to the top of the compartments and apparently down the other side. The diver took a different route hoping to intercept and found to his amazement that he was looking through a hole in the weed a foot or two from him that seemed to have turned completely blue. It was the bass which had doubled back before staying motionless deep in the weed. Intelligence too—or perhaps just cunning—is another word we must add to the list of qualities of these streamlined beauties.

The seething life of this one spot is, it is true, highly concentrated in a small area, but it is typical of the vast marine aquarium that the diver finds around our coasts. Within two miles of the Phoenix and only a few hundred yards from the shore is Bognor reef. At low Spring tides it rises from the water and runs like a great black pathway of stepping stones right across the front of the town itself. Among the weed that decorates the rocks you can see through your mask another well-populated undersea world.

There the little pipefish (*Syngnathus acus*) plays at being another piece of curled weed. There the battered leaders of the black bream (*Spondyliosoma Cantharus*) brings little convoys which go to make up the massive shoals which come inshore in the Spring. Wrasse (*Labrus Bergylta*) curl in and out of the weed curtains. And all that shallow water is alive with life.

Even inside the reef in even shallower water there are still wonderful things to be seen. On a flat sand bottom one fine summer day four of us, Malcolm Todd, John Messent, Penny, and I, saw what looked at first like a three-foot wide blackened sheet of corrugated iron. On closer inspection the iron moved and flew—and a great sting-ray (*Trygen pastinaca*) soared into mid-water and raced away like a great bird.

In just as shallow water you can see the annual mating of the sea-hares (*Aplysia punctata*) . . . No, life in the sea is not confined to one particular place—divers will be the first to tell you so. Many will tell you that in comparison the wonderfully clear waters of the Mediterranean are barren. Probably one should not compare the two—for just as they are different they provide very different kinds of diving enjoyment.

British waters are less inviting and call for just that little more effort. But when our waters are clear, when the sun shines, when the sea is calm, when it happens and it sometimes does . . . Well then!

FORTRESS UNDER THE SEA

by Major Hume Wallace

Major Hume Wallace is Administrative Agent of the British Sub-Aqua Club. Has led many underwater geology expeditions in this country. Is investigating the discovery of a "Roman fortress" under the sea at Selsey Bill. Is the chairman of Kingston Branch of the Club.

Underwater geology and underwater archaeology sound pretty terrifying subjects. But the truth is that due to the present state of ignorance of things underwater, the amateur week-end diver can and does make useful contributions to knowledge in both these fields. What's more he can have fun doing so.

I am dealing with both geology and archaeology here because I have been interested and involved in both. It is in practice difficult to disentangle them because although it is possible to "geologize" without becoming involved in underwater archaeology, the converse is certainly not true. The underwater archaeologist, even if he is only interested in wrecks, must have some knowledge of the geological processes of sedimentation and erosion, and wave and current transport of materials. If he gets interested in drowned cities and harbours, he also gets involved in the geological question of changing sea and land levels. He must try to find out whether a much battered collection of stones is entirely the work of nature or whether, when and how man has played a part. This may mean learning all about the local rocks, soils, beaches and bottom deposits—as well as building materials.

This inter-relation between archaeology and geology is well-illustrated in three of the four following projects in which I have been involved. Only the first of these has been a geological project, pure and simple. It is a nice example of the sort of task that any group of divers should be able to undertake—the observation of the structure of the rocks and the collection of bedrock samples from an area of sea bottom over which they dive regularly.

Kingston Branch of the B.S-A.C. first sampled the delights of diving off the South Devon coast in 1961. We had heard from our friends in Bournemouth, Peter Browne and Frank Brooker, who had been there the previous year, of a submerged peak which came up from the bottom called East Rutts. So we took ourselves to the Plymouth area and made contact with a certain boat-owner. We asked him to take us to this point marked East Rutts on the chart and he duly did so.

That dive was a revelation to us. Never before in our diving in British waters which had all been up-Channel, or when in South Devon immediately offshore, had we found such clarity of water. Then there was the livestock. Fourteen divers between them collected fifteen varying crustacea—all over seven pounds. We had never seen anything like it before and nor, it seemed, had our boat skipper, whose eyes grew rounder and rounder as the catch accumulated on the deck. This, we were to learn, was fatal to our future prospects with him, although we engaged him to take us back there a fortnight later, he was strangely unable to locate the peak we had dived on before, but eventually found another further to the East which we now believe to be that shown on the chart before the present issue, about fifteen hundred yards further towards Bolt Tail.

We had an almost equally successful dive there, this peak being even more spectacular than the last one. It was, in fact, a great slab of marble some ten feet thick and fifty or sixty feet wide rising absolutely sheer sixty feet from the sea bed. In fact it resembled a monstrous tombstone rising from the one hundred and twenty foot sea bottom but its crest had been eroded into a series of sharp pinnacles and crotchets which would have done credit to Barry's work at Westminster.

We know that the peak is marble because that was where our geological work started. The visit two weeks before had aroused my curiosity, this time I had taken the precaution of bringing a hammer and chisel and detach some samples from various points before joining in the hunt for livestock. Here again the whole party did very well.

On the way back towards Plymouth, we noticed a collection of what looked like pot markers and remarked on them. The skipper, being out of ear-shot, his boy then said to us, "Oh, yes—he has had his pots here ever since you were out last time!" We gave up using that boat shortly afterwards as he kept raising his price with every visit and then there was the business that we could never find the same peak twice; not if there was anything to be found on it!

When we visited the East Rutts some years later in a boat out of Salcombe we found our old skipper still working the place we had found for him and when we came up alongside, he triumphantly held a crab about a foot wide above his head and addressed us in broadest Devon—"Lookit here me dears, and you can have 'ee too if you will let us have the wimin for half an hour." The "wimin" in question, two local Salcombe girls, were observed to become somewhat agitated. They later confessed to their escorts that they thought the offer seriously meant and that there was a serious danger that we would accept it. It would seem that the traditions of the Spanish Main die hard among the sea-faring inhabitants of the West Country.

But to return to geology. On examining the samples back in the boat, it appeared that we had found marble, but in order to confirm this, and because I thought they might be interested, since marble is not very common in this country, I took the samples to the Geological Museum at South Kensington. There, I was directed by the uniformed Civil Servant at the entrance to another uniformed Civil Servant at the entrance to the Library where I wrote my name, business and address in the Visitors' Book and was then ushered in where my samples were examined by the Librarian on duty. Deceived by the shape of the largest piece, the tip of one of the pinnacles on top of the peak, she decided that I must have got hold of a piece of stalactite or stalagmite, i.e. calcite, quite ignoring my explanations of where the pieces came from. She eventually consented to take a second opinion and went off to consult the chief petrographer. About ten minutes later she returned and somewhat huffily gave them back saying, "You're quite right they are marble," but displayed no further interest. So I took my pieces away again.

However, it would appear that the Civil Service procedure of the Visitors' Book has its uses, because about five days later I received a very apologetic letter from the Deputy Director, Dr. Peter Adams, who explained that he had been going through the book at the end of the week and came across an entry about a visitor with rock samples from five miles seaward of the Bolt Tail. He had not been given this vital information when the samples had been brought to him for identification as if he had he would certainly have seen me, as the area was one in which he, himself, was very interested. Would I please send or bring the bits back for further examination? As there was a telephone number at the top of this letter I rang up Dr. Adams to ask, politely, what his organization was playing at. This was the beginning of many years of fruitful co-operation, between the Geological Survey and the Oceanographic Institute on the one hand and the Kingston Branch of the British Sub-Aqua Club on the other.

Over the next five years we obtained for them about thirty samples of the bedrock from various points between Start Point and the Lizard. Most of these samples were orientated. This is very important to the geologist in the case of old and distorted rocks such as these, as it enables him to trace from which direction came the thrusts which have distorted them, and he is thus able to build up a picture of past mountain-building earth movements.

So before detaching the rock sample, which should be at least the size of a human fist, from the bedrock with hammer and chisel, the diver should make use of his diving compass and make some marks on the sample which will enable it to be afterwards orientated with regard to direction and the horizontal plane. How this may best be done will depend on the nature of the rock and what is growing on it, but one simple method is to use the saw edge of a divers knife to make some straight scratch marks, but once on the surface these scratches should be emphasized and amplified with crayon or paint before one forgets what they mean.

After the first few trips, when we had proved that we were

capable of delivering the goods, the Oceanographic Institute encouraged our efforts by a small subsidy towards the cost of boat hire. This is a very useful means of persuading a boat-load of divers, most of whom are not the least interested in geology, to dive in areas which will produce results in geology as well as in livestock; for it must be emphasized that our dives were ordinary branch dives on which only one or two people did the geological sampling while the rest followed other interests.

Over the years, the amount of work done by these few individuals as and when opportunity presented itself amounted to far more than that done in the same area by some who mounted special purpose expeditions only to be largely frustrated by the unreliable British weather and their own ignorance of local conditions; while the other method by which the same sort of results could have been obtained, sampling by instruments from a specially equipped surface vessel would have cost many hundreds or even thousands of pounds. So it can be said that the Geological Survey and Institute of Oceanography received very good value for the £25 odd which they paid out in subsidy over several years. Where there is no great hurry to obtain results, this method of employing amateur divers to obtain rock samples and information on the rock structures on an opportunity basis has much to recommend it.

As well as rock sampling, for the Geological Survey, we also began on our own account observations on the submerged beaches and wave platforms which throw light on past sea-levels in that part of the world and I think we are now in a position to say something about the general picture which is revealed. Going from bottom to top we have a very wide and extensive terrace, a plain almost a mile wide in places, in the − 120 to − 130 feet range, which must represent a very long pause in the sea-level, possibly during more than one ice-advance when the sea-level all over the world was lowered by the great quantity of water locked up in the ice caps. This is followed by a very steep and, in places, vertical cliff up to the − 60 foot level, where there is a distinct terrace on some of the submerged peaks and a great many others are cut off completely at this level. Then there is again a rapid rise to − 30 feet and from there a gradual rise to the present low tide level, again a great many

The only picture ever taken of cuttlefish mating in British waters. Shot one evening off Brighton front, the picture shows clearly the zebra striping adopted during courtship. Cuttlefish are usually much harder to see as they are experts at camouflage. The photographer usually needs to stalk them carefully, but Tony Baverstock, who took this picture, reports that on this occasion they were too engrossed in their love-making to notice him. Leica 1F, High Speed Ektachrome, f8/250. Visibility 10 feet; depth 30 feet. PF45 flash bulb.

The Wreck Hunter. Reg Dunton of Bromley Branch probes into a sunken Mulberry unit near Selsey with a lobster "hook". Depth 30 feet, f16/60, natural light, High Speed Ektachrome, Nikonos camera. Kendall Mc-Donald (See Chapter Five).

submerged peaks are cut off completely at – 30 feet or a little above. It must be emphasized that this is a composite picture built up from observation on many sites in the area. Part of the record may well be missing or obscured by recent deposits of sand at any one site.

We were interested to learn from Robin Eden's paper at the Watford "Sea Science '67" Conference that Edinburgh Branch of the British Sub-Aqua Club had followed very closely Kingston's pattern of activities combining lobster gathering with sampling the bedrock off the Berwickshire coast for the Geological Survey, with the very valuable result that the coal measures of North-East England are found to link up with those of the Scottish Lowlands a few miles off the coast. Then on their own account they have gone on to follow a very prominent wave-cut platform at – 60 feet off Berwick to the present sea-level on the Firth of Forth and then to 30 feet above sea level a little further north. This gives powerful support with precise figures, to the theory that the British Isles have tilted up in the north-west and down in the south-east since the melting of the Scottish ice-cap relieved the Highlands of the enormous weight of ice. How this particular terrace relates to those we have found still remains to be seen. It is to be hoped that other branches of the Club may be encouraged to fill in the gap along the West coast, there being not much hope along the East coast where sand fills most of the bottom of the southern North Sea.

THE EXPLORATION OF THE THAMES BED

A couple of years after the start of Kingston Branch's infatuation with South Devon a group of members who were not often able to get away for such long week-ends developed an interest much nearer home in the River Thames.

The leader of the group was Robert Forrest-Webb and the Group's Archaeological Adviser was Dr. Francis Celoria, then at the London Museum, which institution how houses the more important of our finds: the most notable being one of the few mesolithic (Middle Stone Age) maceheads to be found in Britain.

The London Area Scientific and Technical Group of the Club was founded shortly afterwards. Bob Webb and I both joined it, in addition to our own branch, and some of the river dives which followed were officially S. & T. and some Kingston Branch, with some of the same people appearing on both. The main area of operations was a semi-tidal one where the river flows past Kew Gardens from the "London Apprentice" at Isleworth to the Lion Gate at the North end of the Gardens.

The river is tidal for about 8 hours around high tide, but from about 1 hour before low-tide at London Bridge to about 2 hours afterwards when the filthy water which came up from below has flowed out again, the river level is determined solely by the flow of fresh water from further up. This is the time to dive there if one wishes to see anything and avoid being poisoned by filth. The best season is in winter after a dry spell when the growth of algae in the water is at a minimum and there are fewer pleasure steamers rushing up and down.

The important geological point is that the main river channel is cut down into the London Clay but is well lined with coarse flint gravel so that the clay is only occasionally visible. One place where it appears is opposite the Lion Gate at the north end of Kew Gardens where, presumably, the river crosses the out-crop of a slightly harder strata in the clay.

The first time we dived there, Bob Webb emerged shouting: "There are bloody great boulders on the bottom." "A geological impossibility," I retorted, "there is no hard rock within fifty miles of here" and dashed in to find what looked remarkably like Dartmoor granite Tors projecting four or five feet up through the gravel. However, I found that I could stick a knife into them and indeed cut a slice off, which turned out to be just yellow London clay. Also some of the boulders had score-marks two or three inches deep where they had been struck by the keels of larger river craft. They must have received quite a jolt!

This is not the only place where I have observed this underwater weathering of clay to the same rounded shapes, which granite and other hard rocks assume when subjected to long weathering in air. In fact, most clays which are wet all the time behave far more like hard rocks than they do in air where alternate wetting, drying and freezing rapidly reduces any prominent features.

Another, at first surprising, fact which follows from this is the stability of river courses (and navigational channels in the sea) which run through clay. In the case of this particular stretch of the Thames we can say that there has been no significant change in the low-tide course since Roman times. This view, rather surprising in view of the serpentine nature of that course, was forced upon us as we examined the two sub-merged strips of undisturbed gravel on each side of the river between the low-water mark and the recently dredged channel in the centre of the river.

The gravel is coarse, mainly water-worn flints, but included are almost round lumps of chalk which must have been rolled down the Thames or its tributaries from Windsor, Guildford or Dorking. They are well covered with moss and obviously have not rolled for a long time. There too are occasional frag-ments of animal bone and Stone-age artifacts such as our mace-head. Lying on top of the gravel we found water-logged branches and tree trunks and more animal bones (presumably preserved by the lime-saturated nature of the Thames water) and, the important point for the archaeologist, anything heavy such as metal, glass or pottery which has been dropped or thrown into the river for the past two thousand years. A further important point for the archaeologist is that for the most part these objects are lying where they fell. We can say this because the broken pieces of pottery and glass are still quite sharp at the edges, not rounded as they would be if they had been rolled along the bottom with the gravel. Also, there is a noticeable concentration of coins and keys at the places where one would expect to find them—the Ferry Crossings. It is rather pleasant to imagine the changing fashions in bad language as generation after generation dropped their latchkeys into the drink while pulling out their money to pay the ferryman.

Following our first successful results at Kew Ferry, Dr. Celoria persuaded us to extend our operations a little up-river to the site known as Old England at the northern end of Syon House grounds.

The whole Syon river frontage is something surprising to

find in the heart of Greater London—a wilderness where the river is not confined by artificial embankments. At high tide it spreads over the marshy pastures and every few hundred yards there are creeks caused by the receding waters draining back into the river. The river bank and these creeks are lined by marsh-loving trees in which herons and other birds roost and nest in season and, to complete the illusion of a primeval wilderness, the northern end of the grounds is scored with old and new overflow channels of the Syon ornamental lakes. At the time of Dr. Celoria's visit a couple of years before, this was let out to a farmer who allowed large and ferocious pigs free range in the tidal thickets.

This unpromising location had, however, been the site of a pre-Roman and then partially Romanized town or village. This is attested both by local legends and by the work of various archaeologists who have nibbled at it from time to time. It is not surprising that they have done no more than nibble since most of the Roman occupation level is covered by eight feet of stinking black tidal ouse with another two feet of river water on top of that at high spring tides.

Observing the state of the place today, earlier archaeologists naturally concluded that the inhabitants must have lived an amphibious existence in dwellings built up on piles like those today in the Malay Archipelago. Theories were put forward that the earliest inhabitants were migrant Swiss lake-dwellers. This was the state of knowledge when in 1928 Sir Mortimer Wheeler took a larger than usual nibble and with a large gang of navvies dug into an eighty yard stretch of the river bank, at the extreme north end of the droperty. He uncovered what he took to be the remains of a 16th-century flood embankment and below that the foundations of a Romano-British hut.

In spite of the fact that the hut was built on piles, Sir Mortimer concluded that these piles had been driven their full length into the clay and that the house had stood not out in the river raised up on piles but on the river bank with its floor of packed clay enclosed in a frame resting on the piles only six inches or a foot above the surrounding earth, and from this he concluded that the high-tide level must then have been at least fifteen feet lower than it is today.

I had not read Sir Mortimer's report when we first became interested in the place. If I had it would have saved me a lot of puzzling. While the others concentrated on the river bed between the low-tide mark and the dredged channel, I also tried to make some geological sense of the steeply sloping river-bank between the field above and the low-tide mark. A search of the river-bed produced immediate results. For as well as the medieval and modern pottery and glass fragments, which we had found at the other sites (see R. Forrest-Webb *Triton*, Nov./Dec. 1963) we began finding Roman material in quantity. Mainly roof tiles and some very large and thick floor tiles, usually broken. Also five pottery mooring rope weights (illustrated and discussed in my article in *Triton*, Jan./Feb., 1964).

But the river bank above took a little longer to reveal its secrets. Not unnaturally I could make no sense at all of the segment which had been churned up by Sir Mortimer Wheeler and his navvies. But, immediately up-stream from it, the record became plainer but still puzzling. It is, as illustrated in the adjoining sketch. (FIG. 1). The Roman period remains are all

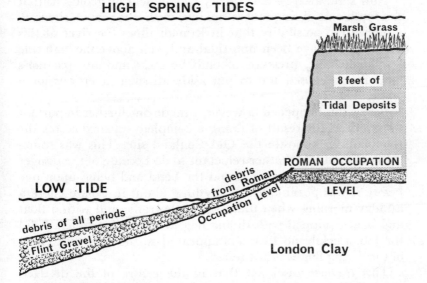

FIG. 1 : Section through Thames bank at "Old England"—Syon Park

concentrated in a three- to four-inch layer of red sandy soil which outcrops in the steep river bank about one foot above the low water mark. Below is a sloping beach of clay with flint-gravel appearing lower down and, above the Roman layer, eight feet of tidal ouse. There was at this point no trace of the artificial embankment mentioned by Sir Mortimer Wheeler. Presumably at this point it lay a few feet further out into the river and had all been washed away.

I began then to have serious doubts about the aquatic village on stilts both on archaeological and geological grounds. Archaeologically it seemed unlikely that Roman buildings sufficiently important to have roof tiles and two-inch-thick floor tiles would be constructed in this manner and geologically the soil of the Roman occupation level looked to me more like a fresh water flood plain deposit than anything that would be laid down in a tidal river such as the grey-black deposits which overlay it which are composed of glauconite, a precipitate caused by the mingling of salt and fresh water, and decomposed London sewage. One can see this deposited on every blade of grass of the overlying meadow following high spring tides.

Now I am aware of the theory widely held by geologists that the south-east of England is sinking, so that it was no shock to visualize the possibility that in Roman times the river at this point might have been non-tidal and well above the high tide level. However, pressure of club business and my partner's fatal illness caused me to put aside all such diversions for a while.

Before this happened however, I made one further important discovery as the result of doing a complete traverse across the river bottom opposite the Old England site. This was something we had been rather reluctant to do because of the danger of river steamers coming round the bend and being upon one before it was possible to do anything about it. So we chose a Sunday morning when there was little traffic and with a float and boat equipped with diving flag to keep off steamers I did the job. Luckily no steamers appeared so the deterrent effect of the diving flag was not tested.

This traverse disclosed that in the centre of the dredged channel there was a natural channel, which there was no need to dredge since it was over fifteen feet deep but still lined with flint-gravel and at the bottom of this "V", the final surprise—a river within a river . . . a river of *sand* three to six feet wide, the surface layers at any rate moving downstream with the current. The existence of sand rivers, often starting opposite the mouths of rivers on land and cutting deep channels in the under-sea continental shelves and slopes has been one of the exciting oceanographic discoveries of recent years. It would appear from what we found that these sand rivers start further up the existing courses of rivers than anyone has so far surmised.

At the beginning of 1967, I was at last able to resume some of my hobby-activities and it appeared that the Old England site was a favourable location to get the precise figure for the rise in the sea-level since Roman times. This had become important in view of Kingston Branch's interest in the sub-merged site of Roman Selsey. The first step was to check my previous impression regarding the nature of the soil of the Roman occupation level, so I visited the freshwater flood plains of Runnymede, Laleham and Sunbury Ait, all meadow lands about four to five feet above the natural (undammed) course of the river at normal levels but every few years they get swamped when major floods occur and a new layer of coarse-grained soil is laid down by the rapidly moving waters. At all three I was able to obtain soil samples which resembled very closely the Roman occupation level at Old England.

With this evidence reinforcing the archaeological considera-tion already mentioned—that tiled buildings would not be erected less than five feet above the normal river level to give a reasonable margin against floods—I felt it safe to conclude that the high-tide level in early Roman times must have been at least fifteen feet lower than today, since eight feet of ouse plus two feet of covering water plus five feet safety margin equals fifteen. But before publicly announcing this conclusion it seemed advisable to read for myself the report on the site by Sir Mortimer Wheeler.

I had heard from Bob Webb and Francis Celoria that Sir Mortimer reported finding a pile dwelling, but either they had not mentioned or I had not appreciated the vital qualification that the structure had stood firmly on the river bank with its floor only six inches or one foot above ground level. It therefore appeared to me that Sir Mortimer favoured the aquatic village theory which I was now convinced was completely erroneous, but if one is to contradict so eminent an authority, it is as well to be sure exactly what one is contradicting. So I did what I should have done long before and rang up Miss du Plat Taylor of the Institute of Archaeology, who is always very helpful to divers, told her the approximate period of the dig, and asked if I could come up and read the report on it.

When I called in that afternoon one of her assistants had the appropriate volume of *Archaeologia* with the place ready marked. I learnt with a mixture of chagrin and gratification not merely that Sir Mortimer and I were on the same side after all, but that we had both independently, at slightly differing sites, his with the complication of the 16th-century embankment remains, arrived at the same figure of fifteen feet plus, for the rise in high tide level. It is this exact agreement which to a great extent offset my anger at the waste of effort on my part caused by failure to read the sources for myself earlier.

Following from all this, I would suggest that we are now in a position to attempt a tentative "history of the river" at that point since the last glaciation. The present low-tide channel must have been cut down into the clay following the last glaciation when the sea level was very much lower than today. Also in the immediate post-glacial period the climate would have been much more severe so that winter freeze-ups would alternate with violent spring floods capable of rolling around the large flints and balls of chalk which now partly fill the channel in the clay. However, at some point in time this transportation of large material must have ceased with the easing of the climate and the rise in the sea-level, causing a backing-up effect on the current. Once stopped for any length of time it would be difficult for this movement of materials to restart since the fine sediment filters down between the stones and (possibly aided by the abundant lime in solution) consolidates into a stiff clay binding the lot together. Finally, the algae forms a sealing film over everything except in the central deep channel where the abrading grains of sand concentrate and cut their own inner river course. We can say that this con-

Spider crabs will camouflage themselves by planting weed on their backs. Here is a good example of this trick. Taken at Kimmeridge with available light over sand bottom Rolleimarin. Depth: 12 feet. HP4, f11/60. Philip Smith.

Above. Divers decompressing after a deep dive off the Dorset coast. The tide was so strong that this shot was taken by Colin Doeg while clinging to the anchor rope with his arm-pit. Calypsophot camera, Tri-X. f8/125. *Below.* The small Mulberry unit which can be clearly seen from the beach at Pagham is a favourite spot for the Sea Lemon slug (*Archidoris britannica*). In the sheltered interior you can often find the frilled lemon-yellow coils of their eggs—and the poor female resting exhausted beside her handiwork. This picture—a black-and-white from a High-Speed Ektachrome colour transparency, taken at f16/60, Nikonos with close-up lens—shows the slug on one of the towing cleats of the Mulberry unit. Kendall McDonald (see Chapter Five).

solidation of the bottom must have occurred by Roman times because we find undisturbed and unworn fragments of glass, pottery and bronze dating back to then. But it could have happened much earlier when there were just not the people about to drop things into the river.

About the beginning of the present era some iron-age men built themselves a village on the banks of the still non-tidal Thames just above its junction with the Brent. Then the Romans arrived and built some more ambitious structures, and one would suppose that they then built some flood defences to protect them from the occasional freshwater floods, since no thickness of freshwater deposits overlies the Roman level. Any banks which they built would be taken over and heightened against the now rising tides by the monks, who held Syon in the Middle Ages, and were everywhere notable builders of embankments and reclaimers of riverside meadows. The last reinforcement and heightening of the defences on this stretch of the bank was probably the building of the 16th-century embankment found by Sir Mortimer Wheeler; the workmen having obligingly dropped sufficient odds and ends in with the fill to enable it to be dated.

But it would seem that the Dukes of Northumberland who succeeded the monks at Syon were not able to maintain these defences against the ever-rising waters which either flooded over or washed away the barrier to flood the riverside fields. Probably when this first happened they were flooded almost every tide, but no doubt by then there was sufficient London sewage to give plenty of solid content to the waters, so the level of the land subject to flooding would rise rapidly until the present equilibrium was reached where only a few floodings at the highest tides are sufficient to deposit the $\frac{1}{10}$ inch per year necessary to keep pace with the rising sea-level.

HUNTING THE CRANNOGS

As a change and a relief from wallowing in Thames-side sewage sludge—a task which many would consider beneath the dignity of a diver, but one which only the diver amongst the archaeologists, with his close fitting and washable neoprene

5

suit is likely to attempt—Francis Celoria invited us to join the Islay Archaeological Survey Group camped on Inchcailoch, "The Island of the Spirit", in Loch Lomond. Three of us went in 1964, Bob Webb, expedition leader, David Gray and myself. Next year Bob could not go and I took charge of the diving party consisting also of David Gray, Roger Howlett and Frances Howell, of Kingston Branch and the Scientific and Technical Group.

In both years our principal task was to look for crannogs. For the benefit of those not versed in Celtic studies, crannogs are artificial islands constructed in ponds or lakes and may be any size from a few yards across to some which, in 16th-century Scotland, were the sites of considerable towns.

According to archaeological discoveries made during the last century as lakes and bogs have been drained, crannog building seems to have started in Ireland as early as 1500 B.C. These earliest crannogs were just round platforms of logs, brushwood, sods and clay, built to serve as bases for typical Bronze Age farmsteads. Presumably at that stage the crannog people were no different from their surrounding Irish neighbours. They just found it safer or more convenient to live that way. However, it would appear that they became specialized and particularly adapted to their aquatic way of life, because all of a sudden in the first two centuries A.D. crannogs appear in the Scottish Lowlands, Welsh Lakes and Somerset Bogs. The very rapid spread of the habit and the fact that the main concentration is on lakes which drain into the Irish Sea suggests that it was the Crannog People who were spreading out rather than that the natives of all these different areas suddenly decided that it would be nice to live that way.

Since nothing survives about this invasion it may be presumed that it was peaceful and that the newcomers, who may well have been related to the itinerant smiths who brought copper and gold from Ireland, pushed up the rivers and streams till they found a suitable piece of cultivable land beside a lake. There they settled with the permission of the chiefs of the local tribes who in these areas would be predominantly cattle keepers practising a little cultivation around their hill-top villages. They would not be interested in small patches of wet bottomland. This is only speculation on my part, but it seems to fit the facts as we know them at present.

Unlike the Scottish Lowlands where many crannogs have been carefully excavated and studied, little was known about any in Loch Lomond or elsewhere in the Highlands when we went there. There was a local belief that certain of the many islands in the Loch were crannogs. A written record exists which says that in the 17th century someone pulled one to pieces and recovered much timber. So for two weeks in two successive years we buzzed around the twenty-mile-long Loch in a variety of craft, often beneath the blazing sun which the Highlands can produce in May and June, so much so that it was a relief when we came to a likely looking islet and could flop out into the clear cold water. There is no doubt that using divers, not necessarily with aqualungs, is much the quickest way of identifying crannogs, but it also helps if some of the divers have some geological background.

We found at first that David Gray and I were having to teach the others what a natural glacial moraine looks like, though they soon caught on. Loch Lomond occupies the trough cut by an enormous glacier, so that glacial moraines, banks of stones deposited at the snout of the retreating glacier whenever it paused, are to be found everywhere.

The numerous islands in the Loch are of three types, solid rock islands which posed no problem, moraine islands and sand-banks which could stand on a base of either solid rock or moraine. It was the moraine islands which sometimes caused difficulty when looked at on the surface since this was often covered with thin soil and vegetation. It was difficult then to decide whether the island was a natural moraine or a man-made pile of stones brought from one. But once one put one's head under water the difficulty disappeared, since crannogs were distinguishable by:

1. Their more regular shape; all the Loch Lomond crannogs we identified had the same basic shape though their size varied greatly. (FIG. 2, *see page 132*).

2. The uniformity in the size of their stones. While moraines are usually a jumble of stones of all sizes from

enormous boulders far too large to be moved by relatively primitive people down to pebbles, the crannogs were composed entirely of stones of a convenient size for loading into small boats, between 6 inches and 18 inches across and there was often a grading towards smaller sizes at the top which was then finished off with a layer of gravel. This is just the reverse of the size grading one finds on a natural shingle beach where the larger stones are pushed to the top of the slope.

3. Where a layer of sand or silt overlay the solid rock or moraine lake bottom it was found to continue *under* the crannog, though sometimes with reduced thickness, i.e. a further thickness of silt had accumulated and overflowed the foot of the crannog since it was built.

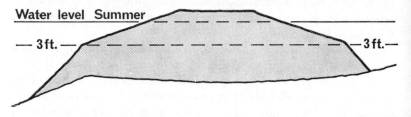

Water level Summer

— 3 ft. —   —3 ft.—

FIG. 2: Loch Lomond. All-stone crannog

It took us some little time to realize that these were the features we should look for, but once we had done so it became a matter of a moment to say "it is" or "it isn't". So, in the time we were there, we were able to examine most of the possible suspects in the Loch—about fifty islets. Out of these we identified five definite crannogs and one natural rock island which had been artificially extended. Not many, but in view of the multitude of natural building sites it is a wonder they bothered to make any.

I shall not go into the details about them here, though we did make rough plans with tape and prismatic compass, because we were working for Dr. Celoria and all this should be coming out in his archaeological reports. The purpose of this section is rather to show what divers can do in this field and to give some hints as to how they should go about doing it.

This then is the best point to bring in the fact that in South-West Scotland, nearer the origin of the Crannog People, there are many hundreds of suspected crannogs awaiting positive identification and rough mapping. Any diver who can use a compass and tape can do this. I was introduced to this area on the way up to Loch Lomond the second year by Mr. A. E. Truckell, Curator of the Dumfries Museum and Secretary of the Dumfries Archaeological Committee.

He had heard of our work at Loch Lomond and was anxious to have some divers look at his crannogs. So I went up a couple of days in advance of the others and stopped off at the pleasant county town of Dumfries, dominated by a steep hill topped by a *camera obscura*, with the County Museum housed in the same building.

The curator seems to be regarded in the neighbourhood as the source of all knowledge, geological, archaeological and zoological, as there was a constant stream of callers, mostly children, bringing for identification everything from curious stones and dead birds to a 13th-century leather shoe found in the peat.

Also there were two members of Edinburgh Branch, Robin Eden (a geologist) and Alan Pendereigh, who was interested in archaeology, whom I had asked to come across as it seemed that there was far too much work in the area for our London-based group alone. Then other members of the Dumfries Archaeological Committee arrived and transported us to Loch Kinder, a few miles south-west of the town at the foot of the thousand-foot high granite mass of Criffell. We embarked in boats belonging to the local angling club and were rowed out to the first suspect islet. As we approached the shape looked familiar to me. Robin Eden, the geologist who had never seen one before, immediately said that it did not look natural to him even though it was made of natural stones like those strewn everywhere along the lake-shore. Once looked at underwater, there was no doubt at all. It was the same sort of thing as the Loch Lomond Crannogs, but with two significant differences, there was no change in the angle of slope three to four feet below the waterline. There was an even 30 degrees slope from top to bottom, and all round the base of the crannog the remains of

very large tree trunks stuck out like the spokes of a wheel (FIG. 3).
They were half buried in the soft lake bottom and the bark and
heartwood had rotted away to leave great hollow tubes, but
what remained was very hard, almost petrified so that the point
of a knife would only just scratch it. The first one I came across
in the rather murky water I thought must be the leg-bone of
some prehistoric monster!

On the way back to Dumfries we paused beside Loch Arthur,
where another suspect crannog was pointed out. It looked
similar but there was no time to investigate it then. Edinburgh
Branch did so later and I understand found it to be almost
identical; a truncated cone of uniform-sized stones resting on
log spokes which presumably helped to keep it from sinking

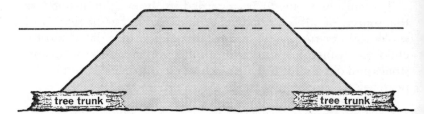

FIG. 3: Dumfries—Lochs Kinder and Arthur. Stone and radial timber

into the soft lake bottom. It would seem, therefore, that in this
region where both glacial stones and timber are abundant we
have a type of crannog intermediate between the log and sod
construction of Ireland and some other parts of the Scottish
Lowlands, and the entirely stone crannogs of Loch Lomond.
The gradual slope of the Loch Lomond structures could be to
deal with the large waves which can develope in the Loch.

Back at Loch Lomond I made a special point of looking for
any trace of radial timbers but with negative results until the
last day. Then we departed slightly from the policy which we
had hitherto observed of searching, observing and measuring
without disturbing our crannogs, since we were not experienced
archaeologists and in any case there just was not time for a
proper excavation.

But by the day before we were due to depart we were getting

into a mood of some frustration. We had found, examined and, in some cases, surveyed five crannogs and one extended natural rock. One of these, Inchgalbraith, was different from the others in that it stood well out by itself in the Loch and had served as the base for the Medieval Castle-of-Refuge of the Galbraiths. This crannog had obviously been extended many times at various points with different types of stone, some of which looked quite recent.

But the other five all stood close to stretches of flat cultivable land, either on sand islands or on the mainland and every fifty to one hundred yards along the shore of these flat stretches were little jetties, twelve to eighteen inches high, made of piled glacial moraine similar to the crannogs. This strongly suggested that each piece of flat land with its crannog was, in fact, a farm on which the means of transport between field and farmhouse was the boat rather than the cart. The following year, I saw a similar arrangement still operating on a sheltered fiord in Denmark where the complex of farmhouse and barns stood partly on the land and partly built out into the water so that the boatloads of hay from the outlying fields could be brought right alongside.

Unlike Inchgalbraith the stone of these fieldside crannogs was all of the same type and without any obvious joins as if it had all been laid at the same time. The cause of our frustration was that we just could not tell when that time was. It could have been 200 or 2,000 years ago. So on our last day we decided to give the nearest crannog, a very small one called The Kitchen, off the north-east end of the flat island of Clairinch, a thorough going-over.

David Gray and Roger Howlett put on aqualungs and grubbed round the base. According to David they lifted and replaced every stone of the bottom tier. Frances Howell and I waded and crawled over the top. We found a few slight depressions under which the stone was stained black which might have been the sites of posts which had rotted away, but otherwise nothing we had not seen before. Then just where the little wavelets were breaking, I noticed something a slightly different shade of red from the red-sandstone gravel which surrounded it. I picked it up. It was a small triangle of pottery

about 1½ inches each side. It appeared to have been the lip of a
pottery vessel with a thickened rim and an inset band of
pattern below it. Though waterworn, it reminded me of
something which I had seen recently, but I was not sure.

Then David Gray surfaced holding a blackened piece of
wood, which he had found under the crannog, the end of what
might have been a pole, but very flattened and rotten. We
returned to camp and sought out Francis Celoria in his work
tent surrounded by the bits and pieces which the land party
excavating the site of the ruined chapel on Iinchcailoch and a
farmstead a few centuries old had found.

I held out my piece of pottery and asked, "Is it . . ."

He looked at it and at me. "It *is* Samian" and he reached for
his pamphlet of Samian patterns. "First or Second Century
A.D."

So my visual memory had not deceived me. Only a few
months before I had seen a museum showcase where laid out
side by side were almost identical examples of ware found in
Britain, Continental Europe and the Roman predecessor of
Pondicherry discovered by Sir Mortimer Wheeler in South
India. And here it was turning up at the other edge of the
Roman World where some petty chieftain living on an island
in a remote lake had acquired it by trade or raid. It meant this
crannog and, possibly the others like it, had been occupied at
the same time as the first wave of crannog building was happening in the Scottish Lowlands.

David Gray's piece of wood was placed in a plastic bag, and
Francis Celoria told us later that it was a soft wood—larch or
pine. It raises an interesting question. Was it just by chance that
a waterlogged tree trunk was lying on the bottom when the
stones of the crannog were dropped; or were a few small pines
cut and laid on the bottom as a ceremonial vestige of what had
been the necessary first step in the building of a crannog in the
bogs of Ireland—a crannogic foundation-laying ceremony?

THE SEARCH FOR ROMAN SELSEY

Did the sea overwhelm a large prosperous Roman town near
Selsey? Have we found a fortress under the sea? These are the

Above. Six feet of camouflaged death. Tony Baverstock took this picture of a huge angler fish, which he found right underneath the diving boat anchored in 20 feet of water under the cliffs at Black Rock, Brighton. After he had taken his pictures, he wanted to see more of the fish—all six feet of it. He says: "Nothing moved except the eyes. I was not prepared to prod it. Stone-throwing proved ineffective until I crept up alongside and dropped a small rock on to the head—at arm's length. The reaction was instantaneous —the fish reared up, turned towards me with enormous mouth showing two rows of teeth. I fled." Calypsophot camera, High Speed Ektachrome, f8/125, visibility 10 feet, PF24 flash. Black-and-white from colour transparency. *Below.* The edible crab loves this sort of hiding place under Swanage Pier. Depth only 5 feet, visibility 10 feet. Camera Exa 1 in case with modified Ivanoff lens and electronic flash, Plus-X, f16/60. Geoff Harwood.

Above. Spotted Dragonet resting on a hard clay and rock bottom in Kimmeridge Bay. Taken by Geoff Harwood using an Exa 1 in case with modified Ivanoff lens and electronic flash, Plus-X film, f11/60. The fish was found by the photographer at a depth of 40 feet; visibility at the time was 12 feet. *Below.* Long-spined scorpion fish at rest. This picture was taken at Tilly Whim, near Swanage, using an Exa 1 in case, Plus-X film, electronic flash and close-up lens, f11/60. Depth: 20 feet. Geoff Harwood.

questions that divers are trying to find out at Selsey, Sussex.

Our work could develop into a major archaeological discovery or it could be just a tantalizing glimpse of what might have been. It all really depends on how much the sea has destroyed and how much it has merely submerged as it advanced. At present we continue to find something new each time we dive—each time the weather and tides are kind enough to let us dive there.

The site stretches from the Mixon Beacon, which is $1\frac{1}{2}$ miles south out to sea of the Selsey Lifeboat Station, $2\frac{1}{2}$ miles to the Malt Owers. So far we have explored only the Eastern end of the shallows near the Mixon Beacon (FIG. 4, *see page 138*).

What we have found there is shown best in Figure. 5. This figure shows the features we have so far definitely established as man-made. These are marked by the heavy shading and shows 300 yards of what we think must have been a defensive wall system. About 200 yards away to the North is an area marked "Quarry".

Here the two bands of hard Mixon limestone, which outcrop all around the Mixon shoal, are underwater, but appear to have been dug back in a series of jagged bays a few yards across. It looks as if separate gangs have been working in each bay. The clay bottom is littered with "quarry scrap"—small and often triangular bits of limestone quite unlike the naturally collapsed slabs one finds on the South face of the Mixon shoal, where the limestone has been undercut by wave action.

Of these two finds, the quarry and the remains of the wall, the quarry, though the less spectacular, is probably the most important. The reason is that the Roman Palace at Fishbourne and the wall we found are both made from similar stone slabs —from our quarry or one close to it. Another reason the quarry is so important is the light it throws on sea levels in Roman times.

The revelation of the connection with Fishbourne was one of those satisfying dramatic events which are not so uncommon in archaeology where discoveries at one side are apt to throw a sudden revealing light on something found at another.

Following first reports of our discoveries at Selsey Mrs. M. Rule, Secretary of the Sussex Marine Archaeological Com-

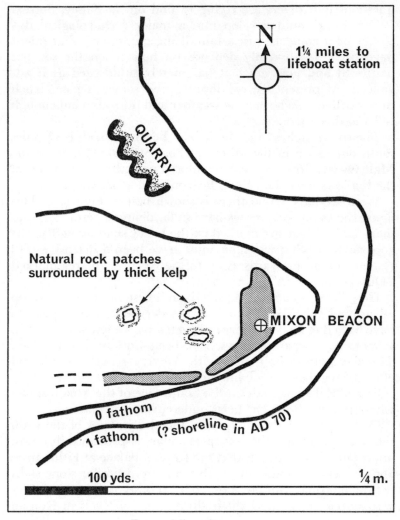

N

1¼ miles to
lifeboat station

QUARRY

Natural rock patches
surrounded by thick kelp

⊕ MIXON BEACON

0 fathom

1 fathom   (? shoreline in AD 70)

100 yds.   ¼ m.

FIG. 4: Mixon Beacon area

mittee, who also supervised the excavations at the Roman
Palace of Fishbourne near Chichester, telephoned me to say
that she had some stone she would like me to see. Luckily I
anticipated the reason and took with me samples of stone from
the Mixon. We were able to match these with the building

stone used for the west wing of the original Fishbourne Palace and the Forum in Chichester, both constructed around A.D. 70.

This "Mixon limestone" is quite distinct and is not known to occur anywhere else in Britain. Since the thickness of the slabs of the Mixon Mound, Chichester Forum and Fishbourne Palace correspond to the bands of natural rock under the Mixon, they must have been quarried somewhere quite close to there, possibly our quarry. The stone from Chichester Forum and the Fishbourne foundations is quite fresh without traces of wave erosion or boring by marine organisms, such as disfigure many of the slabs of the Mixon Mound. This means that it must have been dug from what was then an inland quarry not picked up on the inter-tidal foreshore. For our quarry to be above water for 50 per cent of the time, the sea level would have to be 10 feet lower than it is today and for it to be dry all the time 18 or possibly 20 feet to allow for normal wave height.

For the sort of large-scale quarrying necessary to build Fishbourne Palace and much of King Cogidumnus's new capital at Chichester in the space of a few years, hurried "raids" for stone at low tide would just not have done. One would think that the quarry had to be dry for at least 50 per cent of the time and more probably for 100 per cent bearing in mind that this quarry must have been successfully worked in competition with the quarries at Bembridge, Isle of Wight (Bembridge stone also occurs at Fishbourne though not so abundantly). Bembridge quarries can be worked at all states of the tide and are equally convenient for sea transport to Fishbourne.

Now we have already established that the rise in sea-level on the Thames at Old England is *at least* 15 feet and evidence from London itself suggests that the true figure is nearer 20 feet—one of our Kingston Branch members has seen Roman pile tops that distance below the embankment. If this effect along the line of the Thames is indeed due to the British Isles tilting down towards the South-East as some geologists believe, the effect should be greater still at Selsey, say 20–22 feet, which would make our quarry dry 100 per cent of the time. If we accept the figure of 22 feet, it corresponds conveniently with the present one fathom line on the chart (the tidal range of 16 feet plus 6 feet).

If we now examine the Admiralty Chart of the Selsey area with this in mind something interesting emerges (FIG. 5). If the one fathom line did indeed correspond closely with the shore line in A.D. 70 then we see that the stretch of water called "The Looe" on the chart would be surrounded on three sides by dry land! If the sea level were 22 feet lower these banks would be dry at low tide and only just covered at high. Enough diving has been done by Southsea Branch on these banks for us to be sure that they are not recent sandbanks. In parts they are geologically similar to the Mixon feature with tabular masses of clay and with a harder cap rock with some stretches of boulder banks filling the gaps. So they must have been there in Roman times, though then they were probably larger than today. They may have lost something through current erosion along the

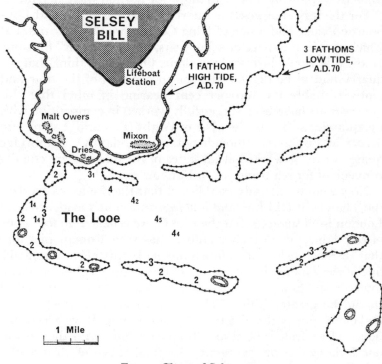

FIG. 5: Chart of Selsey area

sides and they have certainly lost a few feet off the top during the stage when they were only just awash and waves broke heavily on them.

So in Roman times The Looe would have been a stretch of enclosed water similar in scale to Portland Harbour. The shape looks so artificial and so well adapted to providing shelter against the prevailing south-west wind that one is tempted to wonder if that too is not partly artificial. At any rate it would have provided the first sheltered anchorage down-Channel from Pevensey Lagoon. This could hardly help making it a place of commercial and strategic importance. There is archaeological evidence to support this: a Roman road ran due South from Chichester towards Selsey and the Romans in Britain are not thought to be all that addicted to sea-bathing!

Roman coins, tombs and the remains of scattered prosperous houses and their wells found under modern Selsey suggest too that this area was part of the suburbs of a large and prosperous town whose centre must have lain further to the South in what is now the sea. Enough pre-Roman coins have been found also to suggest that this was a thriving trading centre even before the Roman Conquest.

There is also a certain amount of legendary and historical evidence for the post-Roman period. There is a legend that the South Saxons made their first landing at the Owers—and one could certainly not land there today. Then, according to the Venerable Bede, when St. Wilfrid converted these same South Saxons he built his church and monastery in the Isle of the Sea Calf, "surrounded by the sea on all sides except the West". And Selsey remained the seat of the Bishops until the move to Chichester in 1060. It was very common for early missionaries to build their churches inside the walls of deserted Roman towns or fortresses. In this case the place was obviously not entirely deserted since King Ethelwalh presented the Saint with "250 male and female slaves who dwelt in the Isle". Since the Saxons were not given over to large-scale slaving this suggests that they must have been the descendants of the surrendered Romano-British inhabitants of a town, who would not count as freemen and could be disposed of in this casual way.

Some of these tales had been known to me since, as a boy,

I spent summer holidays at Selsey. I had then paddled my kayak out to the Mixon and had been struck by its artificial outline. So, when at the beginning of 1967, I decided that Kingston Branch ought to take up the geological investigation of the Mixon and the submerged cliff on its South face, which had been started by the Scientific and Technical Group in 1963 and continued by Southsea Branch in 1964, I had some hope of finding an archaeological and historical bonus. I was not too hopeful however about the regular bank of broken stone slabs on top of the Mixon in view of the Scientific and Technical Group's failure to find any trace of a foundation. I had come to accept the view that it must have been composed of stone ripped from the edge of the natural rock platform by the waves and then pushed up into a mound in much the same way as Chesil Beach has been formed. However, when describing the site to Dr. G. C. Adams of the Natural History Museum, he put to me the direct question—did I think that stones of the size I described could be so moved by the waves? This started me reconsidering the problem and I then found that the difficulty about foundations disappeared as soon as the problem was approached from the standpoint of the marine geologist rather than as a land archaeologist.

Bearing in mind that the Mixon limestone probably belongs fairly well down in the Eocene series in an area where this period is usually fairly well covered by later soft deposits, it becomes obvious that the same situation would probably have existed here also, so that at least the same thickness of clay and earth which forms the present Selsey Bill would have covered the rock platform.

Few buildings in ancient times would have foundations more than 10 feet deep when situated on firm clay. So, provided that such a depth of soil and clay existed over the rock platform, all that we can expect to see now in the way of building remains, will be the heavier fragments which fell over the cliff edge as the sea advanced as is still happening today. Modern Selsey goes over the edge at the rate of about 1 yard per year. But there is no rock platform and the fragments are soon buried in shingle.

Subjected to such treatment, only the most massive structures such as fortifications, amphitheatres, and so on could be expected to retain anything like their original plan; and what the shape of the Mixon complex suggests in conjunction with its situation, is the S.E. corner of a city, or fortress wall, which had been undercut by the sea when its level rose above the underlying rock platform and could attack the soft material on which the wall stood.

However, all this remained only an interesting speculation until we could demonstrate either that the mound was positively the remains of a man-made structure, or negatively that it could not have been so formed by natural forces alone. So one of the principal objects of our expedition was to carry out a detailed examination and statistical sampling of the stones of the Mound. It was our hope that we would find some stone foreign to the area or some of those big flat tiles that the Romans, or Saxons and Normans who re-used their material, were so fond of putting in as ties or decorative courses.

In this we were disappointed. We could find nothing other than Mixon Limestone or what appeared to be decomposed Mixon Limestone, which is not surprising in view of the fact that we later found that there was a quarry of the stuff only two hundred yards away. But by an analysis of slab thicknesses in comparison with the bed from which they must have come, and by noting that certain other stone which was present in the beds did not appear among the larger stones of the mound we concluded that human selection and deliberate splitting of the stone must have occurred, so the mound could not be the unaided work of nature.

This analysis was published in the Club's Scientific and Technical Newsletter of August 1967, and although an interesting exercise in deduction it proved in the end to be something of a waste of time. We later found enough examples of fully squared stones, and stones altogether too large to have been piled up by the waves for us to be quite sure that the Mound was the remains of a man-made structure. We presume that the comparative rarity of fully squared stone is due to original sparing use. The Romans when building something like a wall would only use it on exposed surfaces, add to this the fact that the mound had been picked over for centuries to build medieval and modern Selsey and neighbouring villages down to 1831 when the practice was forbidden as a coast defence measure.

Some of the records refer to this fetching of stone from the Mixon as "quarrying". But we must bear in mind that by 1831 the hard bands of Mixon Limestone would be almost as deeply submerged as they are today. Also if we examine some of the products of this "quarrying" in the walls of the 13th-century Selsey Parish church we will see that the larger pieces, which have not been reworked, have the typical water-worn cushion shape of the outer stones of the Mixon Mound. Some also display the bottle-shaped burrows of the marine worm *Tholus* so they have obviously been looted from the ruins rather than freshly quarried. What is more some of these obviously water-worn stones are NOT Mixon Limestone. So that it would appear that other stone was also used in parts of the ruins which we have not yet found. We have already said that it is likely to have been a large and prosperous town and so would draw stone from many parts of the world as ships' ballast.

What now of our plans for the future? We will obviously try to follow the walls further Westwards from the Mixon. We have already seen from the air that they do continue though partly buried in sand. We still don't know whether they are the walls of our anticipated port town or of a "Saxon Shore" type fortress like Pevensey which it much resembles in outline. These fortresses were generally constructed as purely military and naval establishments separate from existing towns. If this is the case we can expect to find our civil port further to the West.

We are also hoping to find the actual docks or quays both of the military fortress, if that is what it is, and the commercial port. If these were situated on an inlet or dug back into the land there is a good chance that they and the surrounding buildings will be in a better state of preservation than the outer walls. There is a fair chance that they may have sunk below water level before the advancing shore-line reached them, so they will have been submerged without having first gone over the edge of the cliff. That this can happen is proved by Alexander McKee's work at Church Rocks a few miles to the West (*see* Chapter Two).

So we have great hopes, but realizing them will be slow work since the area to be covered is enormous and the time one can dive there limited. The only slack water is for half an hour before low tide. The rest of the time a fantastic current rushes across everything. Also with any wind other than North visibility goes to nothing, and getting a low tide at a reasonable time of day, the right weather and a week-end to coincide takes a lot of luck.

We can also hope to solve some of the mysteries of ancient artillery by noting the size and distribution of the stone balls which litter the seabed to the south of the Mixon. They closely resemble in size and shape known ballista or catapult balls found both inside Pevensey Castle and buried in the ground outside the east end, where the original entrance to Pevensey Lagoon is presumed to have gone through underneath the present car-park. I was able to acquire the broken half of a ball dug up under that car-park which matched exactly for size and shape, though made of a different stone, a ball we had raised from 80 feet of water at the bottom of the Selsey cliff off the Mixon. But the relation of this to existing information on ancient artillery is going to take a lot of research and may even entail learning Greek, since the Greeks seem to have revealed or pretended to reveal more of their military secrets than did the Romans, and those moderns who have endeavoured to make sense of these revelations have come up with some pretty curious and contradictory conclusions.

As an ex-gunner I feel that I might well take a hand when I am too old for diving. In the meantime I must get on with the Mixon . . .

CAMERA UNDERWATER

by Horace E. Dobbs

Horace Dobbs is a specialist in the use of radio-isotopes and a prize-winning underwater photographer. Author of books on diving and photography underwater. Former Scientific Officer of Oxford Branch, now lives in Yorkshire. Builds most of his equipment himself.

MOST of us think that underwater photography is a modern branch of photographic art. Yet the records show that the first underwater photograph was produced over 100 years ago. And what is even more interesting is that it was taken off the English coast.

William Thompson was an engineer. He constructed an underwater housing for a whole-plate camera. It took the form of a massive metal box fitted with a glass porthole through which the picture was taken. The camera was sealed inside the case which was then attached to a stout iron tripod. The complete assembly was cumbersome and very heavy. Indeed Thompson must have had a difficult job of manhandling it over the side of his rowing boat, and lowering it into the water in Weymouth Bay one still, clear summer's day in 1856. The drop shutter was operated with a piece of string from the boat. The exposure time—10 minutes!

When Thompson reopened the housing in his darkroom he found that some sea water had leaked in. Nonetheless he persevered and developed the photographic plate to obtain a passable record of seaweed, and sand.

Thereafter Thompson seems to have faded from the underwater photographic scene, and it was the French zoologist Professor Louis Boutan who progressed underwater photography to such an extent that he was able to write a book about his experiments and findings. In 1900 his book entitled *Underwater Photography, and Progress in Photography* was published, in French. In the final chapter he predicted that one day underwater photography would become a popular pastime. I am sure that most of Boutan's contemporaries must have viewed this prediction with scepticism; especially when one considers the heavy standard diving equipment the photographer had to wear, and the colossal size and weight of underwater photographic equipment at the time. They probably dismissed this far-fetched idea with a good-natured shrug of the shoulders, and wondered what next to expect from this eccentric professor who spent so much of his time experimenting under the sea. Yet today underwater photographs are taken almost everywhere you find a group of divers. So much for the sceptics!

Many excellent pictures and films, taken in British Waters, appear at exhibitions such as the International Festival of Underwater Film held in Brighton. Such presentations are proof that despite the difficulties in the not-so-clear waters off the British Coast good results can be obtained if the limitations are appreciated, and the correct techniques are adopted.

CINÉ OR STILL?

The majority of people taking up underwater photography are divers first and foremost. They often have little knowledge of photography, but find the underwater world so seducing that they want a permanent record of their sub-aquatic activities. I think that most of them would agree that still photography appears simpler than ciné photography, superficially at least. It has been my experience, however, that it is frequently possible to produce good movie sequences under conditions in which it would be difficult, if not impossible, to produce reasonable still pictures. There are a number of points, therefore, that the undecided photographer should consider before committing himself to taking still or motion pictures.

The ciné photographer can create a mood. Once an audience is captivated by the movements, and perhaps also by the accompanying music and sound effects, they become less critical of picture definition. The photographer can therefore sometimes get away with a picture quality that would be intolerable in a still photograph. With a ciné camera it is possible to pan across a subject (FIG. 6). This enables the ciné photographer to get much closer to his subject, thereby reducing the loss of definition due to cloudiness in the water. The large depth of field inherent with the short focal length lenses fitted to amateur ciné cameras reduces the need for accurate focusing; in fact the depth of field of the wide angle lenses fitted to 8 mm cameras is such that a fixed focus lens is adequate for most purposes. Finally, it is also possible to purchase for a modest price a ciné camera with a coupled exposure meter—a so-called "magic eye". This ensures that the film is always correctly exposed despite the directional differences in light intensity that are encountered underwater.

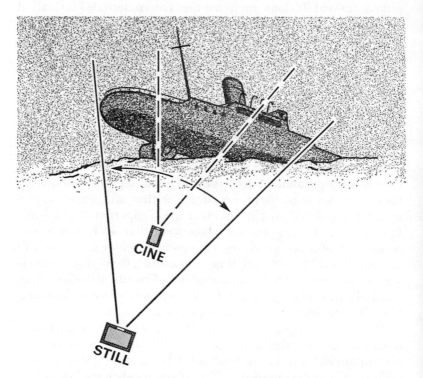

FIG. 6: The ciné photographer can pan across a subject that would be impossible to cover in a single still photograph due to limited visibility underwater

Super-8mm Cameras

The current trend in amateur ciné camera design is towards models that use Super-8mm gauge film. The frame size of Super-8mm is larger than that of standard Double-run 8mm. Other things being equal, therefore, the Super-8mm gives a higher quality picture.

An undesirable feature (from the underwater photographers' point of view) of the use of Double-run 8mm cameras is the need to open the camera and switch spools half-way through a 50-foot run of film. This requirement is eliminated when a Super-8mm camera is used, for the film is supplied in continuous 50-foot lengths.

Further advantages with Super-8mm cameras are the ease and speed with which the film (which is supplied in preloaded cartridges) can be changed—an important consideration if you have to change the film in a small boat that is pitching heavily.

Although the tremendous number of Standard 8mm cameras in current use virtually guarantees the continued production of suitable film, this gauge is becoming obsolete, and a person setting himself up with ciné equipment for the first time is seriously advised to consider purchasing Super-8mm equipment.

UNDERWATER CAMERAS

Unfortunately, the selection that is currently available to the diver of cameras designed specifically for underwater use is very limited.

The Siluro is virtually a waterproof box camera, and comes complete with flash. It takes the 120 size of film, but suffers the severe limitations inherent with this class of camera. Its lack of versatility renders it unsuitable under most conditions encountered in waters off the British Coast.

The Calypsophot was designed by Cousteu's team, and was originally made in France. Although it is still sometimes possible to buy this camera the manufacturing rights have now passed to a Japanese company who produce the camera, with a few modifications, under the trade name of Nikonos.

The Nikonos undoubtedly presents the diver with simplest approach to underwater still photography. It can be used above and below water without modification. The camera uses standard cassettes of 35mm film, and incorporates a focal plane shutter which enables the shutter speed to be varied from 1/30 to 1/500 sec. The standard camera is fitted with an f2.5, 35 mm focal length lens sealed behind a flat glass porthole that prevents the lens from coming into direct contact with the water. The body of the camera is made from pressure- and corrosion-resistant materials, the controls passing through water-tight "O" seals. "O" rings are also used to seal the components of the camera that come apart when the film is loaded. All of the controls are operated by simple movements that are easily accomplished underwater. Yet the Nikonos is only slightly larger than the non-reflex 35mm cameras in common use for above-water photography. A diver can easily hang the camera round his neck when preparing for a dive. During the dive the camera is no more of an encumbrance than a camera would be to a climber—say. The diver can adopt the same attitude to photography that he may above water, i.e. if a good subject turns up he can photograph it. If not—well it is not much trouble to take the camera anyway.

The same attitude cannot be adopted if one takes the other approach to photography, which requires enclosing the camera in a housing. This approach requires firstly loading the camera into its case, and checking that all the controls are operating satisfactorily. A camera in a housing is a more bulky affair, and the effort of trailing it around underwater on the off-chance that a good photographic subject will materialize hardly warrants the effort. Such a procedure is worthwhile only if the diver has a specific photographic objective.

SUPPLIES

The selection of underwater equipment available for both ciné and still photography is constantly changing. The diver wishing to acquaint himself with the current designs and supplies cannot do better than consult the latest catalogues.*

Those wishing to use a specific make of camera for under-

* Available from Lillywhites Ltd., Piccadilly Circus, London, S.W.1. and Aquasnap, 158 Oulton Road, Stone, Staffs.

water purposes may also find it worthwhile contacting the manufacturers, or their British distributors, to establish if an underwater housing is available.

For cinematography the use of a wide-angle lens is advisable, even in clear water. In British waters it is essential. So when buying a housing for a camera that requires a supplementary lens to convert the standard lens to a wide-angle make sure that the housing is large enough to accommodate the additional lens.

The advanced photographer with a critical approach to the subject will only be satisfied with the quality of pictures available from large format cameras. For still work a Rollei-marin housing, encasing a Rolleiflex camera with a wide-angle lens which takes 12 pictures on 120 film is recommended. The 16mm Bolex camera fitted with the 10mm focal length lens inside the Paillard Bolex underwater housing, is an admirable combination for the ciné photographer, particularly if he wishes to use his material for television.

Pressure Compensating Housings

There are three basic types of underwater camera housing. The simplest of these consists of a container with an opening which is sealed with a rubber diaphragm, often in the form of a glove. The camera is attached to the inside of the vessel, and the lens "looks" through a glass or Perspex window. Many variations on this basic theme have appeared over the years. Boutan described a housing with a balloon connected to it to act as a pressure compensating device as long ago as 1900.

The principle of these housings is simple. As the diver descends the air inside the housing is allowed to contract with the increasing pressure—the change in volume being accommodated by the movement of the diaphragm. Thus large pressure differentials are not developed, and the rigid part of the housing can be of relatively light construction.

The major disadvantage of this type of housing is the limited depth at which it can be used. At a depth of 33 feet the amount of air enclosed in the housing must decrease to half its volume on the surface if the pressures inside and outside the case are to balance. As a general rule about 30 feet is the maximum depth to which such housings can be taken with safety.

The advantage of housings of this type is their general purpose nature. Thus a single housing of this type can be used for a variety of cameras, as the controls are operated manually through the diaphragm.

Pressure Resistant Housings

The most widely used camera housings consist basically of a pressure resistant box, into which the camera is sealed. The force exerted on such a housing, which maintains atmospheric pressure inside, can be considerable when it is taken to quite modest depths. For instance, the total force on a 9-inch cube at a depth of 33 feet is over 3 tons. And this force doubles when the case is taken to a depth of 66 feet. Rigid housings must therefore be of very robust construction if they are to withstand stresses of this magnitude.

Most commercial housings designed for specific cameras are made of an aluminium alloy, and are fitted with a plate glass porthole through which the pictures are taken. The cameras are normally operated via control rods that pass through seals (usually "O" rings) in the casing. Many ingenious devices have been developed to translate the simple reciprocating and rotary movements of the external controls to the delicate, and sometimes complex movements necessary to operate the camera.

Amongst the finest examples of rigid cases are the Rolleimarins. The top of each housing incorporates a prism which enables the diver to view the reflex screen, even from a swimming position. In addition there is an external framefinder, that can be adjusted to correct for parallax. All of the camera controls can be operated externally. Models 1, 2 and 3 are available for earlier Rollei cameras. The latest version, Model 4, accepts the Rolleiflex 3.5f camera without meter. The advantage of this model over the earlier models is that it will accept a filter as well as a close-up lens. The earlier models accepted one filter only.

In addition to housings made for specific cameras, a number of general purpose rigid cases are available that can be modified by the supplier or the customer to suit a particular camera. In addition there are suppliers who will design and fabricate a housing to a customer's special requirements.

Above. Ole Nosey! That's what Geoff Harwood called this prize-winning picture of a pipefish taken at Swanage at a depth of 30 feet. In visibility of 20 feet, he used an Exa 1 in case, modified Ivanoff lens, electronic flash, Plus-X film and exposure of f11/60. *Below*. Fish-and-chip shop habitués will know this one as "rock salmon". Divers and fishermen know it's a dogfish. This youngster was photographed at Abereiddy, South Wales, using an Agfa Flexilette in case with close-up lens, electronic flash, Ekta-chrome-X, f11/125, black and-white from colour transparency. Depth: 30 feet. Geoff Harwood.

Divers returning to the boat with their catch. This unusual shot from below was taken in 15 feet of water using the mirror of the surface as a back-cloth. Lobsters are taken by hand after being tweaked into the open by the small hook held in one of the diver's right hand. The lobster he is holding in his left is unable to use his claws when he is held firmly behind the head. Exa 1 in case, Plus-X film, f8/60. Geoff Harwood.

Do-it-Yourself

Those with a very limited budget may resort to building their own camera housings. Many excellent cases have been constructed from prefabricated containers such as pressure cookers, and fuse boxes. If a conveniently shaped vessel is not available the d-i-y enthusiast can construct his own box from materials such as fibreglass, marine ply, or Perspex.* Construction kits and aids such as complete control rod assemblies are available.

Most commercial underwater housings, complete with camera, are negatively buoyant. A buoyant camera on a neck strap is annoying and potentially dangerous if it keeps floating up in front of the diver. Larger cameras that are hand held are also more convenient if they are negatively buoyant. The diver can park his camera temporarily on the sea bed leaving both hands free for such a purpose as adjusting his aqualung harness. It is sometimes necessary to attach weights to home-constructed cameras in order to achieve the desired degree of negative buoyancy.

Automatic Internal Pressurization

The most sophisticated (and expensive) camera cases are automatically internally pressurized. This principle which is normally restricted to housings for large 16mm and 35mm ciné cameras, is utilized to obviate the engineering problems associated with the fabrication of large pressure-resistant vessels. Such a housing is therefore connected to an air cylinder via a pressure reduction valve (similar to a diver's demand valve) that automatically maintains the pressure inside the case slightly above the ambient pressure. As the cameraman descends, air flows from the small external high pressure cylinder into the housing. If the housing has a slight leak, air bubbles out—no water leaks in. As the diver ascends, the internal pressure is reduced by escape of air from the housing via a pressure relief valve. By embodying the principle of automatic internal pressurization housings of relatively light construction can be taken to considerable depths without increasing the strain upon them.

---

* Full details on underwater camera case construction are included in *Camera Underwater* by H. E. Dobbs (Focal Press).

FILMS

The underwater world is "soft" in photographers' jargon. On a bright sunny day on land the big difference in the light intensity reflected by parts of the subject in the shade, and areas in the sun gives rise to pictures of high contrast—and the lighting is said to be "hard". This difference between light and shaded areas is greatly reduced when the same subject is taken even a small distance below the surface of the sea, and it becomes progressively smaller the deeper the diver goes. And the pictures the diver obtains become "softer".

How can the photographer hope to obtain crisp bright pictures under these lighting conditions? Selection of the most suitable film helps. The contrast of photographic images varies with the speed of the film, and as a general rule the faster the film speed the lower the contrast. From the underwater photographer's point of view it is unfortunate that film speed and image contrast are related in this way, as he needs to increase the brightness of the photographic image as much as he can. Thus a slow speed film is indicated. But in addition to being diffused by water, light is also absorbed. And the reduced light intensity often imposes upon the photographer the need to use a high speed film when natural lighting is the sole source of illumination. The choice of a film is therefore a compromise. The rule observed by many photographers—whether using black and white, or colour—is to use the slowest film commensurate with the anticipated light intensity.

Rule 1—Use a slow film whenever possible

Black and White, or Colour?

The photographer setting out with the specific purpose of producing black-and-white prints should obviously use monochrome film stock. The choice between monochrome and colour is more difficult, however, if the photographer is not quite sure to what end he ultimately intends to put the final product.

Colour negative film is intended for use when coloured prints are the desired end product. It is worth remembering, however, that it is possible to print directly on to black and white printing paper from colour negative stock.

Colour reversal film, i.e. film intended to produce a positive colour image which is normally viewed as a transparency, cannot be printed directly on to black and white paper. It is necessary to produce first a monochrome negative. As this negative can be produced from slow speed film it is possible to obtain an image with good contrast from a relatively "flat" transparency.

Rule 2—When in doubt use colour

Those who might dispute this rule I would refer to inspection of the colour and black-and-white sections of the Brighton Festival of Underwater Film. On more than one occasion I have seen a transparency win a prize in the colour section; and a monochrome print of the same picture has won an award in the black-and-white section.

LIGHT AND THE UNDERWATER PHOTOGRAPHER

Photographers need light. And a knowledge of just what happens to light when it gets underwater will help the photographer to understand and overcome some of the problems he faces.

Light from the sun is both reflected and refracted when it strikes a water surface. The light that is refracted into the water can be regarded as useful light for the underwater photographer. The light that is reflected is wasted. The percentage of light taking these two alternative routes is dependent upon several factors. If the sea is absolutely flat the proportion of the light lost due to reflection from the surface increases when the sun is low in the sky (FIG. 7). This is demonstrated by the dazzle from car headlamps on a wet road. When the sea is choppy the angles at which the light strikes the water at mid-day varies. And overall, less light penetrates the surface than when the sea is flat. Small suspended air bubbles also reflect light back towards the surface, causing an additional reduction in intensity.

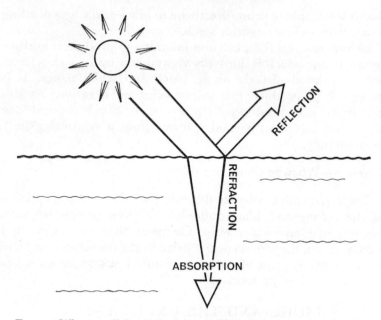

FIG. 7: When sunlight strikes the surface of the sea some light is reflected back into the atmosphere, and some refracted into the water. The light intensity underwater is reduced with increasing depth due to absorption by the water

> *Rule 3*—The brightest pictures are obtained close to the surface when the sea is calm and the sun is high in the sky

The light that penetrates the air-water barrier changes its character in two ways:

(1) It becomes more diffuse, and its intensity decreases due to absorption and scattering by the water and suspended particles.

(2) The colour balance changes due to selective filtration of red colours by the water itself. In addition other colour changes may occur due to the action of coloured materials dissolved or suspended in the water.

The relative contribution of these two factors to the overall change in character of the light depends upon the location and the prevailing conditions. Red colours are always rapidly absorbed, however, and virtually no natural red light penetrates below 20 feet (FIG. 8). So if the photographer wishes to record bright red colours he must take additional light with him.

Rule 4—To get good colour pictures below 10 feet use flash—the ciné photographer must use lamps, of course.

Suspended particles such as sand and plankton are the primary factors regulating the visibility in British waters. Their cumulative effects can be considered akin to hanging a brown-green curtain in front of the camera. This hypothetical curtain becomes progressively thicker as the separation of the subject and the camera increases, until the subject is completely obscured at the limit of visibility. In order to reduce the effects of suspended particles to a minimum the photographer should always get as close to his subject as possible (FIG. 9, *see page 158*).

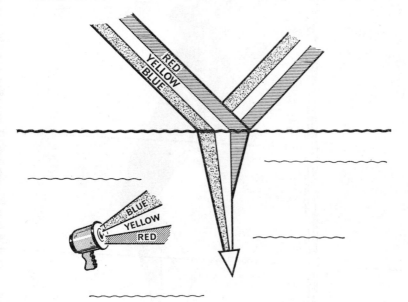

FIG. 8: When white light passes through water the colour balance changes due to preferential absorption of colours. To obtain a full colour range the underwater photographer must take an additional source of illumination with him

Fig. 9: The best conditions for underwater photography, where natural light is the sole source of illumination, are close to

Rule 5—Never let the distance between the major subject and the camera exceed one third of the visibility.

We have observed that light rays may be refracted, or bent, when they pass from air into water. Light rays can also be bent when they pass from water into glass. As a result the field of view of the camera is less underwater than it is above water. This effect unfortunately works against the diver by making the lens of his camera behave like a telephoto lens (FIG. 10). The diver must therefore increase the separation between himself and his subject to attain equal coverage of the film. It is possible to counteract this effect by using a hemispherical porthole of special design in the camera housing. This method is seldom used, however. The telephoto effect can be off-set most simply by using a wide-angle camera lens.

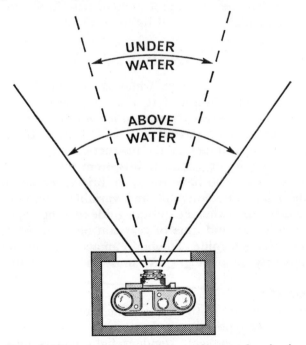

FIG. 10: When a camera inside an underwater housing is taken into the sea the field of view is decreased, and a standard lens behaves like a telephoto lens

An external framefinder fitted to an underwater camera, or a camera housing, should be designed to indicate the reduced field of view. The dimensions of the front frame should be smaller for underwater pictures than that used for above-water viewfinding.

The underwater photographer using an external framefinder should also be aware of the need to compensate for parallax. This effect becomes more pronounced as the separation of the axes of the lens and the viewfinder move further apart. The correction for parallax varies with subject distance, and can be corrected for if the back sight of the viewfinder is made adjustable.

If the camera viewfinder (inside the housing) can be seen by the diver, the parallax correction is reduced, and the correct field of view is indicated. Similarly the image seen on the screen of a single lens reflex camera gives a true indication of the photographic image recorded by the camera.

EXPOSURE

The light intensity above water is so reproducible under general specified conditions that an exposure guide can be tabulated. The exposure chart supplied with films is sufficiently accurate for most purposes—even with colour. If the photographer carefully abides by the instructions he can be assured of at least fair, if not perfect results, from the point of view of exposure. Those who have dived in British waters, however, will know how unpredictable and variable conditions underwater can be. Any tabular exposure guide relating depth, above-water conditions, and time of year can be regarded at best as only a very rough guide. To obtain an accurate measure of the light intensity the photographer must use an exposure meter.

Exposure Meters

Light meters are of two types. The most widely used are of the reflectance type—that is they measure the amount of light reflected by the subject. Incident light meters measure the intensity of the light illuminating the subject. The choice is a matter of personal preference. But we shall only consider the

Dahlia on the seabed. This picture shows a dahlia anemone (*Tealia felina*) under Swanage Pier. The depth was 12 feet and visibility 10 feet. Camera: Exa 1 with modified Ivanoff lens and electronic flash, Plus-X film, f11/60. The filtering mechanism of the mussels can be seen quite clearly. Geoff Harwood.

Man's mistakes are soon covered completely by the sea and the life in it. This picture shows a diver probing into the weed-covered remains of the S.S. *Jebba*, which ran aground in March 1907, close to Bolt Tail, Devon. Calypsophot camera. Plus-X film, f4/125. Horace Dobbs.

more widely used reflectance type—which are generally better suited for underwater use.

The Sekonic underwater exposure meter is admirably suited for sub-aqua use. It is expensive however, and many photographers resort to using a standard less expensive meter in a housing.

If a Perspex camera housing is used the most convenient method of encasing the exposure meter is to locate it inside the camera case alongside the camera. Small underwater housings, usually manufactured from Perspex, are available for specific makes of meter such as the Weston Master. Some of these meter cases are fitted with an external control that enables the meter to be adjusted underwater.

A screw-cap jar, with a stout lid fitted with a good seal can be used as a makeshift exposure meter case. However, such a jar should not be taken to very great depths because of the dangers of leakage and implosion.

The needles of some exposure meters indicate the camera stop directly. The cases for such meters do not need external controls if the photographer presets the film speed on the meter and is prepared to use a single shutter speed. In cinematography the shutter frame speed is seldom altered, and when filming at 16 f.p.s. or 18 f.p.s., the correct aperture is indicated if the shutter speed setting of the exposure meter is set to 1/30 sec.

Some exposure meters express the reflected light from a subject in terms of an exposure value (EV), to which some cameras can be set. Once the camera is set the light reaching the film remains constant if either the shutter or the diaphragm settings are altered.

Although some light meters are better suited to underwater use than others, most can be used with a little ingenuity. The divisions on the scales of most meters correspond to a single stop. When the exposure meter cannot be adjusted underwater the diver can set up his camera to give the correct exposure when the meter needle indicates a specific division on the scale. When the needle does not set at this point the photographer merely has to count the number of divisions between his reference point and the actual reading. This corresponds to the

6

number of stops he must adjust his camera diaphragm to obtain the correct exposure.

Very compact exposure meters costing £2–£3 are available. These are quite suitable for colour photography, where a slow film speed, of say 64 ASA, limits natural light photography to bright conditions. Such meters are usually insensitive to the low light intensities found below 30–40 feet in British waters where black and white films are normally used if natural lighting is the sole source of illumination. At these depths more sensitive, and expensive meters must be used.

Technique

When evaluating exposure, point the meter directly at the subject, and observe the reading. For shots taken horizontally, or with the camera pointing slightly downwards a reading thus obtained will indicate the correct exposure. If the subject is above the cameraman, and well away from him, the light actuating the meter will be derived mainly from the relatively bright upper waters. If the photographer exposes his film accordingly his subject will be under-exposed and will probably appear as a dark silhouette against a light background. The resultant picture may be very dramatic. If, however, the photographer wishes to produce a picture with details in the shadows he should either take a reading close to the subject, or make the necessary allowances, i.e. open the diaphragm by 2–3 stops.

If you are taking colour transparencies, and plan to print them in black and white, the best prints are obtained if the film is correctly exposed. Much better black and white prints can be obtained from a transparency that has been slightly under-exposed than one that has been over-exposed. So when in doubt about exposure under these circumstances it is better to tend to under-expose than to over-expose reversal film.

FOCUSING

One of the first effects observed by the novice diver is that underwater objects appear both larger and closer. The reason why objects look closer is due to the refractive index of water being greater than that of air. The fact that the refractive index

of pure water is 1·33 need not worry the underwater cameraman, but he must take into account the resultant apparent
nearness effect when focusing. The problem can be understood
best if the photographer thinks of the lens of his camera as
behaving like his own eye. An object 4 feet away from the diver
looks to be 3 feet distant, and the eye is focused accordingly.
The camera also sees the object similarly, and should also be
focused at the apparent distance of 3 feet, not at the real
distance 4 feet.

The apparent (focusing) distance can be determined by
dividing the real distance by the refractive index of water, i.e.
1·33. The same answer is obtained by calculating three-quarters
of the real distance. For example if the real distance is 4 feet,

the focusing distance $\dfrac{4}{1\cdot33} = 4 \times \dfrac{3}{4} = 3$ feet.

The depth of field, which is the separation of the nearest and
furthest objects that are in focus, becomes smaller at wide lens
apertures, and also decreases rapidly when the camera moves
closer to the subject. Most photographers can estimate distances
greater than 4 feet with sufficient accuracy to ensure correct
focusing. But at distances of less than 4 feet, where the depth of
field may be only a few inches, estimation of the separation of
the camera and the subject is critical. One way of accurately
determining such distances is to use an underwater ruler, or
"focusing stick". This is a stick 4 feet long calibrated to represent 3 feet.

An above-water rangefinder in an underwater housing would
be subject to the same optical effects as a camera in an underwater case, and would give the correct reading if it could be
manipulated and read. Such a procedure is seldom practical,
however.

Geoffrey Harwood, a well-known underwater photographer
in British diving circles, uses an ingenious system for accurate
focusing for close-up work. In principle it is akin to the method
devised by Barnes Wallace to enable the aircraft to fly at a
specified height over the reservoir at Günne in the famous
"Dam Busters" raid on the Möhne Dam led by Wing Commander Guy Gibson.

Geoff uses an electronic flash unit in a Perspex case hinged to the front of his camera housing. A torch producing a powerful pencil beam is located alongside the flash tube, and another torch is positioned alongside the camera. The torch beams are exactly perpendicular to the fronts of the housings. The torches are adjusted so that the spots from the two beams coincide with the centre of the field of view of the camera at a specific camera-to-subject distance (FIG. 11). This distance can be measured accurately above water, and converted into the underwater focusing distance by dividing by 1·33. With the camera focus preset to this distance Geoff moves the camera towards the subject, and when the two spots coincide he presses the shutter release, knowing that the focus is accurate and that his subject is in the middle of the field of view. Any movement of the subject or the camera case is frozen because of the high speed of the electronic flash.

ADDITIONAL LIGHTING

We have already noted that both the quality and the quantity of light decrease with increasing depth underwater. To compensate for these losses the diver must take an additional source of illumination with him. For the photographer taking still pictures, who has only to illuminate his subject for a fraction of a second, the problem can be resolved relatively easily by the use of flash. For the ciné photographer a supply of additional lighting of sufficient magnitude to produce an effective increase in the light intensity over even a modest area poses problems. Kilowatts of power are necessary to illuminate areas greater than a few square feet. This entails taking power via heavy cables from a generator on the surface to powerful lamps encased in robust underwater housings. For close-up work where the area illuminated is small and the source of light can be situated close to the subject, sufficient light can be derived from battery operated underwater lamps. Suitably encased quartz-iodine lamps powered by accumulator batteries give a high light output. Recently, however, when filming in 16mm off the Cornish Coast I found that five Ikelite underwater lamps mounted on a wooden frame provided sufficient light to illuminate an area of approximately 1 square foot with the

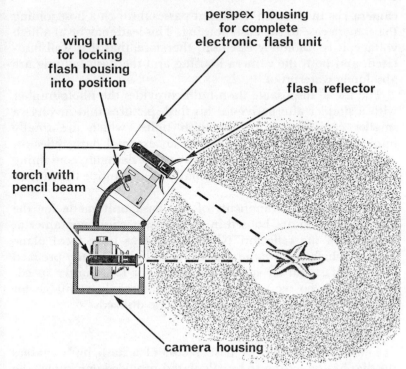

perspex housing
for complete
electronic flash unit

wing nut
for locking
flash housing
into position

flash reflector

torch with
pencil beam

camera housing

FIG. 11 : The principle used by Geoff Harwood for ensuring accurate focusing and framing. The beams of light from the two torches only coincide
when the subject is at the correct distance from the camera, and in the
middle of the field of view

lamps at a distance of about 1 foot 6 inches from the subject.
The lens aperture at 24 f.p.s. using Kodak 4x film which is
rated at 400 ASA for tungsten light, was f 1·9.

Flash

The still photographer can use either disposable flash bulbs,
or electronic flash, to provide additional lighting. Present trends
in miniaturization have reduced the size of electronic flash
equipment. And it is now a more practical proposition to house
such units than it was a few years ago when they were much
bulkier. An electronic flash unit is normally housed in its own
separate underwater case. The flash unit is connected to the

camera via an electrical lead that passes through a hose joining the camera case to the flash housing. This lead may be at a high voltage, it is absolutely essential, therefore, that it is well insulated, and both the camera housing and the flash housing are absolutely waterproof.

The use of disposable flash bulbs provides the photographer with a simpler alternative for his flash pictures that involves a smaller capital outlay. The flash bulbs, which are totally immersed in water, are located in an external flash reflector, and are changed by hand. The body of the flashgun, containing the electrical components, is normally located inside the camera case.

The electrical components of the flash unit made for the Nikonos camera are housed in a small watertight container at the base of the reflector. Nikonos cameras have focal plane shutters which require the use of special bulbs, usually prefixed by FP, if fast shutter speeds are used. For low shutter speeds (e.g. 1/30–1/60 sec.) bulbs that are commonly available for use with non focal-plate shutters can be utilized.

Flash Factors

The guide number, or flash factor of a flash bulb enables the diaphragm setting to be calculated provided one knows the separation of the camera and the subject. The flash factor varies with the type of flashbulb, the film speed, and the shutter speed. The aperture setting for correct exposure is derived by dividing the flash factor by the distance between the camera and the subject. For example, a stop of f16 is indicated if the flash factor is 48 and the camera-subject distance is 3 feet. The guide numbers quoted by the bulb manufacturers apply to average conditions above water, with the flash reflector located above the camera, and the flash providing the sole source of illumination. Underwater it is necessary to correct the flash factor to compensate for the considerable light losses due to absorption by the water, and the general lack of reflecting surfaces. As these are variable the degree of correction to apply is a matter of experience, and a subject for experimentation. As a general rule, however, dividing the normal guide number by 4 or 5 gives a reasonable correction.

Particle illumination effect

When the reflector is near to the camera small particles suspended in the water close to the lens are very intensely illuminated. As a result they are out of focus, and appear as unsightly blotches on the final print, or colour slide. This is a common defect on flash pictures taken in British waters. It can be reduced, if not completely eliminated, by extending the reflector arm, preferably towards the subject (FIG. 12).

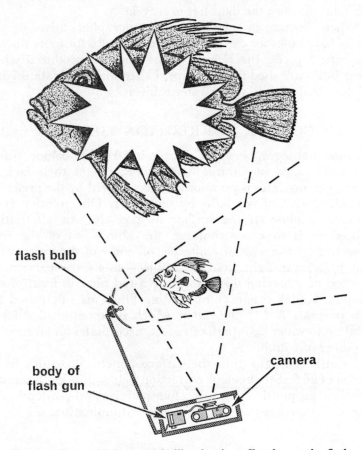

FIG. 12: To avoid the particle illumination effect locate the flash reflector as close to the subject as possible

> *Rule 6*—To avoid the particle illumination effect position the
> flash reflector close to the subject.

Coated flashbulbs

Flashbulbs for use with colour film above water are usually
coated blue to absorb the excessive red colours. Water preferen-
tially absorbs red colours, and therefore acts as a correction
filter to the light emanating from clear flashbulbs when they
are used underwater. The degree of correction depends upon
the total distance the light has to travel.

When shooting in colour some photographers advocate the
use of blue bulbs for close-ups, and clear bulbs for more distant
subjects. I prefer the richer colours that are produced when
clear bulbs are used for close-ups. I therefore advocate the use
of clear bulbs for all underwater subjects.

COLOUR CORRECTION FILTERS

Some photographers are disappointed with colour transparencies taken in natural lighting because of their lack of
bright colours. This is yet another effect caused by the preferential absorption of red light by the water. One solution is to
remain as close to the surface as possible. An alternative
procedure is to counterbalance the absorption of the reds
absorbed by the water by filtering off some of the excess blue
just before the light from the subject enters the camera. A
method of achieving this is to place a red filter in front of the
camera. Kodak colour compensating filters are often used for
this purpose. A CC 50R filter, which is recommended for a
total underwater light path of 12 feet, necessitates an increase in
exposure of 1 stop.

So little red light from the surface penetrates to depths in
excess of 20 feet that colour correction below this depth is not a
practical proposition. For full colour pictures at these depths the
photographer must use supplementary illumination.

DIVING EXPEDITIONS

Time and Location

One of the characteristics of British waters is the variability of the conditions. The underwater visibility is one of the primary factors affecting the quality of the final photographs. Before setting off on a photographic expedition therefore, it is worth while trying to determine at what time the conditions at the diving site are likely to be most favourable.

If you are going to dive in or near a harbour or estuary the best time to dive is on a rising tide near high water. The incoming tide, which usually brings with it fresh clear water from the open sea tends to hold back the dirty water that may be running into the diving area. As the tide falls conditions usually deteriorate as the murky water flows out towards the sea.

As a general rule the conditions most suited to photography are also those best suited to diving in general, thus all of the divers will benefit from any efforts made to dermine the most favourable conditions. The strong tidal streams encountered at some sites well off shore round the British Isles often dictate diving times, which are restricted to slack water at high or low tide.

When diving in unfamiliar waters it is worth consulting local charts when selecting a diving site. Areas where there are rocky outcrops rising from the seabed are usually much more rewarding from a photographic point of view as they are normally centres of a high underwater life density. They provide much more interesting and photogenic backgrounds than flat sandy areas.

> *Rule 7*—Try and arrange to arrive at diving sites close to shore well before high tide. Always be the first into the water.

Once a crowd of divers get into the water the conditions for photography always deteriorate. Although they may not actually touch the bottom the turbulences set up in the water by the divers' fins invariably disturbs sediment of one form or another, and results in a clouding of the water. The magnitude of the effect, and the speed with which it clears, depends upon local factors such as the nature of the sea bed, and the speed of the current, etc.

I recall on one occasion diving in a bay off the Yorkshire coast on one of those rare days when the water was exceptionally clear. I suddenly discovered to my annoyance that I had lost my exposure meter. I turned round, and despite the fact that I had been swimming very gently I could see a trail of sediment suspended in the water behind me. It was almost as clear as the vapour trail left by a high flying aircraft. I easily retraced my movements by swimming over the trail. I soon recovered my meter which was lying on a rock glinting in the sun.

Fortunately on that occasion I got my pictures before the insatiable lobster hunters and spear fishermen invaded the pitch. One of those philistine "sportsmen" even speared a little lumpsucker fish that I had made friends with earlier.

A case for a case

Underwater camera housings, and cameras with flash attachments are very vulnerable to damage. For this reason they should always be kept in a box when not in use, particularly on board a boat.

When filming with the Oxford Underwater Research Group, I always insist that our 16mm camera, which is housed in a Perspex case, stays in its box until I am in the water and ready to take it. When the dive is completed I hand the camera back into the boat and ask that it be immediately returned to its box. This practice is based on a lesson that I learned the hard way during my early underwater photographic days.

I was sitting quietly in a boat waiting for my turn to go overboard—the proud possessor of a new home-made camera housing complete with flash attachment. A companion diver, who had earlier become known to me affectionately as "Conger 'Ead" (and whom I must admit was not distinguished for his genteel deportment) was standing in the boat. Suddenly the boat lurched. "Conger 'Ead" fell backwards onto the seat beside me, which he had occupied earlier but was now the repository for my pride and joy—my new camera and flash gun. As he touched down the bottom of his air cylinder made contact with my flash unit with the power of a steam hammer. Accelerated by a few verbal obsceneties he rapidly removed his loathsome body, with its attached air cylinder, from my presence, to reveal the reflector dish of my flash gun, tortured and distorted, swinging pathetically from the camera housing on an electrical lead. It was only my gentlemanly upbringing and the thought of what might have happened if his cylinder had landed on the camera case itself that quelled my desire to dispense similar punishment to "Conger 'Ead's" head.

Buoyancy

The most interesting photographic subjects are often found on, or near, the seabed. Before taking his pictures the photographer must focus and measure the light intensity, etc. Whilst he is doing this he does not want to drift away or lose sight of his subject. It is convenient therefore, if he can rest lightly and comfortably on the bottom until his photographic equipment is properly set up. This state of affairs can only be obtained satisfactorily if he is negatively buoyant. A photographer who is positively buoyant will find that he has to expend a considerable amount of effort keeping down, and the efforts he makes in doing so will often frighten away any underwater animal life he was hoping to photograph.

> *Rule 8*—When diving and photographing aim to be slightly negatively buoyant.

In the ideal situation the diver can adjust his buoyancy to suit his needs of the moment. A diver wearing a FENZY-type lifejacket can do this. The diver-photographer with such equipment can enter the water well over-weighted, and adjust the volume of air in his jacket to bring himself to neutral buoyancy for normal underwater swimming. When a subject is spotted he can deflate his lifejacket and kneel firmly on the bottom whilst setting up his equipment and taking his pictures. When he has got his shots he re-inflates his lifejacket to bring himself once again to neutral buoyancy—and he can swim off in comfort and safety to continue his dive.

PHOTOGRAPHIC TECHNIQUES

Perspective Distortion

Earlier we noted that one of the most important rules in underwater photography is to get as close to the subject as possible. When observing this rule it is important to keep the whole of the subject at approximately the same distance from the camera, if possible. For if part of the subject is excessively close to the camera it will appear disproportionately large in the final print.

Exaggerated perspective seldom produces pleasing results. The photographer taking a picture whilst swimming close behind another swimmer will find that the divers' fins will appear large, and his head will appear small in the final picture. When filming companions the ciné photographer should position himself such that the line of movement of the other divers is across his field of view.

Spear fishermen seldom object to a little photographic deception, however, and for maximum ego boost they should be photographed behind their impaled prey, which can be held at arm's length on the end of a spear directed towards the camera (FIG. 13).

Silhouettes

"Contre jour" is the expression used by photographers to denote a photograph taken with the camera pointing towards the light source. Such pictures are often taken to produce dramatic effects. And in clear water the same approach can be adopted by silhouetting the subject against the surface of the sea. A picture from the seabed of a diver descending, or ascending the anchor rope with the hull of the boat visible on the surface is a popular and often successful theme for this type of shot.

Filming Techniques

Many situations that would yield only poor still photographs can be exploited to provide interesting ciné sequences. The ciné camera can be used to present the diver's eye view of the underwater world. A sequence taken at eye level as the photographer glides over a kelp bed will give the impression of flying

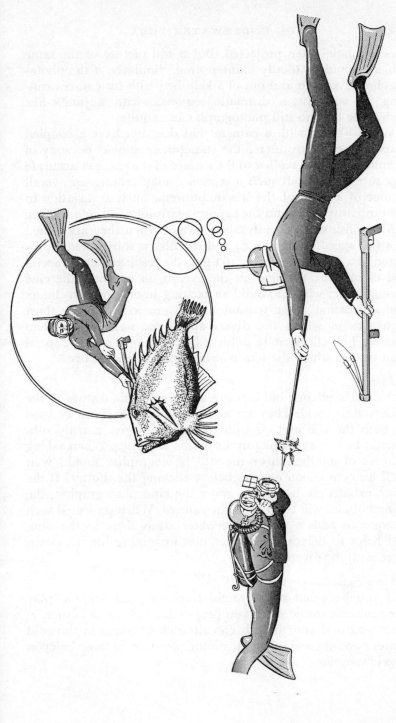

FIG. 13: Spear fishermen seldom object to perspective distortion

over a jungle when projected. But a still picture of the same subject would be totally uninteresting. Similarly, if the photographer dives into and out of a kelp bed with his camera running he will obtain dramatic sequence with a jungle-like undertone that no still photograph can capture.

When filming with a camera that does not have a coupled automatic exposure meter the cameraman should be wary of panning from the seabed to the surface of the sea. For accurate exposure throughout such a sequence may require an overall change of 4 stops of the iris diaphragm. Such a variation in light intensity is beyond the exposure latitude of all colour films.

Many fish swim rapidly underwater. When they are filmed at a fast speed, i.e. 24 f.p.s., and the film is subsequently projected at a slower speed, i.e. 16 f.p.s., the result is more graceful and often more pleasing on the eye. If, in contrast, the ciné photographer wishes to build an exciting James Bondish climax into a situation, more tension can be created by using short sequences in which the divers appear to swim faster than normal. This effect can be achieved by filming at a slower speed than that at which the film is projected to the audience.

Bubbles

A diver's exhaust bubbles are a characteristic feature of the underwater world. They are also photogenic, and can be used by both the still and ciné photographer to give a truly subaquatic feel to a still picture or a ciné sequence. When taking pictures of another diver the still photographer should wait until his companion exhales before clicking the shutter. If the diver exhales as he passes under the ciné photographer, the rising bubbles will boil round the camera. When projected such a sequence adds a truly underwater atmosphere to the film, and helps to delude the viewer into imagining himself down there with the divers.

A Final Rule

If you have not put a sound track on your film do play some suitable music when you project the film to an audience. Then you and your friends can sit back at home in the cold winter evenings and relive the diving pleasures of those halcyon days of summer.

AROUND BRITAIN UNDERWATER

by Leo Zanelli

Leo Zanelli is Deputy Diving Officer of the British Sub-Aqua Club. Former honorary Diving Officer of the Metropolitan Police "C" Division, now diving officer of Westminster Branch.

THE water surrounding the United Kingdom covers some of the finest and most interesting underwater scenery in the world. Compared to the luxuriant vegetation of the sea off the West Country and the West coast of Scotland, the Mediterranean sea bed is bald. Admittedly the sea is more variable—indeed, at times downright unfriendly—and colder than the Med., but this is of little import to the serious diver. It is the scenery that counts.

That first sentence will no doubt be met with a little scepticism, but it is true. To make my point, let's embark upon an underwater tour of the U.K. For convenience I have utilized four maps from the Stanford series of Coloured Charts for Coastal Navigators—Nos. 16, 13, 12 and 9. The reason for this selection is simple; these maps comprise the areas that I have dived in most. I have strayed off course once or twice, to nearby sites that I think will prove of interest to the reader.

To keep the record straight I must admit that, although I have dived at most of the following sites, I have not visited them all. Much information on Scotland has been provided by my friends in the Scottish Sub-Aqua Club, and Lieutenant George Wookey, M.B.E., R.N.

CHART 16

Chart No. 16 encloses a vast area: the whole coastline of Ulster; east Eire down to Dublin; Anglesey; Snowdonia; the

Isle of Man; and South-West Scotland. You could stick a pin almost anywhere on this chart and almost certainly pierce a superb diving site with clear water, wonderful underwater scenery, and nearby wrecks for added interest. But it is no area for the pampered "holiday" diver; to venture into these cold, swirling waters you need hair on your chest and a genuine interest in diving. Should you possess these attributes you can be sure of really superb diving.

Anglesey is almost surrounded by clear water—"almost" because of the muddy, shallow Menai Strait—and is rapidly becoming the Mecca of Midland divers. There are excellent facilities here for sub-aqua swimmers.

The most heavily dived spot at the time of writing is in Penrhos Bay at Porth y Garan which, according to my Welsh dictionary should mean "Ferry of the Stork"—I always wondered where it started from! A mile out at sea from Porth y Garan a rock, Maen Piscar, breaks the surface at low tide. It is essentially a boat dive with a slack water period of half an hour. The main attraction is a number of small wrecks scattered about the base. There are two more popular sites in Penrhos Bay, Raven's Point and Porth Dafarch, both inundated with divers at week-ends. The S.S. *Missouri* was wrecked off Porth Defarch, and the remains can be reached from shore over the rocks, or by boat. The west end of the bay is rather inaccessible, which is just as well because nasty races lie offshore.

At Holyhead several wrecks are accessible from shore, some off the beach and others from the breakwater. Air is obtainable from Holyhead Boatyard, Newry Beach, telephone: Holyhead 2568. The chaps at the Boatyard will give you the data on the wrecks. You will need a boat from Holyhead if you fancy a dive on a wreck farther out; the S.S. *Primrose Hill*, off North Stack. Again, nasty races offshore. Cemaes Bay and Bull Bay are also popular, accessible sites.

The picturesque town of Moelfre is the site of Anglesey's most famous wreck, the *Royal Charter*, which went down in 1859. Charles Dickens wrote about the wrecking in *The Uncommercial Traveller*. A more modern rendering is in *The Golden Wreck*, by Alexander McKee. The *Royal Charter* was returning from

Australia, an actual treasure-ship with nearly half a million pounds worth of bullion in her holds. Most of it was recovered, but some remained unsalvaged. I must confess that my only visit to the site of the wreck was caused by the lure of gold. The site is accessible, only a few yards offshore, in about twenty feet of water. Visibility underwater was 6 feet—poor for this side of Anglesey—and I feverishly searched the bottom for signs of that great vessel, but to no avail. Wicked fingers of rock thrust upwards, and I shuddered to think of what the hull of the *Royal Charter* must have looked like after the sea had ground her on them. Only half a mile away, also close inshore, lies the 650-ton *Hindlea*, wrecked a hundred years later.

Traeth Bychan lies between Moelfre and Benllech. From the Harbour House J. Leyland-Smart provides air, equipment, boats and accommodation. An excellent site for a holiday with a safe sandy beach for the children. Telephone: Cressington Park 3027 or Anfield (Liverpool) 2884.

Red Wharf Bay looks attractive (access via Porth Uongdy) but is in fact much too shallow for diving.

Whenever the sea surrounding Anglesey is inclement, there is plenty of freshwater diving inland. And if you head back over the Menai Bridge to the mainland, the lakes of Snowdonia, provide varied conditions. Lake diving is rather dull compared to the sea, but conditions are more stable. Currents are negligible and you can always get a dive in—which is more than can be said of the sea.

Mind you, although lake-diving can be dull it can also be surprising. I well remember a visit we made to a high-lying lake, Melynllyn, to collect plant specimens for the National Museum of Wales. Melynllyn is over 100 feet deep, with a sloping, dreary, featureless bottom, and pitch black at maximum depth. Moreno, Tony and I snorkelled slowly back at the end of the dive clutching plastic bags full of plants, and plastic writing tablets covered with data, as the only reward for our efforts. As we congregated, almost ashore, we were joined by George, who had wandered away earlier. We commented on the fact that there was little of interest in Melynllyn. "Yes," replied George, "except for that 'plane over there."

The silence was electric as three pairs of eyes tried to follow

the direction of George's inclined head. On being assured that
he was not joking, we took off again, three pairs of fins splash-
ing dementedly, looking something like a Mississippi paddle
steamer race. George was right. In only a couple of feet of water
twisted, broken metal lay scattered over the rock-mud bottom.
As we dived deeper the pieces of wreckage got larger until at
70 feet, we came upon the main fuselage. At this depth the
remains were bathed in a dim lighting something like moon-
light. It was very eerie and cold. Using my underwater camera
at its widest aperture and slowest speed, I tried a few shots
which, fortunately, came out with forced development. We
lifted a buckled plate with a red white and blue roundel
affixed, which George assured us was a peace-time combination
(in the war period it was red and blue).

We are still curious as to the history of our "wreck". I wrote
to various authorities explaining our find and requesting any
details they might have. Only one replied; to the effect that
my letter was being passed to the relevant department. At the
time of writing it must have found a snug pigeon-hole, for that
was two years ago.

By the way, Melynllyn is a drinking reservoir and permission
must be obtained if diving is contemplated. You would also
need a Land-Rover or similar vehicle for the rugged trek.

One of the finest lakes for diving is Llyn Llydaw, halfway up
Snowdon. The water is a beautiful turquoise with fabulous
visibility often exceeding 40 feet. There is an outlet pipe to the
nearby power station situated by the hut off the causeway,
which must obviously be avoided. When work was being carried
out on the causeway a dug-out canoe was found in shallow
water, evidence that the bleak shore was inhabited in some long
forgotten era. Llydaw is nearly two miles in length and at the
western end is nearly 200 feet deep.

If you park the Land-Rover (yes, you will need one here too),
on the far side of the causeway, a quarter mile slog up a rugged
track will lead you to the highest lake on Snowdon, Glaslyn.
About 120 feet deep, Glaslyn is an impressive sight with Yr
Wyddfa, the summit of Snowdon, towering above. The water
is identical to that of Llydaw with the same soft light-coloured
sediment bottom. I was in a group which made, I believe, the

first (and probably only) dive in Glaslyn. We were ostensibly looking for a legendary monster that was slain nearby and the body disposed of in the cold Glaslyn water. We placed a float and shot-line in the middle and used this as a fixed point for searching. We didn't find the monster but George (the same one) lost a flipper—it's a long, hilarious story for which, unfortunately, I have not the space here—and I lost a thermometer. So if you should happen to be diving in Glaslyn, please keep an eye open!

Not all the Snowdonia lakes require a rugged vehicle. The A498 runs alongside Llyn Gwynant, you can park here and plop straight into the water. If you find a weight-belt—it's mine! Gwynant is no more than 28 feet deep at the far side to the road, but has some interesting vegetation and is a useful site for a dive-picnic, as is a sister lake, nearby Llyn Dinas.

Llyn Cwm-y-ffynnon is a tough walk over the back of the Gorphwysfa Hotel on the A4086. A relatively shallow lake, it is more suited to snorkelling.

Llyn Geirionydd is a long drive over farm tracks, but a car can make it. On a dive there we found the bottom strewn with old-fashioned lemonade bottles—the kind that has a glass marble as a stopper. A reporter from the *North Wales Weekly News* theorized that they were thrown in by the crowds who used to attend the annual bardic ceremonies there in Victorian times. We just about cleared them out, but you might still find the odd one or two.

A few don'ts—don't dive in Llyn Ogwen (shallow, unexploded shells); Cwellyn (deep and lightless); Llyn Crafnant, Llyn Elsi, Llyn Cowlydd (reservoirs). And don't forget, every lake belongs to someone. Get permission before you dive.

The Irish coast is increasing in popularity—and with good reason. Dublin Bay is large; about 7 miles wide from Dalkey to Howth, and thrusting 7 miles inland. Visibility tends to be poor in the immediate Dublin area but improves, with stronger currents and deeper water, towards Dun Laoghaire. The Irish Sub-Aqua Club at 127 Lower Baggot Street, Dublin, will put you in touch with the current source of air. I have dived on several wrecks far out in the bay; all well broken up, but still worth a visit. Of course, I missed the best one—or so they say—

the M.V. *Leinster*, sunk in 1916 and lying nine miles out.

Lambay Island, farther north, is the site of the S.S. *Tayleur*; wrecked over 100 years ago and still worth seeing. It is essentially a boat dive which is just as well because the island is privately owned. My friend Tony Morelli salvaged several bottles, with corks still intact, from the *Tayleur*. At his Dublin home he enthusiastically invited me to join him in a tasting, but I had to decline. After all, the label was missing! and although it might have read "Chateau Lafite 1860", it might equally have been labelled "Turpentine" or "Cyanide". When I pointed this out Tony's enthusiasm suffered a rapid decline. At a later date I heard that he had indeed opened a bottle and sampled some of the contents. He said that it was clear, the colour of sherry, and tasted strange! It was probably a corked bottle, he should have sent it back!

There are several more wrecks around Lambay, all dived on regularly. A nearby pub, The Brook, at Portrane, Donabate, houses a collection of artifacts lifted from the *Tayleur*. This is well worth a visit if only to refill your cylinders with Guinness!

Carlingford Lough is really a deeply indented bay 9 miles long and two miles wide at the throat. On the main Carlingford is shallow with a dreary mud bottom, but on the seaward side of Greencastle, rocks predominate and 100 feet can be plumbed—but visibility is still not much. Visibility, depth and currents all improve outside the lough and there are at least three wrecks known and dived on.

Ardglass lies north of Dundrum Bay. Diving is carried out in the harbour (ask permission of the harbour master) and south of the harbour, where 50 feet can be reached from shore. The bottom has attractive rock gullies at this site but on the main the area is rather muddy, although the vegetation breaks the monotony.

There is a site nearby named Cannon's Hole, with easy access from shore. It was here that Robert and Maureen Trouton of Belfast Branch found many cannons at the site of a previously un-recorded wreck.

Strangford Lough is open to the sea at the southern end. It is long (about 18 miles) and 100 feet deep in places. The bottom is muddy and uninteresting and visibility is poor. There is a wreck or two about, but Strangford is really only useful if you are in the area and in a hurry. If you have some time and are motorized, it would be better to head farther north. The narrow neck of the lough, at ebb tide, is dangerous.

Belfast B.S-A.C. meet at 2 Alexandra Park Avenue, Belfast, on Monday nights at 8 p.m. Belfast Branch own their club-house, which boasts a compressor room, kitchen, photographic dark room, cylinder store, and chart and lecture rooms. An enterprising and busy branch (they also publish the *Ulster Underwater News*). You could do no better than pop along and ask their friendly advice about diving in the area.

It was Belfast who found the wreck of the *State of Louisiana*, a 2,000-ton passenger liner which went down off Larne nearly 100 years ago. I am told that it was found at the foot of Hunter's Rock in 80 feet of water. But you had better ask them.

The island of Rathlin, although surrounded by strong currents, is a very popular area. Essentially boat diving. A number of wrecks lie around, and a really good dive is—or was— H.M.S. *Drake*, a 14,000-ton cruiser torpedoed in 1917. I say was, because there were plans to blow her up as a danger to shipping, and I hear that this has indeed been carried out. Also around is the *Loch Garry*, now lying upright, on an even keel, under 100 feet of water. An excellent dive when conditions are right. Despite its popularity Rathlin Island has not been thoroughly explored.

Portrush, near the Giants Causeway, possesses clear water and varied underwater scenery; excellent diving from shore or boat, although the current can be strong. Somewhere around here are the remains of the Spanish Armada ship *Girona*, a full account of which is given by Roger Jefferis and Kendall McDonald in their book, *The Wreck Hunters*.

From here, map 16 crosses the North Channel to Scotland. The Rhinns of Galloway is a pick-shaped peninsula, jutting out from Wigtown. At the south end resides the Mull of Galloway, a site that is dangerous and spectacular. The underwater cliffs plunge vertically down through 200 breath-taking feet of water, and dangerous currents reside offshore. This site is only for very experienced divers, and you will need a good boat and local skipper.

A lot safer is Burrow Head, at the other end of Luce Bay, varied diving can be obtained for all grades of experience.

Luce Bay, sandwiched between the two, is generally rather sandy and shallow. But the area is not exactly over-dived, and the bay covers a large area, so there might be some very good spots here.

Diving in South-West Scotland revolves around an inland site—Glasgow. It is from here that G.M.T. Diving, 520 St. Vincent St., Glasgow, C.3. dispenses air and a vast range of equipment. You can telephone G.M.T. at City 3916 during business hours. Outside business hours you can 'phone Bill Gourley at WES 2578 if you have any particular problems.

There are two sites farther north that have been in the news and are of particular interest. So I hope you won't mind a little diversion, for they both lie off our map.

Tobermory Bay sits snug near the north shore of the island of Mull. Much has been written about the Tobermory Treasure, and most of it is presumed, merely legend. But in fact a ship from the Spanish Armada did go down here. Several expeditions have brought up artifacts that prove this beyond doubt. Whether it had any treasure aboard is still open to discussion, but it is there, in the harbour, and only several feet offshore. By now of course, you are wondering why, if the wreck is so close. . . . The answer is that over the years it has settled in the soft harbour mud to the extent that it is now completely covered. The actual site is a frustrating dive; the monotonous mud bottom is desolate and bare. The wreck—and possible treasure—lies only a few feet below you; and although the barrier is only soft mud, it might as well be a concrete wall of the Bank of England.

Perhaps you are among the many who saw that hilarious film, *Whisky Galore*, or read Compton Mackenzie's novel on which the film was based; but few are aware that the story was basically true.

Eriskay is a small island in the Outer Hebrides, just south of South Uist. It was off Eriskay that the S.S. *Empire Politician* was wrecked in 1940. This in itself is not remarkable, but the *Politician*'s cargo—several thousand cases of whisky, brandy and liqueurs—certainly is. Apart from the entertaining tales handed down regarding the Customs attempts to track down illegal "visitors" to the wreck, no more was heard of the ship until twenty years later.

In 1960 Lieutenant George Wookey, M.B.E., with two other R.N. divers, located the wreck and salvaged—trust the Royal Navy—many bottles of drinkable whisky. Five years later Reg Vallintine—the most indefatigable, adventurous diver I know —visited the *Politician* with Scottish B.B.C. and salvaged, strangely, several bottles of whisky. The extra five years had not improved it. Reg states that it was revolting. However, for the venturesome I am assured that there are many bottles left. And if the vintage is not up to scratch the sea around the island boasts visibility up to 40 feet and prolific flora and fauna.

During his visit Lieut. Wookey's group took part in an eight-mile underwater tow from Benbecula to the Monach Islands. He reported that the underwater scenery was some of the best and most interesting he had ever seen. And as he has experienced diving in New Zealand waters, among other exotic areas, you can appreciate the compliment.

There are countless opportunities for the explorer in the wild, wonderful Scottish waters. Scapa Flow with the scuttled German fleet and H.M.S. *Royal Oak*. Gulberwick Bay in the Shetland Isles, where two gold-covered Viking ships were wrecked in 1148. Hundreds of islands off the west coast have never seen a solitary diver's bubble. And despite the rugged conditions it is a lot more exciting than getting in the queue by the pier of Somewhere-on-Sea to be among the thousands who are already choking the water.

We have one area left on map 16—the Isle of Man. Boasting clear water, safe diving, and excellent diving facilities, the I.o.M. is also a perfect holiday resort for the wife and kids. There are many fine diving sites on the island, with the advantage that you can nearly always find a spot sheltered from wind and tide.

A complete diving holiday can be arranged from the Isle of Man Sea Sports Co., including accommodation, transport to and from diving sites, air, equipment, and even an underwater camera. If you can't manage a full week, Sea Sports will arrange a diving week-end by charter flight. They are at

Marine House, Strand Road, Port Erin, telephone Port Erin
3032. In addition there are two sites where air is provided;
The Marine Biological Station at Port Erin will charge cylinders up to 3,000 p.s.i. during office hours, and the same hours
apply at the Fire Service, Murray House, Douglas. It is essential
to give both advance notification of your arrival. The former
will also assist you with any scientific queries you may have.

Visibility around the island is up to 100 feet—excellent by
any standard. Boats are plentiful, and many of them are
equipped with echo sounder. The average depth available when
diving from shore is about 50 feet. Generally speaking the north
stretch of coast from Peel to Ramsey is not dived. The water is
shallow and far better sites abound. Port Erin is one of the best
sites on the island, with sheltered diving in the bay and marvellous water out by boat. A car can be parked right at the
edge of the sea and within a few yards 50 feet of clear, interesting water is available. It has the added merit of being a good
site on which to unload the family.

There is a small island to the south—the Calf of Man. Although the diving (boat only) is very good, with a fair sprink-
ling of wrecks, the Calf is a bird sanctuary owned by the Manx
National Trust, and permission must be obtained should you
contemplate landing. Dive at slack water only, for the currents
are very strong.

CHART 13

The area enclosed by this map is undoubtedly the most dived
in the U.K. There are numerous compressor stations, often
offering equipment and other services in addition to air. It is
also a popular holiday area, which makes it that much easier
for the diver who has a family to consider.

The north coast of Cornwall, although excellent, is not
popular with amateur divers. This is because the sea on this
side is more unpredictable because it is exposed to the bruising
Atlantic rollers. There is also, compared with the south, a lack
of diving services and facilities.

My only dive at Land's End was approached with a combination of awe and respect. I don't know why the former, probably
because as you looked out to sea you were doubly aware of the

immense body of water out there. Apart from a few rocky islets, it is thousands of miles to the nearest land with the sea, in places, several miles deep. Respect came easily because the immediate waters are dangerous, with strong currents allied to the rough Atlantic swell. Although the road runs almost to the cliff edge, access is not easy. It is really better to dive by boat, when you can visit the interesting—or so I am told— Longships rocks a way out. The rocks are saddled by a light-house with an occulting (work that one out) light.

Anyway, back to Land's End. Underwater, I fully expected to see breathtaking, dramatic scenery while vicious currents whirled me about. In fact, I was rather disappointed, the luxuriant weed-covered bottom was attractive, but not drama-tic, and the current pulled steadily. But twenty minutes later the tide was really on the move and we had to get out quick. To explore this site one should be an experienced, well-trained diver.

Penzance is a diver's paradise. Air, boats, equipment, are all available, along with clear water, attractive underwater scenery, and wrecks in profusion. Watersports, Albert Street, telephone Penzance 4157, are the sub-aqua specialists here. Watersports have three large stationary compressors which will pump to 3,000 p.s.i.g., but are normally set to cut off at 2,000. They also have a portable compressor on road wheels, which is set to pump up to 2,200 p.s.k.g., and has a free air displacement of 15 c.f.m. which is available for hire for remote sites. In addition to air, Watersports provide a full range of diving facilities including boats. I don't know how many wrecks there are in Penzance Bay, but it cannot be far short of two dozen, ranging from a small minesweeper to a battleship. Enough to satisfy the most fastidious wreck-diver.

Porthleven is a small, quiet resort, with a harbour. It was right inside this harbour, in fact facing the old Fishmonger's Arms, that the barque *William* was driven ashore with the loss of only one life in 1769. You can dive from the beach. The bottom is sandy but quite interesting with a large variety of fish life. If the fish are your main concern swim east towards Looe Bar, where H.M.S. *Anson* was wrecked. For myself, I prefer the more attractive rocky scenery west, in the direction of Tre-wavas Head.

Good diving is available at Gunwalloe, where you can park the car right on the beach. And adjacent Poldhu Cove, although you have to get out a bit to find real depth. Some large turbot have been speared in the vicinity.

If you charter a boat even better diving can be had in this area. Porth Mellin is where to get the boat. Mullion Island is a favourite site but I prefer the less visited Vradden Rock, off Predannack Head. A useful site for bass and red bream. Nasty races flow off Lizard Point, which is avoided by boats. Do the same, there are plenty of better, safer sites around.

Falmouth is an excellent holiday resort with a large harbour containing many wrecks. I have seen divers going in off the beach, but from this entrance it is better to snorkel. Boats are available in Falmouth so make the most of it. Sailing directly out from St. Antony Head Light, heading towards Porthkerris Point, takes you in a line directly over two wrecks. The far one is the S.S. *Caroni River*, well smashed up by depth charges as a danger to shipping. St. Antony Head itself is a very good boat dive. Depths in the immediate vicinity only average 20–30 feet, shelving steadily to 45 feet. Air is available from Visack Marine, Customs House Quay, Falmouth.

Porthscatho is a charming, picturesque village. You can get a good dive in from the excellent beach and even launch a small boat. The water is clear and the bottom is rocky with sand patches. The best diving is obtainable when the wind is from the west, as Porthscatho lies open to the east. Depths are shallow (12 feet) near shore but the bed slopes down quite rapidly to 40–60 feet.

Porthloe is an attractive fishing village set in a rocky inlet in the cliffs of Veryan Bay, diving can be carried out from the small beach, or a dinghy launched. Conditions are best when the wind is from the west. If you have a local boat and skipper, a visit to Gull Rock at the west end of the bay will prove rewarding, but if you are after really big fish move farther along to The Whelps, on the seaward side. The depth on this side is 50 feet, sloping rapidly down to 100. Dodman Point, at the other end of the bay, has nasty races flowing offshore, and is best avoided.

Mevagissy boasts two harbours, an outer, and an inner one

which dries at low tide. One of the most colourful little ports in Cornwall, it is a very popular holiday resort. Shore dives can be embarked on from several sites, but anglers are prolific and you must beware the hook and line.

St. Austell Bay is an excellent diving area for several reasons. The bay has good diving, averaging 25 feet deep near shore to 50–60 feet in the middle. Tidal streams are relatively weak in the bay although—as with all the Cornish coast—it is best not to presume that this is always so; and a south wind can rough things up a little.

You can dive from shore at Porthpean and Polkerris with the former, in my opinion, the better dive. Boats are available and even better diving is available farther out. In Charlestown, St. Austell Divers, telephone St. Austell 4855, supply air and provide an equipment hire service. Air is also available at the Cornish Diving Centre, 7 Ropehaven Road, Tregonissy, telephone St. Austell 4511.

Polperro is probably the most famous of the "picture postcard" Cornish fishing villages. The deluge of tourists make things a little difficult, but it is possible—just—to get some good diving in. At the season's peak it is sometimes difficult to get a good shore dive in, better to charter a local vessel and skipper, although these are snapped up early by anglers.

Whitsand Bay is an excellent dive all over. Mind you I haven't been in at the western end—there is something in the charts about it being a danger area from rifle fire. There is often a heavy surf, so be careful about shore diving.

Snug in the south-east corner of Whitsand Bay lies the most dived-on wreck in England—the *James Egan Layne*. The *Layne* sits upright, on an even keel, in 90 feet of water. A mast breaks the water and affords a direct route down. A 7,000-ton Liberty ship, torpedoed in 1944, she is a remarkable sight and dive. A swim along the promenade deck (did Liberty ships have promenade decks?) resplendent with anemone and ghostly davits, is a memorable experience. The hold, with caution, can be entered, or you can pop over the gunwale and drop vertically down a wall of gorgonia coral to the sandy bottom sprinkled with starfish. I have lost count of the number of times I have visited the *J.E.L.*, but the experience never palls. The last time I dived here I remember thinking that there could not possibly be a single item left for a souvenir—it is nothing to find 4–5 diving boats moored around the mast—when John Betts drifted past me with several items of crockery. You will need a boat, and this is easy to obtain in Plymouth. Salvage work has recently been undertaken and you should check before diving as the Receiver of Wreck, Plymouth, has warned that the wreck is dangerous.

Around Plymouth diving by boat can almost always be carried out owing to the enormous breakwater lying between Cawsand and Bovisand Bay. There is plenty of variety. The inner side of the breakwater boasts depths in excess of 150 feet, with a mud-rock-seaweed bottom. Off the seaward side the marine life is much more prolific, although more exposed, with visibility that can exceed 30 feet. There are wrecks well broken up around the breakwater but you will need a local man to point them out. A. Birchly operates a 36-foot diving boat from Plymouth which can take you to all the sites, including the wrecked iron-screw barque *Nepaul*. And also supply air. Air is also available from Plymouth S-A.C. c/o 57 Mutley Plain, telephone Plymouth 68657, and B.O.C. Maxwell Road, Prince Rock, telephone Plymouth 63047.

Provided there are no novices in your group, charter a boat and local skipper and take a trip to Eddystone Rocks. There is possibly no better dive in English waters; the rocks climb abruptly from depths, in excess of 120 feet and are inhabited by very large bass, conger, pollack, sea urchin, and sometimes shark. The visibility is fabulous with scenery to match. Steep rock valleys woven with sand tracks and large fronds of curling seaweed. Then again, many vessels have been wrecked on Eddystone. . . .

There is a camping site at Stoke Beach (near Stoke Point), run by Plymouth Co-operative Society. The beach offers a really good shore dive with rocky gullies and sandy fissures, wrasse, mullet, and pollack. Average depth for a shore dive is 35 feet. The visibility is often good enough for underwater photography.

Thurlestone is a useful site for a shore dive. I usually go through Thurlestone Village to a car park. You can splash in direct from the beach on to a rocky, weed covered bottom. There are several other sites around here, but this is the only one I know.

Hope Cove is tucked in the south-east end of Bigbury Bay, inside Bolt Tail. Turn off the A381 at Malborough. The bottom is rock and sand with flatties and shellfish. You can park the car—but get in early for there is not much space.

Rounding Bolt Tail, we come to Ramillies Cove, the site where the 90 gun man-o'-war H.M.S. *Ramillies* was wrecked in 1760. This is essentially a boat dive and the *Ramillies*—or what is left of her—is privately owned, so no souvenirs, please. A short distance away a Spanish Armada vessel, the *San Pedro el Mayor*, was wrecked near the Shippen Rocks. Rusting boilers and plates nearby indicate another wreck, the 4,000-ton mail-boat *Jebba*.

The first two wrecks are well documented in *The Wreck Hunters*. The area itself is an attractive dive with weed covered rock gullies persisting some way out to sea.

Out at sea, halfway between Bolt Tail and Bolt Head, the 3,600-ton S.S. *Maine* lies on shingle in 120 feet of water. A superb dive, the *Maine* is owned by Torbay Branch B.S-A.C., who will supply full details including a sectional drawing if you are interested.

Salcombe Estuary provides good sheltered diving, but there are plenty of boats buzzing around and care must be taken. There are many excellent dives available if you have a boat, and and there are several for hire. Princess Diving Holidays, White-strand, Salcombe, will provide accommodation on board a moored 110 foot ex-M.T.B. with daily diving trips, Sunday to Friday, on the M.F.V. *Princess*. Air is available at Salcombe Motor and Marine Engineering, Central Garage.

Lying deep (150 feet) off Prawle Point is another Torbay-owned wreck, the 2,900-ton *Riversdale*. A very good dive for the experienced only. Contact Torbay Branch if you are interested.

There are a couple of good beaches in Lannacombe Bay, but it is difficult to find, and parking space is so limited that you will probably have a half-mile walk from the car.

Hallsands lies at the south end of Start Bay. There is a car park at the cliff top and it is only a couple of hundred yards down to the shore. The underwater scenery is attractive with plenty of fish and an average depth, from shore, of 30 feet. At its worst when a north-east wind is—or has been—blowing. A caravan site is situated nearby.

CHART 12

Slapton Sands, in the middle of Start Bay, is a dangerous area for swimmers and divers. There is a strong undertow and powerful currents sweep across, so it is best avoided. You are not missing anything, for the underwater scenery is very dull and dreary.

Blackpool Sands is approached through Stoke Fleming and makes a good shore dive. The underwater shelves steadily providing an average depth of 30 feet, with plenty of marine life. If you intend to go farther out, do so by boat in case you hit the tail-end of the Slapton Sands undertow. There is ample space for parking the car behind the beach.

Dartmouth and the immediate area is not—compared with surrounding waters—noted for good visibility, particularly at ebb tide when the River Dart comes rushing out quickly. There are, however, plenty of wrecks a way out; and boat hire is no problem.

St. Mary's Bay is a useful site for the whole family. A holiday camp lies adjacent. A short walk through the camp and down to the beach will land you in attractive water. A friend of mine used to hunt monkfish here, for they are apparently prolific from here to Berry Head. Monkfish are slow and ungainly, needing no great skill to spear. But the skin, if you can find someone to treat it, makes a useful covering for articles. In days gone by it was frequently used instead of leather to cover elegant sword scabbards and handles. The flesh is of little use, but there is a central white core that is cooked or smoked and eaten in the West Country as Brixham Ham, although I have never tasted it. Average depth is 25 feet.

Berry Head possesses strong tidal streams and is best avoided.

Brixham is an excellent shore dive. Off the breakwater in the harbour when the sea is rough, or from the beach on the opposite side in better conditions. It is off this beach that I have caught several crabs in excess of five pounds, this alone makes it worth a visit. The scenery is very attractive and prolific in marine life. Several years ago I was squatting on the beach preparing to dive when stalwarts of Chelsea Branch marched past displaying a 7-foot monster conger they had just speared. Honestly, I had to rush quickly, into the water, before I lost my nerve! You can park the car nearby. In the harbour watch out for very heavy boat traffic. Air is available from Divers' Store, The Quay, telephone Brixham 2027 (Mr. Lister) or 2530 (Mr. Dunfold).

Tor Bay is a very good area. There is little current and the underwater scenery is very attractive. With air and boats and plenty of sites for shore dives, it would be easy to spend a diving holiday without venturing out of the bay. For shore dives, depths average 25 feet, while even in the middle of the bay 40 feet would be about maximum. The following sites lie in Tor Bay: Meadfoot has a car park, sandy beach, rock-sand bottom with plenty of flatties, but no great depth. Shag Rock is about 300 yards off Meadfoot Beach with plenty of fish to tempt the spear fisherman. Thatcher Rock is a boat dive. A very good site for fish such as bass, mullet, flatties. It should be dived only at slack water. Depth 30 feet. Air is available from Torbay Divers, Number 10 Store, Beacon Quay, Torquay Harbour, 8 p.m. Torbay Branch meet in the Corinthian Lounge of the Royal Torbay Yacht Club, Haldon Pier, Torquay Harbour every Monday evening from 8.30 to 10.30. Visitors are welcome to drop in, when you can get first-hand information on the diving scene.

I have a very soft spot for Babbacombe Bay, for this is the site of my first sea dive in British waters way back in, well, way back. Not for me the normally clear Devon water; the vis. was about 4 inches. I inched my way fearfully—and feet first—down the anchor chain flicking out a tentative flipper once in a while and praying I would touch bottom. The photograph being displayed by the skipper of a shark caught off nearby Anstey's Cove the day before did not help. It has never been as bad since. Babbacombe is a good site with a car park adjacent, but it really does get crowded in the summer. Heavy boat traffic.

Maidencombe is a useful shore dive. The bottom tends to be too sandy for real interest, but shell fish and flatties make up for it for some people. Average depth 20–25 feet. There is a car park, and a camping site, nearby.

Dawlish boasts 1½ miles of excellent beach, but you have to swim out a little to get some depth. About two miles out from Clerk Rock the wreck of the *Gallicia*, a 5,900-ton cargo vessel sunk by mine in 1917, lies in 50 feet of water. Although well broken up, the *Gallicia* still stands 12 feet proud of the seabed. Well fished by anglers, the marine life is prolific. Smaller boats can be hired at Dawlish, but if you are venturing out it is better to charter something more substantial, with a local skipper, from Teignmouth.

The River Exe is rather shallow and sandy, which usually mucks up visibility in the immediate area. And at ebb and flow the tides race through the estuary at well over 3 knots. However, there are reasonable sites for shore dives about. Snug against the west side of Straight Point, Sandy Bay has a slowly shelving beach with rocky outcrops out towards the end of the point. There is a caravan site adjacent, and the beach gets very crowded at the peak of the season. On the opposite side of the point, Littleham Cove is less sandy and often produces better visibility, although you will have to hump your gear over a small path down the cliff. I have never been out by boat off Exmouth, but boats can be chartered from the harbour, and exploration should prove rewarding.

Otterton Point provides good diving, but mainly by boat (from Exmouth or Sidmouth) as the Otterton Ledge, which dries at low tide, extends a long way out to sea. The bottom is sandy with many rocky outcrops, and prolific marine life. The sea around here gets rather rough when a south-east wind blows. For a shore dive, the beach at Budleigh shelves steeply into water housing bass and conger. The beach is shingle, resulting in better-than-average visibility. There is a car park just behind the beach. Tides are not usually swift—but watch that south-east wind.

Sidmouth is a useful source of boat hire; with good diving sites around. There is a site a couple of miles east of Sidmouth—I think it is called Weston Beach—which is far enough to avoid

Exotic looking fish in sordid surroundings. The tin can, newspapers and bottle tops are part of the underwater scenery under the Palace Pier, Brighton. Fish is a John Dory. Legend says that the black mark on its side is the thumb-print of St. Peter when he caught this fish in the Sea of Galilee. Leica 1F in Lewis Photomarine case, Kodachrome 1, PF45 flash, f4/25, depth: 25 feet, 15 feet visibility. Black-and-white from transparency. Tony Baverstock.

The nose of a killer. This close-up of the head of a conger eel was taken inside the Pagham Mulberry using an Agfa Flexilette in case with close-up lens and electronic flash, f11/125, Plus-X film. Geoff Harwood (see Chapter Five).

The ones that got away—pictures that will make rod-and-line fishermen weep. Mullet are normally shy and off like a flash at the sight of diver. Another extraordinary thing about these pictures—they were the first ever taken underwater by Colin Doeg. Tri-X, f8/500, Calypsophot camera. The weight, seen hanging from a rock, in the bottom picture, had been lost by a rod-and-line fisherman and just happened to be there. Pictures were taken near Swanage.

the crush of anglers. The journey to the beach is a hard slog, perhaps too hard. It is best to hire a boat when the attractive underwater scenery off the beach can be explored. If you do hire a boat, the spear fisherman in particular will find some good hunting around Hook Ebb Rocks.

Beer as a diving site is enough to set any diver's pulse racing. Unfortunately the liquid lapping the shores of Beer Beach and Beer Head, although very divable, is salt water. From the beach, a shore dive can venture right out to the head. The bottom is rocky and weed covered, but is rather shallow at low tide. Nearby Seaton can be covered at the same time, as it rests in the same indentation on the map. Although there are interesting underwater ledges directly off Seaton, my favourite spot is the long beach under Haven Cliff, east of the river. The beach is pebble and sand, and seems exposed to the elements, and in fact the waves do roll in when the wind is southerly, but when the wind is offshore you can get a good dive in, for tidal currents are usually weak. The last time I dived here, the expedition numbered around 60, mostly divers! Cylinders and other assorted equipment lay stretched out until you could hardly see a pebble for diving gear. About 200 yards out a rocky ridge provides most of the diving. Boats can generally be hired in Seaton.

Lyme Regis is a useful area for diver and family, with a safe, sandy beach and weak tides. There is a picturesque harbour, the Cobb, where the Duke of Monmouth landed in 1685. The beaches in summer are really too crowded for shore diving, but boats are available and there are some good sites out at sea. The 3,000-ton *Baygitano* lies wrecked in 50 feet of water about 1½ miles south-west of Lyme Regis. Sunk by torpedo in 1918, the *Baygitano* is broken up but still a very interesting dive. The remains stand about 10 feet high on the seabed, and is a popular site for anglers.

Chesil Beach stretches from Bridport to Portland Island for 18 bleak, bold, impressive miles. The beach is sandless, comprising shingle from end to end. At the Bridport end the pebbles are the size of a broad bean, increasing gradually in size until, culminating at Chesil Cove snug against Portland Island, they are stones about 4 inches in diameter. The increase in size is so

7

uniform that you could almost tell your position along the beach by measuring the particles. Another curious feature is the underwater extent of the shingle. I have dived off Bexington Beach and followed it down to a depth of 35 feet before a soft bottom took over, while at the Portland end it ceases at only 10 feet. Lying open to the south-west, surf and a heavy swell operate when the wind is from this quarter—in fact the heavy swell sometimes comes in any wind. The beach shelves sharply providing deep water very quickly and the water is often clear enough to take excellent underwater photographs.

The main difficulty at Chesil Beach is one of access, in all its eighteen miles I don't suppose there are more than a half dozen spots that one can easily reach. A car can be parked behind the beach at Bexington, and this is a rewarding site for a shore dive. Chesil Cove is also of reasonably easy access, while other sites— although I have not dived at these—are Cogden Beach, approached through Swyre, and Burton Freshwater (caravan site) approached via Burton Bradstock. Boat diving is difficult as there is little or nothing to hire. If you want a boat dive you will have to charter one from Bridport Harbour.

At Weymouth, air, boat, and equipment are available from Ron and Joy Parry at Sub-Aquatics, 43 Walpole Street, Weymouth, telephone Weymouth 6712. I have had many pleasurable trips around Portland and Weymouth with Ron—he knows the area well and can dump you on several worthwhile wrecks. In fact my first dive in this area was off Ron's boat. We dived, I think, on a wreck called the *Himalaya*; a mere shell but well preserved.

As I swam along the stern, in remarkable visibility, the water suddenly became thick with fish of one particular species— wrasse I believe, but in my excitement I could not be sure in retrospect. I have never—before or since—seen such a concentration of fish, it was like swimming through a sardine can. The creatures would dart a foot or two away as the bubbles burst from the exhaust of my regulator, then, in the silence of inhalation, drift inquisitively to within inches of my mask. Consequently I held my breath until I was going purple, swimming through the mass and actually bumping into some of them. On surfacing we excitedly told the following divers, of the marvellous sight below. They entered the water some ten minutes later and dejectedly reported visibility less than eight feet with not a fish in sight. As I have said, British waters are variable.

Durdle Dor makes an excellent dive, but unfortunately it is such a long slog back up the cliff that a shore dive just isn't worth the effort. If you can get a boat from nearby Lulworth Cove the situation is different and you will be well rewarded.

Chapmans Pool is a bit of a climb from the parking space on the cliff top, but when the weather has been calm with no wind or, at worst, north-east winds, then it is well worth a visit. It was at Chapmans Pool that I saw an eleven-pound turbot caught. This in itself is not remarkable—they have been speared or hooked at over twice that weight; but the manner in which this turbot was caught is rather unusual . . .

I was diving with Jim and Tony, rejoicing in the marvellous visibility (Chapmans Pool, in this respect, is very good or very bad). We were out near the entrance of the pool when Jim checked air gauges then started to lead the way back to shore. I had no more usable film in the camera, so I surfaced and unloaded it on the snorkel cover. Descending once more I saw that Tony was carrying something that on first glance seemed to be a circular tray, but which was in fact a nice fat turbot. I was of course certain that the fish was dead; after all, they just don't allow you to pick them up by hand. Tony saw me staring and gave an uncertain shrug; he was as puzzled as I was.

The weird procession, Jim leading the way and Tony following, holding the turbot on each side—or is it edge?—and looking for all the world like an underwater waiter, proceeded for about five minutes. We arrived at shore on the east side, where the water is about 12 inches deep and very rocky. Jim scrambled to his knees and whipped out his mouthpiece; he intended to tell Tony not to lift the turbot out of the water. But too late.

Mister Turbot had indeed been very much alive, apparently enjoying his free trip, but on being lifted out of the water he promptly gave a somersault and flopped back into the sea. Jim reacted swiftly, whipping out his Heinke standard diver's knife—a formidable-looking weapon at the best of times—and, hurling himself across Tony's half elevated body—and knocking him flat on his face in the process—he transfixed the turbot at its edge. This was no easy prey, the turbot wriggled free and sped through the shallow water past Tony's head, now partially submerged. Undaunted, Jim threw himself back in the opposite direction over Tony's prostrate body. From a few yards away I watched horrified as Jim hurled himself time and again like an international goalkeeper while the knife flailed the air and water. I could see myself trying to explain Tony's multiple wounds to the coroner.

At last they triumphantly landed the fish, thereby posing several questions: Who caught it? Even though it ended up in Tony's car, the argument continues. Why did it not object to being picked up and carried through the water? Perhaps a marine biologist would know the answer. And the turbot? Well, the following morning Tony's wife disposed of it in the dustbin —she said it smelt. If the ensuing row had ended in divorce it might have been said to represent rough justice.

Swanage Bay is easily the most dived area in Dorset. The bay is sheltered from all but south-east winds and provides varied diving up to a depth of 40 feet. Its popularity is due in no small part to the presence of Divers Down, 10 Park Road, Swanage, telephone Swanage 3536. Divers Down have a changing room and show room on the pier along with an enormous glass tank for training when the sea is too rough. Here is provided air, equipment and equipment hire. Five-day courses are run from Monday to Friday and accommodation can be arranged.

Poole Bay, as long as you keep clear of the Poole Harbour side, is a vast stretch of diveable water with depths up to 60 feet. The bottom is well studded with rocky outcrops and prolific fish life. The only outcrop I have dived on is the Outer Poole Patch, about 3 miles east of Poole Harbour. Commencing at a depth of 40 feet and reaching to within 15 feet of the surface. The rocks, or rather "patch" was inhabited by some of the most brilliantly coloured wrasse I have ever seen. Unfortunately I only had black-and-white film in the camera. Boats can be chartered in Poole Harbour and air is obtainable from Carbery Engineering, Southbourne, telephone Bournemouth 43243.

Christchurch Bay is similar to Poole Bay, except that depths are no greater than 40 feet. Boats are obtainable from Mudeford (at the mouth of Christchurch Harbour), but when out in the boat keep well away from the Christchurch end of the bay, which is very shallow.

At the eastern edge of the map, the north-west tip of the Isle of Wight, the Needles, juts into the picture. On a more detailed map such as the Admiralty Chart L (D5) 2615 there are a lot of dotted circles marked with a depth and indicated by the abbreviation "WK". This means wreck, and the profusion of them indicates dangerous water—which it is. The most famous wreck here, which I believe has never been found, is that of the *Insurance*, a forty-gun vessel that sank in 1753. It was carrying the Governor of Jamaica and, it is said, large sums of money.

CHART 9

This map, at the west edge, starts at Selsey Bill, just missing the sea off Portsmouth Harbour. It was in this area, Spithead, that H.M.S. *Mary Rose* was sunk in 1545. Actually sunk is not the correct description—committed suicide is more apt. The *Mary Rose* was performing manœuvres under the land-based gaze of King Henry VIII when, for no apparent reason, she heeled to one side, overturned completely, and plunged to the bottom.

There is not space here to enter the conjectures as to why she sank, but an important point is that she was not smashed up in any way and at the spot where she sank the bottom is soft and muddy. There is a chance that she is buried, nearly complete, in the mud. If this is the case, and it is possible to salvage her in the same manner that the Swedish ship *Vasa* was raised and is now preserved, the remains would be of great interest to historians. The sinking is gone into in great detail in *History Under the Sea*, and, most importantly, in Chapter Two of this book.

Back to the map. Littlehampton is useful both as a holiday resort and diving base. Boats are available but expensive as anglers are prepared to pay high prices for a good boat. It was out from Littlehampton, at the Kingsmere Rocks, that I saw a conger about a hundred yards long. Well, perhaps not quite that long, but I was about to peer into a hole on the seaward side of the rocks when this massive head slid out, only inches from my face mask. I clung petrified to the mouth of the hole as this endless body oozed out. Either the shock numbed my reactions and it seemed to empty out for minutes, or it really was a hundred yards long, but as visibility was no more than eight feet I shall never know. I am only glad I didn't stick my hand in the hole, and even more so that I didn't put my head in!

Approximately 9 miles out from Shoreham lies a virtual convoy of wrecks, casualties from two wars. The many vessels are recorded as having been sunk in this area but to my knowledge none have been found, although the distance out mitigates against regular exploration. Both my attempts to survey the sea bed here were thwarted by inclement weather.

There are many sites of interest in the Brighton area. Air can be obtained from Brighton and Worthing Branch B.S-A.C., who also own a sturdy boat, a 45-foot-long diesel cruiser complete with echo sounder, ship-to-shore radio and covered accommodation. This vessel—the *Blue Dolphin*—will take 20 divers and is available for charter complete with skipper and crew. For details of air or boat phone the Diving Officer, D. Cullen, at Shoreham 2318.

I have not dived at Newhaven since the new marina was built, although I hasten to add, it has been circumstances, not the marina, which caused my absence. Nevertheless I can vividly remember the excellent diving I participated in. Most of it from Rex Golder's M.V. *Miss Conduct*. I think Rex is no longer there, but boats are available—and necessary—for the wrecks lying several miles out. In any area you are lucky if you can obtain the services of a local skipper who dives or caters for divers. In Newhaven the man to contact is P. Carpenter, c/o The Manager, Harbour Tavern, Transit Road, who will provide a good boat and skipper—probably himself—and supply profuse data on diving in the area.

Several people have assured me that you can get a good dive direct off Seaford Beach, and the chart seems to bear them out.

For myself, the nearest I got to Seaford was about 4 miles directly out on the wreck of the *Celtic*. We had chartered a boat from Newhaven, having been assured that no boats were available at Seaford—although this situation may have changed now. The same sources informed me that the best diving in this area was off Cuckmere Haven (it's not on this map, but is marked on Admiralty Chart (L(D5)1652) which is the indentation east of Hope Point, provided you don't mind a long walk (about a mile) to the sea. If you fancy yourself the athletic type—have a go. For myself, I have a painful memory of lying exhausted in the car park at the top of Durdle Dor and swearing that if I ever again had to walk more than fifty yards to the water I wouldn't dive, and a mile is slightly more than this limit.

From Beachy Head eastward the sea, in my experience, becomes more unreliable both regarding visibility and conditions at the surface. But even when visibility is bad, a boat trip a few miles offshore will often produce clear water.

Pevensey Bay is where William the Conqueror landed in 1066. But the underwater swimmer will probably be more interested in less historical facts, such as the location of Roberts Sports, where air to 2,250 p.s.i. can be obtained along with equipment for sale or hire. The telephone number is Pevensey 259. The bay comprises a shingle beach and is approached through Wallsend. Of more interest to the spear fisherman, the attraction is bass and flatfish.

The area several miles off Hyde Flat, just west of Folkestone is marked with "Numerous sunken wrecks". I haven't tried it, so I don't know how true it is, but I do have some sad memories of Folkestone. It was July 1962, and I was an excited member of a team assisting Byron Cowie to swim the Channel underwater. This had never been done despite several attempts and, in fact, some experts were already saying it was impossible. We took off from Cape Gris Nez in bad weather, it would have been better to wait a day or two, but finances were low and it was now or never.

Conditions were so bad that I never thought we would complete more than a couple of miles, but we managed Byron's supply of air every half hour and slowly he ploughed across the

Channel. But although Byron was going well, sea-sickness was chopping down the pool of supply divers like the plague. Soon, out of a total of eight divers there were only three left to take down the supply of air and food (boiled sweets) at regular intervals. Unfortunately for me, for I had to make the decisions —I was in charge.

I had just finished one change-over and was sitting exhausted on deck when Ron Chamberlain, who did a magnificent job handling the equipment, jarred me with the observation that it was getting dark and, with only three tired divers and the sea getting wilder, there was the probability of a nasty accident. If a diver was swept away when it was dark it would be impossible to find him. I waited until the dusk was really setting in, but the sea was getting worse. At night, divers would actually be risking their lives on each dive. Reluctantly I sent Garry down to bring Byron up. Byron was still going like a bomb and, understandably, was annoyed and disappointed at being hauled up—he was more than half-way across. A disconsolate band of divers disembarked at Folkestone, but we were already making plans for the next attempt. We knew it could be done.

Two days later, to our consternation, the newspapers carried the story of Fred Baldasare, an American. Submerging at Cape Gris Nez, Fred surfaced at Folkestone to become the first person to swim the Channel underwater. But we all knew that it could have been Byron Cowie.

The rest of map 9 comprises water that is very variable and dangerous, particularly the area between Deal and the Goodwin Sands. And the visibility is usually nothing to write home about.

The map just misses the north coast of Kent, which is a pity for along this stretch lies the site of what is possibly the only Roman wreck known to date. The site is Pudding Pan Rock, several miles out at sea between Whitstable and Herne Bay. Anyone interested in sub-aqua swimming will hear the story many times over, so I will not indulge in annoying repetition here. Many expeditions have tried to find the wreck—or what remains of it—without success. There was one such mass attempt in May, 1961, which made headlines in the *Whitstable Times*. Decca set up three observation stations—one at Whitstable, the other at Hampton and Reculver, so that if anything was found of interest it could be pinpointed within a few feet. I had never dived the area, so I wangled myself into the diving team.

I had been told that the maximum visibility one could expect was in the region of 8 feet, but on 7 May 1961 it was nearer 4 inches as I went down roped to my old buddy Moreno. We found that if we swam with our masks scraping the bottom we could just see a few inches of seabed. Imagine our excitement when we stumbled across hundreds of broken pottery fragments. Carefully selecting handfuls of the larger pieces, we jubilantly surfaced to display our find.

But be warned. The seabed comprising Pudding Pan Rock is covered with natural stone that, at depth, looks just like pottery fragments!

For divers requiring equipment, air, boats or information, the Whitstable Diving Co., 38 Oxford Street, Whitstable, Telephone 3593, is the place to go.

DIVING INTO
THE FUTURE

by Colin McLeod

Colin McLeod is a vice-president of the British Sub-Aqua Club.
He was recently made an honorary life member, the highest
honour the Club can bestow—in this case for his services to the
Club and diving. He represents Britain on committees of the
World Federation.

THE whole history of diving has been revolutionized by the
development and perfection of the aqualung. We are now in a
state that would be undreamed of by those pioneers of the
undersea world who walked the bottom in leaden boots
attached to the life-giving surface by tubes down which the
precious air was pumped (for certain kinds of heavy work this
same helmet dress is still the most useful). But the day of the
free diver is with us. More, the day of the free amateur diver is
with us. All we have to decide is the way that amateur diving
should go.

No one wants to take the sport out of diving. This is one joy
that the demand valve and air cylinder have given us. Every
man is his own Livingstone, Scott, Rhodes, Shackleton. Every
diver making his own discoveries in his own undersea jungle,
plain, desert, mountain, valley, lost city, sunken wreck. This is
what the aqualung has given us—the chance to become explorers again without having to travel to some far-off land. For
all the best parts of the land have been explored, but the best
parts of the sea are yet to come.

In this book you have read of men and women who are
diving with a purpose. Diving to find out something or diving
to see what no scientist has ever seen before.

They are diving to some purpose, but what of the non-diving
scientists who study fields that are intimately concerned with
the sea. Are they using this new force, these new eyes? Those
who are, are few and far between.

202

In the chapter of this book by Dr. David Bellamy you have read how 250 people willingly gave up hours of their time to do a survey of seaweed growth and the effect of pollution. It seems fantastic that few other men of science are prepared to use so many willing hands and eyes—belonging to people who can penetrate and see where the non-diving scientist can only grab and grope from the surface. What holds them back? One can only hope it is only a lack of knowledge of the presence of such a force of trained divers and not some stupid academic pride.

In Britain we would like to think we lead the world with our diving training. And so we do. Now we need to penetrate a shade further. And to do this we cannot rely on our own skills. Most divers cannot afford the time to be marine biologists, archaeologists, ecologists.... Most have enough trouble earning their livings and satisfying their own curiosity about the things they see below the surface of the sea.

What an opportunity for a marine scientist! All he has got to do is to tell this diving work force exactly what he wants and they will do it, if it is within their powers.

With "Operation Kelp" (see Chapter Four) it worked. With other operations it can be done too. The evidence for this comes not only from Britain, but also from the United States. There, as in this country, early enthusiasm for the underwater world was largely confined to spear fishing.

World Beneath the Sea, a book produced by the National Geographic Society, describes what happened then in America:

"One day in 1960 in the office of Dr. Lionel A. Walford, director of Sandy Hook Marine Laboratory in New Jersey, a group of divers appeared and demanded something to do.

"He put them to work on a number of projects. 'From this nucleus of enthusiastic volunteers came the American Littoral Society, organized in 1961,' Dr. Walford said. 'As amateur naturalists they have accumulated much new information about fish. Of course they've needed guidance and training and we're happy to give it to them when time permits.'

"Now, six years later, the Society has about 2,200 members, representing every state. The 700 divers among them count and tag fish, observe other underwater life and report back to the Society.

"John R. Clark, a member of the laboratory staff and president of the Society said: 'Every year a group of Arizona divers goes faithfully to the Gulf of California and makes a fish count, similar to the Audubon Society Christmas bird count. If the group continues monitoring year after year, its reports could reveal a conservation or a pollution problem in time to remedy it before serious damage is done.' "

In this country there seems no reason why this sort of work could not be done by divers, but the scientists have to guide and advise. Such a link with scientific organizations is very much in the minds of the General Committee of the British Sub-Aqua Club, though they have had some experience of lack of support for scientific work. The formation of Scientific and Technical Groups within the Club did not function very well due to the shortage of divers with enough technical qualifications.

Now Scientific and Technical Liaison is carried out by a member of the Executive Committee of the Club. Spurred on by the success of "Operation Kelp", the Club plans more mass operations of this kind.

And it has already notched up some striking successes in the scientific field. The formation of the Committee for Nautical Archaeology would never have come about if it had not been for the enthusiasms of British Sub-Aqua Club divers.

The Committee for Nautical Archaeology is basically a mixture of archaeologists and divers. Represented in the committee are the National Maritime Museum, British Museum, Science Museum, Institute of Archaeology, London University, Society for Nautical Research, the British Sub-Aqua Club, and the Council for British Archaeology.

They lay down their aims as:

1. To promote research into all material aspects of nautical archaeology in the sea, lakes, rivers, and on the land.
2. To organize a wreck survey in and around the British Isles, noting such wrecks as are of historical and technical importance and which would repay detailed study.
3. To promote the training of nautical archaeologists work-

ing on land and underwater, to promote good standards of recording and excavation, and to encourage the publication of results.

4. To act as a channel of communication between field archaeologists, divers, local historians and related scientists.

5. To maintain files of wrecks, ports, harbours, and other nautical sites of archaeological interest both at home and abroad.

6. To compile a bibliography of books and articles relating to nautical archaeology.

7. To keep a list of specialists in all fields of related research, and of selected local representatives who will be informed of the committee's activities and who will advise the committee on local developments.

Chairman of the Committee is Mr. George Naish of the National Maritime Museum. Secretary is Miss Joan du Plat Taylor, who, with her sympathetic understanding of the problems of the diver, did so much to bring about the formation of the committee. The address is: c/o University of London, Institute of Archaeology, 31–34 Gordon Square, London, W.C.1.

Now the first School of Nautical Archaeology has been set up at Swanage and suitable archaeology students are taught to dive and to deal with the problems of underwater surveying and recording on an "ancient wreck" near Swanage Pier. To help with their wreck survey round the coasts of Britain the Nautical Archaeology Committee has appealed to all divers for help.

Divers who find wrecks are asked to supply the following information:

(a) Date the wreck was discovered. Ship's name if known.

(b) Name of finder and address.

(c) Exact position of wreck from chart references, bearings, and a tracing of the chart showing its position in relation to the land.

(d) Depth of the wreck, including state of the tide and time when depth was recorded.

(e) Whether the wreck is wood or iron.

(f) Estimated size of the wreck or area covered by debris with length, breadth, and height.
(g) Estimated age of the wreck.
(h) Sketches or photographs of any fittings of the ship.
(i) What is visible.
(j) Conditions on the site such as currents, seabed, weed, etc.

A typical example of the sort of thing that the Committee for Nautical Archaeology encourage is provided by the discovery of a Roman stone anchor just outside Lulworth Cove, its recovery and final display at the National Maritime Museum. This is believed to be the first discovery of such an anchor round our shores. Certainly it is the first discovery of its kind in Britain by a diver.

The story of the anchor starts with a gala organized by Bromley Branch of the British Sub-Aqua Club at the New Ladywell Baths, Lewisham. Branch divers were asked to bring along objects they had recovered from the sea for static displays in the foyer. Among the cannon and portholes, shells and corals on display one archaeologically-minded diver noticed a pottery cone with a hole in the centre of the "nose". He guessed that it was Roman from having seen similar pottery on dives abroad. The diver to whom it belonged, Albert Greenland, said that he had found it outside Lulworth Cove and would be delighted to take it to Joan du Plat Taylor for identification.

The pottery cone turned out to be an unguent bottle from the Roman occupation period and Greenland was encouraged by the Committee to carry out further dives in the area to discover whether his find was flung overboard because the neck was broken off or whether it was part of a Roman wreck. Either way it was incredible that such a fragile object had not been smashed to pieces during the centuries.

The importance of this find cannot be too highly stressed. Experts to whom it was shown tentatively placed it as Mediterranean-made. This would seem to indicate a ship that had sailed all the way from there, but a short cross-Channel shipping traffic route could obviously not be ruled out.

More importantly all the experts said that they had not seen one like it in this country and added that they thought the nearest place such a type had been found was near Cologne. Would further dives in the area produce more surprising finds?

Greenland did dive again in the area and to his own astonishment as much as anyone else's he saw a large stone, buried under rock and shale, but with enough clear to show that a hole was bored right through it. From photographs he had seen and descriptions he had read it seemed remarkably like a Roman stone anchor of Mediterranean type.

A small expedition—of three divers—was formed to raise the anchor for fuller examination. The divers were Albert Greenland, Mike Greenhaugh and John Humphreys.

John Humphreys wrote the following report for *Snark*, Bromley Branch's magazine—for the amusement of his fellow divers not as a scientific treatise!

"Friday morning saw us down at Lulworth, carting the inevitable load of gear on to the beach. Sun brilliant, water like a lake. Having no engine and not being able to hire one, we started paddling out towards the inviting sea. We could see the bottom of the cove clearly 30 feet down all the way out. Outside the cove the tide was running and our wet suits were soon wet all right—with sweat—in our efforts to propel the inflatable dinghy in a straight line. Al and Mick had made a rough fix of the location a few months before, so we anchored and played out our safety line and buoy.

"We dived in pairs looking for an old iron anchor which was remembered as being near the artifact. The water was beautifully clear, visibility about 30 feet.

"The current made things rather hard so we had to conduct the search up stream, then back to the inflatable's anchor—pick that up and let the lot drift down tide, stick it in the rocks and search again. The depth was 50 feet and all of us were very negatively weighted although we were wearing the normal amount of weights for each of us. This was due to the fact that just outside the cove a lot of fresh water mixes with the sea. As a result when we surfaced it had to be up the anchor line!

"After three hours of diving, rowing and searching we were getting a bit dubious about finding the artifact, but suddenly Mick spotted the old iron anchor, tied a line to it and surfaced still holding on. Al and I dragged ourselves into the inflatable and rowed like lunatics to get to him and get a buoy tied to the end of his line. Now we had a spot marker, so we re-anchored, went down the line and found our artifact not six feet from the old iron anchor!

"The last of our air was used gazing in triumph at our find. In the boat we got a good fix of our exact position in case the buoy was cut or lost. During all this work Al's camera on the surface and mine underwater were used.

"We paddled back to the shore weary but happy, Mick had even caught a decent crab, but we were too lazy to cook it and eventually gave it away. We had used 300 cubic feet of air, so after we had dragged all the gear back to the van and changed we went to Weymouth for more air and some nosh. . . .

"Saturday morning we set out again, weather still perfect and the underwater visibility even better. Our buoy was still in place. Down again—this time even faster with our loads of hammers and chisels. We carefully excavated round our find and at one stage feared that the hole did not go right through (this would have ruled out the stone anchor theory) but eventually all the muck was cleared. This time the current was helpful in clearing all the 'gunge' we created. We attached two large kitbags to the eye and started inflating from our mouth pieces. No luck. We got the two-and-a-half hundredweight stone to stand up but the bags leaked so badly that as fast as we put air in it got out. We had been several hours in and out of the water by then so we decided to call it a day. We thought we would get some thin plastic bags and use them to line the kitbags. Off to Weymouth again for air and Ron Parry offered us the use of a 40-gallon drum.

"We cleaned and freed the bungs on it and took on another 300 feet of air. This time we managed to rig up a light in the tent so we ate our grass sandwiches, grass soup and drank our grass coffee (ever been camping?) while we planned the next day. We were trying to film the whole operation in both reversal film and negative film as I had made arrangements to send the negative film to the B.B.C. and I wanted the reversal film for myself. Of course every shot we planned went wrong and I came back a very humble underwater cameraman! We decided that if we dived earlier we should get some slack water so we talked till three and were up at six—exhausted.

"Down to the Cove again on Sunday morning, sun brilliant and visibility underwater up to 40 feet. Buoy still intact and no current. Our 40-gallon drum which we had towed out we planned to sink slowly and film all the way down. What a hope! After getting a few shots of it being flooded, I paused to wind the camera and it dropped to the bottom like a stone. Just as I started to film the drum being manhandled along the bottom into position the camera case flooded half-way up the camera. Up the anchor line like a lunatic, dump the camera in the boat, drag off my lung, hang it on the transom, scramble madly into the boat to drain the camera case. As I was doing this Mike came up to see what was happening.

"I'd just drained the case when I realized that my set had gone—bottle, harness, valve, the lot into 50 feet of water! Poor Mick eventually interpreted my enraged screams and dived to look for it. He returned about six minutes later—triumphant.

"I could not decide where the camera case had leaked so we dived again to give Al a hand at strapping the drum to the artifact. We got it into position and started inflating. This time things went well, except that I emptied the contents of my lung into the drum instead of into me and had to surface hastily to get another bottle—and the camera to get a shot of it rising to the surface. Fast as I was, the drum complete with anchor nearly beat me to it. After appearing to be just getting buoyant, it suddenly started for the surface and there was no holding it. If our assumptions of its origin were correct there it was back to the surface through which it had plummeted some 1800 years ago.

"It was so unwieldy that we soon decided that we had not a hope of paddling it back across the rip which was starting again, so we hailed a fisherman with a dinghy and outboard and asked for a tow. Poor dinghy—there it was towing our inflatable and all our gear, two divers and our stone suspended six feet below the surface, and with me hanging on behind on snorkel trying to guide him to the beach by the deepest route.

"The fisherman got us to within 30 yards of the beach, where we attached a line and with the help of a dozen stalwart holiday-makers we started to heave it ashore. There had been considerable interest in our activities all along, but we had never said what we were doing. As the stone emerged from the water blank stares were the order of the day. These stares changed to hoots of laughter when we said what we thought it was!

"I must admit that we then began having doubts, but settled down lovingly guarding and photographing our find until the arrival of Mrs. Pat Baker (the Director of Marine Archaeology for the South Coast). She was very excited upon seeing it and after measuring, drawing and photographing it from every angle found it very similar to previous finds in the Mediterranean. . . ."

This report has been quoted at some length because, apart from its humorous side, it does show the need for determination in such an operation and that underwater work is far from easy.

It also shows that amateurs, far from getting in the way of the expert, can be employed in useful work of this kind. In the field of archaeology this is being realized but other fields of science seem slow to take their opportunity.

Certainly the British Sub-Aqua Club is not lagging behind in its efforts to help in this field. The Duke of Edinburgh Prize for Underwater Science is awarded annually to the member or group of members of the Club who have undertaken, published, or completed an important project in the underwater field.

In recommending projects to the Palace the selection committee, made up of leading scientists, underline the Club's intention that the Prize should be open to all classes of divers interested in the scientific challenge of the world undersea. Winners in 1965 were the Cambridge University branch of the Club for work carried out on the day and night behaviour of fish, sea-cucumbers and other sea creatures.

This sort of stress on the scientific application of diving by the British Sub-Aqua Club is one way in which the future of amateur diving is being influenced and guided. The Club at the same time fully recognizes its responsibility for continuing to teach and practise safe diving methods.

Amateur aqualung diving is the fastest growing sport of all in this country. It is also important that the sport side of diving should remain in existence. For it is from the ranks of the sporting divers that many of the future scientists of the sea will emerge.

From those diving scientists will come tomorrow's answer to many of today's world-wide land problems. From the sea—and the diver—the best is yet to come.

B.S - A.C. Branches

If none of these branches is conveniently situated, intending
members may join the General Branch administered from:
25 Orchard Road, Kingston-on-Thames, Surrey

Aberdeen (67): J. Fraser, West Brimmondside, Kingswells, Aberdeen.

Banbury (74): R. C. Llewellyn, Unicorn House, Bloxham, Banbury, Oxon.

Barnsley (95): M. A. Glover, 11 Tennyson Avenue, Mexborough, Yorks.

Bath (33): R. Minns, 85 Bloomfield Drive, Bath, Somerset.

Bedford (89): G. S. Potter, 11 Griffin Street, Rushden, Northants.

Belfast (30): Miss H. P. McGuire, 104 Lansdowne Road, Belfast, N.1.

Bermondsey (42): T. E. Holman, 8 Copperfield House, Dockhead, London, S.E.1.

Birmingham (25): Mrs. K. Mason, 39 Swindell Road, Pedmore, Stourbridge.

Blackheath (188): J. Martin, 155 Ampleforth Road, Abbey Wood, London, S.E.2.

Blackpool (4): Miss A. J. Barber, 19 Dalby Close, Ribbleton, Preston, Lancs.

Bognor (27): Mrs. Dawn Piper, Top Flat Pembury, Richmond Road North, Bognor Regis, Sussex.

Bolton (84): Alan MacIvor, 20 Lovat Road, Bolton, Lancs.

Bournemouth (6): J. B. James, 89 Badpole Road, Strouden Park, Bournemouth.

Bradford (44): Miss W. G. Walton, Barnsley Cottage, Charlestown, Baildon, Yorks.

Brighton & Worthing (7): Miss Shirley A. Hill, "Espinet", 150 Littlehampton Road, Worthing, Sussex.

Bristol (3): W. J. Locke, 11 Mendip Road, Portishead, Nr. Bristol.

Bromley (26): M. Inch, 5 Hilary Close, Erith, Kent.

Burnley (143): R. Goth, 5 Laund Road, Baxenden, Accrington, Lancs.

Cambridge (240): H. C. Townsend, 14 Princess Drive, Sawston, Cambs.

Chelsea (45): Mrs. Lilian Stokes, 82 Urmstone Drive, London, S.W.19.

Coventry (58): J. A. Watkins, 18 Hanson Way, Sharnford, Leicestershire.

Crawley (148): S. W. Bartley, 9 Hermits Road, Three Bridges, Crawley, Sussex.

Croydon (23): D. J. Jessup, 1 Sibton Road, Carshalton, Surrey.

Darwen (47): J. H. Pendlebury, 30 Church Lane, Farington, Nr. Preston, Lancs.

Deptford (M7) (236): I. S. S. Surridge, 143 Trundleys Road, Deptford, London, S.E.8.

Derby (72): L. A. Brown, 3 Queensland Close, Mickleover, Derby.

Doncaster (75): J. E. Matthews, 63 Chekstone Avenue, Bessacarr, Doncaster.

Durham City (104): R. Hogarth, 17 Rowley Crescent, Esh Winning, Co. Durham.

East Anglia (11): John P. Anson, 9 Seafield Close, Great Yarmouth, Norfolk.

East Cheshire (100): Mrs. S. Hamer, Brooklyn Cottage, Holly Vale, Mill Brow, Marple Bridge, Cheshire.

East Lancs. (2): W. D. Stephenson, "Dale Edge", 2 Dalamere Avenue, Whitefield, Manchester.

East London (15): A. W. Hayden, 21 Salcombe Road, London, E.17.

East Yorks. (176): Miss P. Land, Somerville, North Marine Road, Scarborough, Yorkshire.

Edinburgh (21): Lt.-Col. Gordon-Rogers, O.B.E., T.D., 23 Corstorphine Hill Crescent, Edinburgh, 12.

Falmouth (214): V. D. Pentecost, 64 Killigrew Street, Falmouth, Cornwall.

Folkestone (106): Mrs. M. Armstrong, "Cinque Port", 163 Sandown Road, Deal, Kent.

Furness (61): E. Lowther, 28 Gloucester Street, Barrow-in-Furness, Lancs.

Grimsby (37): J. R. Elston, 5 Haile Road, Humberston, Lincs.

Guildford (53): M. Douglas, Leander, Manor Road, Farnborough, Hants.

Gwynedd (71): Miss I. R. Beamer, 23 Llwyn Onn, Rhos-on-Sea, Colwyn Bay, N. Wales.

Halifax (48): Miss Joan M. Longbottom, 10 Ingle Dene, Hebden Bridge, Yorks.

Hampstead (179): D. M. Bailey, 481A Finchley Road, Hampstead, N.W.3.

Harlow (141): Mrs. D. Johnson, 14 Vicarage Wood, Harlow, Essex.

Harrogate (39): S. Clarke, 21 Castle Close, Killinghall, Nr. Harrogate.

Harwich (54): G. K. L. Cousins, Flat 1, Post Office Buildings, Gt. Yeldham, Nr. Halstead, Essex.

Holborn (130): C. G. J. May, 45 Westmoreland Road, Barnes, S.W.13.

Hounslow (55): B. J. Gooding, 5 Church Stretton Road, Hounslow, Middx.

Huddersfield (18): K. Flinders, 15 Red Doles Road, Fartown, Huddersfield.

Hull (14): G. A. Wright, 46 Seafield Avenue, B.O.C.M. Village, Hull, Yorks.

Ilford (49): R. F. Davison, 41 Selbourne Road, Cranbrook, Ilford, Essex.

Ilfracombe (86): N. Hutchinson, Flat 1, Fort Hill House, Goodleigh Road, Barnstaple, N. Devon.

Isle of Man (76): J. P. Colby, The Hollies, Spring Valley Road, Douglas, Isle of Man.

Keighley (117): B. Stubbs, 2 Reservoir Place, Mountain Queensbury, Bradford, Yorks.

Kingston (17): R. M. Turner, 62 St. James Road, Sutton, Surrey.

Leamington & Warwick (217): Mrs. K. I. Herbert, 17 Cowdray Close, Leamington Spa.

Leeds (115): Miss M. E. Eckersley, Flat 7, 220 Chapeltown Road, Leeds, 7.

Lincoln (109): A. C. Temperton, 29 Minister Drive, Cathedral View, Cherry, Willingham, Lincoln.

London (1): Miss J. Stokoe, 10 Westbourne Grove Terrace, London, W.2.

Lunesday (138): R. Hargreaves, 36 Norton Road, Morecambe, Lancs.

Luton (105): Mrs. O. Fidler, 9 Lawn Gardens, Luton, Beds.

Matlock (121): Mrs. M. Hallan, Oker House, Oker Side, Matlock, Derbys.

Medway (59): M. J. Varney-Burgh, 76 Townley Road, Bexley Heath, Kent.

Merseyside (5): W. M. Smith (5) 17 Davenham Road, Formby, Lancs.

Mexborough (41): G. Calderbank, 6 Woodside Avenue, Wath-on-Dearne, Nr. Rotherham, Yorks.

Newham (168): T. F. Barwick, 2 Markhams, Stanford le Hope, Essex.

Newport & Cardiff (35): A. R. Bunn, Henllys House, 30 Garth Road, Cwmbran, Mon.

Northampton (13): Miss R. E. Starmer, 28 Sandhills Road, Whitehills, Northampton.

North Gloucestershire (80): D. D. Millar, Parrington Stinchcombe, Dursley, Glos.

North Staffs. (12): W. J. B. White, Hilltop, 9 Liverpool Road E., Church Lawton, Stoke-on-Trent.

Nottingham (16): G. Aitken, 19 Walk Mill Drive, Linby, Notts.

Oxford (34): Miss A. Symons, Bramblefinch, Boults Lane, Old Marston, Oxford.

Penzance (116): R. H. Trethowan, 26 William Street, Cambourne, Cornwall.

Perth (218): G. Leishman, Shalimar, 12 Unity Terrace, Perth, Scotland.

Plymouth Sound (164): G. Jensen, 34 Fairview Avenue, Laira, Plymouth.

Pontefract (190): Mrs. P. Hudson, 30 Baden Powell Crescent, Pontefract, Yorks.

Reading (28): G. Vance, 131 Overdown Road, Tilehurst, Reading, Berks.

Redditch (248): D. C. Williams, 1 Marlpool Drive, Redditch, Worcs.

Scarborough (83): The Secretary, Scarborough Branch British Sub-Aqua Club, 25 St. Mary's Street, Scarborough, Yorks.

Sheffield (36): Mrs. M. A. Allen, 5 Newhall Avenue, Wickersley, Rotherham.

Solihull (264): James M. Reid, County Borough of Solihull, Education Office, 99 Homer Road, Solihull, Warwicks.

Southampton (139): M. Elliott, 1A Forest Meadow, Crawte Avenue, Farley, Hants.

Southend (22): R. T. Hall, Rustana, Lancaster Road, Rayleigh, Essex.

Southsea (9): Mrs. J. S. Millgate, 23 Jubilee Avenue, Paulsgrove, Portsmouth.

Swansea (99): Peter D. Meehan, 586 Clydach Road, Ynystawe, Swansea, Glam.

Swindon (46): J. E. Hamilton, 11 Springfield Road, Swindon Old Town, Wilts.

Tamworth (137): E. S. George, 13 Borough Road, Tamworth, Staffs.

Taunton (10): A. C. Charlton, "Lorien", 11 Stoke Road, Taunton, Som.

Thornton Heath (210): P. J. Smith, 44 Dixon Road, South Norwood, S.E.25.

Tees-Side (43): A. B. Croft, 33 Fairwell Road, Stockton-on-Tees, Co. Durham.

Torbay (8): E. A. Colling, 14 Lower Fowden, Elbury Cove, Paignton, S. Devon.

Tunbridge Wells (149): Miss L. Gamlyn, Swan Hotel Garage, London Road, Tunbridge Wells, Kent.

Tyneside (114): C. B. Settle, 67 Edwins Avenue, Forest Hall, Newcastle-upon-Tyne, 12.

Wakefield (77): R. Manning, 115 Ravenhouse Road, Scout Hill, Dewsbury, Yorks.

West Bromwich (151): T. Bailey, 33 Lilac Avenue, Streetly, Sutton Coldfield.

West Lancs. (153): Mrs. D. J. W. Newsome, 11 Burnside Avenue, Blackpool, Lancs.

Westminster (159): L. Zanelli, 81 Long Lane, London, N.3.

York (50): K. C. Cousins, 26 Bridge Road, Bishopsthorpe, Yorks.

OVERSEAS BRANCHES

Arlington N.J. (220): F. A. Vogel, 1557 Deer Run Drive, Manasquan, N.J. 08736, U.S.A.

Blantyre (243): W. A. L. Apps, P.O. Box 393, Blantyre, Malawi, Central Africa.

B.S-A.C. de Panama (262): Susan B. McCarthy, P.O. Box 372, Fort Gulick, C.Z., Panama, U.S.A.

Cape Town Assoc. Divers (212): Mrs. H. Micsky, P.O. Box 4178, Cape Town, South Africa.

Durban Assoc. Divers (200): The Secretary, Associated Divers, P.O. Box 3396.

Hillside-Rhodesia (163): Rhodesian Sub-Aqua Club, Box H.G.2, Highlands, Salisbury, Rhodesia.

Indianapolis-1st U.S.A. (154): T. T. Haver, 6001 Compton, Indianapolis 20, Indiana, U.S.A.

Jamaica (51): Jamaica Sub-Aqua Club, 71 Lady Musgrove Road, Kingston, Jamaica.

Limassol, Cyprus (258): Harry Morewood, A.R.I.C. (NE), R.A.F., Episkopi, B.F.P.O. 53.

Montego Bay, Jamaica (192): Miss D. Titterington, c/o Montego Bay High School for Girls, Union Street, Montego Bay, Jamaica, W.1.

Napier NZ Pacific Divers (244): H. Reese, 35 Morgan Avenue, Marewa, Napier, New Zealand.

Salisbury-Rhodesia (63): The Secretary, Salisbury R. Branch, B.S-A.C., P.O. Box 3532, Salisbury, Rhodesia.

Saulte Ste. Marie (175): R. J. Hamilton Rte.I, Box 238A, Saulte Ste. Marie, Michigan, U.S.A.

Transvaal (235): N. L. Heatlie, P.O. Box 666, Johannesburg, South Africa.

Trinidad (129): A. Oliver, c/o Myerson Mouldings Ltd., P.O. Box 111, Port of Spain, Trinidad, West Indies.

SPECIAL BRANCHES

Adriatic (178): The Custodian, Adriatic Sub-Aqua Club, APO New York 09240, USAF/USN.

A.E.E. Dounreay (119): J. Gilmour, 6 Scaraben Court, Thurso, Caithness.

A.E.E. Sellafield (94): E. C. Carnall, 71 Gosforth Road, Seascale, Cumberland.

Aquatic Group (180): Mrs. D. R. Shiers, 11 Epping Way, London, E.4.

Aston University (241): K. B. Higgs, 65 Wootton Crescent, St. Annes, Bristol.

Awali (261): B. Mountain, P.O. Box 39, Awali, Bahrain, Arabian Gulf.

Battersea & Chelsea Colleges (123): Miss S. P. Rodgers, Fulmar Drive, Gerrards Cross, Bucks.

B.E.A. Silver Wings (146): J. W. Brinsden, 111 Long Lane, Stanwell, Staines, Middlesex.

Berlin Inf. Brgd. Group (203): Capt. R. W. M. Eagle, 38 Fd. Sqn., R.E., B.F.P.O. 45.

Borough Polytechnic (186): D. F. W. Hawes, 79 Tarnwood Park, Court Road, London, S.W.9.

Boston & Horncastle School (215): Secretary, Sub-Aqua Club, Boston & Horncastle Grammar School, Boston, Lincs.

B.P. Meadhurst (181): R. Tunesi, 12 Napier Road, Ashford Common, Middx.

Bradford City Police (195): J. Hayhurst, Central Police Station, Town Hall, Bradford, Yorks.

Bristol Aeroplane (88): N. Besant, 3 Bromley Drive, Downend, Nr. Bristol.

British M.A.R.C. (209): O. R. Tooke, 11 Wordsworth Close, Grantham, Lincs.

British Timken (73): K. R. Labraham, The Red House, High Street, Flore, Northants.

Cambridge University (52): C. J. Wakefield, Trinity Hall, Cambridge.

Croydon Technical College (187): M. K. Todd, 23 Hillcrest Road, Orpington, Kent.

De Haviland-Bolton (101): F. J. Lloyd, 26 Crescent Avenue, Ashton-in-Makerfield, Wigan, Lancs.

Dhekelia (120): Lt. Watson, R. B. (D/476664), 58 Sqn. R.C.T., B.F.P.O. 53.

Ebbw Vale Swimming Club (263): D. Brian Druce, "Fair Holme", 57 Stonebridge Road, Rassau, Beaufort, Mon.

Ekon (234): J. Buckingham, 3 Oxhey Avenue, Bushey, Herts.

Episcopi J.S. (150): Cpl. A. J. Jode, No. 1153, Marine Craft Unit, R.A.F. Akrotiri, B.F.P.O. 53.

Exeter University (246): P. T. Stone, 8 Wonford Road, Exeter, Devon.

Farelf (152): 58627 Captain A. Lane, 200 (Singapore) PRO Coy. R.M.P., c/o GPO Singapore.

Flint College (167): Miss S. H. Roberts, Longwater, Llanbedr, Ruthin, Denbighshire.

1st Bn. The Sherwood Foresters (257): Capt. A. C. French, LAD R.E.M.E., 1 Foresters, B.F.P.O. 17.

Ford Motors (227): T. J. Davenport, 3 Minister Court, Minster Way, Hornchurch, Essex.

Granada Aquanauts (253): Mrs. E. Riddell, "Wraxall", 122 Palatine Road, Didsbury, Manchester, 20.

H.M.S. Caledonia (184): Lt. M. T. H. Richards, H.M.S. Caledonia, Rosyth, Fife, Scotland.

Hull University (245): N. V. Sills, Downs Hall, Northingate, Cottingham, Hull.

Ilford Films (177): T. W. Blake, 48 Westwood Road, Seven Kings, Ilford.

Imperial College (64): The Secretary, I.C. Underwater Club, Imperial College Union, Prince Consort Road, London.

Leeds University Union (124): The Secretary, Leeds University Union Sub-Aqua Club, c/o Leeds University Union.

London Fire Brigade (250): J. A. T. Hissex, 32 Fryston Avenue, Addiscombe, Surrey.

London Hospitals (254): J. Dent, 6 Churton Place, London, S.W.1.

London Inter-Varsity (208): Miss J. A. Greenaway, 34 Kensington Gardens Square, London, W.2.

London Scouts (20): W. Best, 78 Chaucer House, Churchill Gardens, London, S.W.1.

London University (69): Miss G. M. Waite, "Maythorn", Westville, Kingsbridge, South Devon.

Loughborough College (165): The Secretary (B.S-A.S.), Loughborough College Branch, c/o Mr. Millard, 74 Holt Drive, Loughborough.

Loughborough University (238): F. J. Rees, 101 Hainton Avenue, Grimsby, Lincs.

Marconi Basildon (219): Mrs. M. N. Fawkes, 8 Goodwood Close, Thundersley, Benfleet, Essex.

Massey-Ferguson (185): M. Moss, 34 Cressage Road, Walsgrove Road, Coventry.

NAC-SAC (Naval Air Command Sub-Aqua Club) (66): R. W. Crocker, 51 Monglgath Avenue, Falmouth, Cornwall.

Nee-Soon (228): Nee-Soon Sub-Aqua Club, c/o Mrs. S. Pollitt, 35 Jalan Kemuning, Sembawang Springs, Singapore, 27.

Newcastle University (249): Miss P. M. King, c/o Dove Marine Laboratory, Cullercoats, Northumb.

New Cross Institute (102): V. Quick, 25 Gladstone Road, Farnborough, Kent.

Northampton College (70): Sub-Aqua Club, c/o Union Society, St. John Street, London, E.C.1.

Oxford University (169): R. S. Tranchant, Merton College, Oxford.

Penang Swimming Club (225): The Secretary, Scuba Section, Penang Swimming Club, 517 Tanjong Bungah, Penang, Malaysia.

R.A.A.F. Butterworth (230): 221250 Corporal Wright, M. K., Base Squadron, Butterworth, Malaya.

R.A.F., Akrotiri (107): 507595 Flt. Lt. McFadzen, I. L. Station Sick Quarters, R.A.F. Akrotiri, B.F.P.O. 53, Cyprus.

R.A.F. Benson (156): Sgt. Bertola, c/o P.F.O. Section, R.A.F. Benson, Oxford.

R.A.F. Binbrook (224): Secretary, Sub-Aqua Club, R.A.F. Binbrook.

R.A.F. Changi (265): 573197 Flt. Lt. Taylor, D. A. J., Fairy Point Officers' Mess, R.A.F. Changi, G.P.O. Singapore.

R.A.F. College (193): Flt. Cd. C. J. Long, Junior Mess, R.A.F. College, Cranwell, Sleaford, Lincs.

R.A.F. Cottesmore (232): Fg. Off. D. G. Bennett, R.A.F. Cottesmore, Oakham, Rutland.

R.A.F. El Adem (201): The Secretary, R.A.F. El Adem Sub-Aqua Club, B.F.P.O. 56.

R.A.F. Falmouth (174): The Sub-Aqua Club, 1102, M.C.U., R.A.F. Falmouth.

R.A.F. Finningly (211): Flt. Sgt. J. Dromey, Sgts. Mess, R.A.F. Finningley, Doncaster.

R.A.F. Gan (126): Officer in Charge S-A.C., Officers' Mess, R.A.F. Gan, B.F.P.O. 180.

R.A.F. Geilenkirchen (110): TO680741 Sgt. Cheyne, J. C. E., Sgts. Mess, R.A.F. Geilenkirchen, Germany, B.F.P.O. 42.

R.A.F. Gutersloh (221): N523518 Cpl. Walker, D. A. Air Traffic Control, R.A.F. Gutersloh, B.F.P.O. 47.

R.A.F. Halton (247): Cpl. Steward, G., 87 Longecroft Avenue, R.A.F. Halton, Nr. Aylesbury, Bucks.

R.A.F. Lynham (231): Flt. Lt. Warren, T., 511 Sqdn., R.A.F. Lyneham, Wilts.

R.A.F. Malta (213): F/O Dainty, Officers' Mess, R.A.F. Hal Far, Malta, B.F.P.O. 51.

R.A.F. Marham (171): Fg. Off. J. W. G. Pethard, R.A.F., 77 Officers' Married Quarters, R.A.F. Marham, King's Lynn, Norfolk.

R.A.F. Muharraq (242): SAC Nigel Green, 208 Squadron, R.A.F. Muharraq, B.F.P.O. 63.

R.A.F. Newton (255): KO681365 Ch./ Tech. Pugh, K. P., 64 Trenchard Close, Newton, Notts.

R.A.F. Nicosia (216): Fl./Off. W. L. Grundy, Officers' Mess, R.A.F. Nicosia, Cyprus, B.F.P.O. 53.

R.A.F. Scampton (189): F/O D. K. Rickard, Officers' Mess, R.A.F. Scampton, Lincs.

R.A.F. Seletar (98): Cpl. B. R. Fenton, E.L.E.S., G.C.E., 390 M.U., R.A.F. Seletar, Singapore.

R.A.F. Stafford (252): Mrs. J. Parry, Lytell Geste, Sherwood Crescent, Market Drayton, Shropshire.

R.A.F. Tengah (134): The Sec., Tengah Sub-Aqua Club, c/o Station Post Office, R.A.F. Tengah, Singapore.

R.A.F. Waddington (251): Flt. Lt. Ades, Officers' Mess, R.A.F. Waddington, Lincoln.

R.A.F. Wildenrath (207): Miss J. E. Dorman, W.R.A.F. Block (47), R.A.F. Wildenrath, B.F.P.O. 42.

R.A.F. Wyton (161): The Secretary, Sub-Aqua Club, R.A.F. Wyton, Huntingdon.

R.M.A. Sandhurst (202): The Secretary, Sub-Aqua Club, R.M.A. Sandhurst.

R.S.A.S.R.G. (91): K. J. Levings, 20 Hampshire Road, P.O. Greendale, Salisbury, Rhodesia.

Ruislip & Northwood Swimming Club (206): P. Zelepuken, 10 Oakfield Avenue, Kenton, Middx.

Scientific & Technical Group (158): D. R. Gray, The White House, Green Street, Sunbury-on-Thames, Middx.

Selo Brentwood (237): G. S. Scarff, 29 Ardleigh, Basildon, Essex.

S.E.M.E. Bordon (233): The Secretary, S.E.M.E. Sub-Aqua Club, S.E.M.E., Bordon, Hants.

Seremban Garrison (259): 23512665 Cpl. Ford, D. I., 17 Div/Malaya Dist. Pro. Coy. R.M.P., c/o G.P.O. Seremban, Malaysia.

South Shields Volunteer Lifeguard (222): R. D. Osborne, 255 Quarry Lane, South Shields.

S.T.C. Basildon (204): R. Taylor, 77 Pondfield Lane, Ingrave, Brentwood, Essex.

St. John's Singapore (223): N. Fanning, 97A Singlan Road, Singapore, 15.

Thorncliffe (256): Miss B. P. Neves, 162 Industry Road, Darnall, Sheffield, 9.

Vickers Armstrong-Hurn (82): M. Davies, 12 Jubilee Road, Parkstone, Poole, Dorset.

Walton Liverpool Tech. College (260): A. E. Gibbons, 5 Barton Road, Walton, Liverpool, 9.

Woolwich R.I. (162): T. H. Simms, 347 Old Farm Avenue, Sidcup, Kent.

Wycliffe College (68): C. Ellis, Windrush, Wycliffe College, Stonehouse, Glos.

Zoology Dept. U.C. Swansea (239): D. A. Jones, Dept. of Zoology, University College of Swansea, Singleton Park, Swansea.